Theatre, Exhibition, and Curation

G000078085

Examining the artistic, intellectual, and social life of performance, this book interrogates Theatre and Performance Studies through the lens of display and modern visual art. Moving beyond the exhibition of immaterial art and its documents, as well as re-enactment in gallery contexts, Guy's book articulates an emerging field of arts practice distinct from but related to increasing curatorial provision for 'live' performance. Drawing on a recent proliferation of object-centric events of display that interconnect with theatre, the book approaches artworks in terms of their curation together and re-theorizes the exhibition as a dynamic context in which established traditions of display and performance interact. By examining the current traffic of ideas and aesthetics moving between theatricality and curatorial practice, the study reveals how the reception of a specific form is often mediated via the ontological expectations of another. It asks how contemporary visual arts and exhibition practices display performance and what it means to generalize the 'theatrical' as the optic or directive of a curatorial concept. Proposing a symbiotic relation between theatricality and display, Guy presents cases from international arts institutions which are both displayed and performed, including Tate Modern and the Guggenheim, and assesses their significance to the enduring relation between theatre and the visual arts. The book progresses from the conventional alignment of theatricality and ephemerality within performance research and teases out a new temporality for performance with which contemporary exhibitions implicitly experiment, thereby identifying supplementary modes of performance which other discourses exclude. This important study joins the fields of Theatre and Performance Studies with exciting new directions in curation, aesthetics, sociology of the arts, visual arts, the creative industries, the digital humanities, cultural heritage, and reception and audience theories.

Georgina Guy is Lecturer in Theatre and Performance in the Department of Drama, Theatre & Dance at Royal Holloway, University of London, UK.

Routledge Advances in Theatre and Performance Studies

For more information about this series, please visit: https://www.routledge.com/Routledge-Advances-in-Theatre--Performance-Studies/book-series/RATPS

Theatre, Exhibition, and Curation
Displayed & Performed

Georgina Guy

Routledge
Taylor & Francis Group

NEW YORK AND LONDON

First published in paperback 2019

First published 2016
by Routledge
52 Vanderbilt Avenue, New York, NY 10017

and by Routledge
2 Park Square, Milton Park, Abingdon, Oxon OX14 4RN

Routledge is an imprint of the Taylor & Francis Group, an informa business

Library of Congress Cataloging-in-Publication Data

Names: Guy, Georgina, author.
Title: Theatre, exhibition, and curation: displayed and performed / by Georgina Guy.
Description: New York; London: Routledge, 2016. |
Series: Routledge advances in theatre and performance studies; 46 |
Includes bibliographical references and index.
Identifiers: LCCN 2016004398 | ISBN 9781138832879 (alk. paper)
Subjects: LCSH: Performing arts—Exhibitions. | Artists and theater—History—21st century. | Arts, Modern—21st century.
Classification: LCC PN1575 .G89 2016 | DDC 791—dc23
LC record available at http://lccn.loc.gov/2016004398

ISBN: 978-1-138-83287-9 (hbk)
ISBN: 978-0-367-18877-1 (pbk)
ISBN: 978-1-315-73571-9 (ebk)

Typeset in Sabon
by codeMantra

For Sam, who enables me to do more.

Contents

List of Illustrations

Acknowledgements

While writing this book I have been supported and invigorated by a field of thinkers whose inclusivity, creativity, and care has sustained and inspired both me and this project. I am grateful to Ben Piggott at Routledge for hearing my work and for inviting me to imagine its possibilities in book form and to Liz Levine for her positive commitment throughout the publication process, as well as to my anonymous readers for their close attention to and understanding of this project and the considered and thoughtful nature of their reports and recommendations. I would like to thank very much indeed the artists who have generously given permission for the inclusion of images as details of their work within this book: Frank Auerbach, Marie Cool and Fabio Balducci, Tacita Dean, Trisha Donnelly, Michael Elmgreen and Ingar Dragset, Tim Etchells and Hugo Glendinning, Dora García, Pierre Huyghe, and the Philadelphia Museum of Art on behalf of Mary Stevenson Cassatt. These figures hold a special place in my project and are integral to, rather than illustrative of, the thinking and ideas expressed therein.

A significant proportion of work towards this project was undertaken during my time at King's College London and I would like to give special thanks to that particularly astute group of performance scholars – Kélina Gotman, Theron Schmidt, and Lara Shalson – as well as more broadly across the Department of English and to those colleagues and advisers who have taken a marked interest in my professional development, including Josephine McDonagh, Sonia Massai, Mark Turner, and Patrick Wright. I am very grateful to the Arts and Humanities Research Council (AHRC), UK, for their support of my doctoral research, as well as to Patrick Ffrench and Freddie Rokem for their perceptive and encouraging engagement with those materials on which this project builds. Sincere thanks also to Stuart Dunn, who has provided valuable advice and feedback on this project in its various stages of development, as well as practical assistance with the development and implementation of the digital methodologies addressed in Chapter 4.

This book is moreover testament to the support of my colleagues and friends in the Department of Drama, Theatre & Dance at Royal Holloway, University of London, and I would like to particularly mention Dan Rebellato, Bryce Lease, Helen Nicholson, and David Williams who have welcomed me with such exuberance into this dynamic context for scholarship and conversation, as well as Emma Cox and Libby Worth who kindly and with great sensitivity read and commented on this work in its final stages. I would also like to acknowledge the enriching frameworks provided by the theatre and performance field in the UK, and expressly the London Theatre Seminar, the Theatre and Performance Research Association (TaPRA), and the Departments of Drama, Theatre, and Performance at Queen Mary, University of London and the University of Roehampton, for providing spaces in which to share ideas and encounter wonderful thinking.

To Joe Kelleher, a friend from Leeds (or thereabouts) who more than once took the time to read chapters of this book and to tell me what he found therein – thank you. From another dear friend and mentor, Alan Read, who has been a great supporter of me and of this project since its beginning, I borrow the ampersand of displayed & performed and much more besides, not least the advantage of his counsel, inimitable energy, and enthusiasm. Finally, to my parents, Susan Beerling and Malcolm Guy, for their boundless support and vivacity, and to my husband, Sam Thomas, for being with me in such great spirit through the writing of this book and in everything, I am more thankful than I can say. It is your blissful environs that make all things possible.

A short article detailing the digital methodology and visualisations on which Chapter 4 of this book reflects appears as 'Out of Sync: Curation, Participation and Reactional Pathways' in *Performance Research* 16:3 On Participation and Synchronisation (2011): 89–93.

Introduction
Displaying Performance

This act of growing into the image, a condensation of live movement into the arresting square of photographic light, introduces a new mode of performance into the history of visual art.

—Peggy Phelan[1]

The exhibition is a dynamic context in which established traditions of display and performance interact. It is a framework in which, in recent years, performance has grown, an arrangement wherein it has flourished and shown vigorous life, not only 'live', re-performed, and photographed, but displayed and made object. In this act of growing, of becoming vitally united, into the exhibition frame, there occurs a condensation, a means of appearing more intensely, and a conversion of state between the displayed and performed. As performance develops in this context, it acquires more and more influence over the domain of display. The square of the white cube becomes a tool for determining the faithfulness of the artificers' work, a guiding principle for the identification of other operations which might count as performance. To condense is to exclude all but the quintessential, to press together objects and ideas to produce a concise amalgamation or new form, in this case an expanded practice of performance introduced *by*, or at least in close relation to, the accumulating history of visual art.

This book traces a specific moment in the artistic, intellectual, and social life of performance. In order to pose significant questions of performing and visual arts practice, and its most recent transformations as they occurred between 2007 and 2012, my discussion examines contemporary intersections between two traditions elucidated here as the displayed and the performed and reframes these terms within a reconceptualised theory of exhibition. At its centre is an effort to unfix thought, critical and creative, from the spaces and categories in which it can sometimes appear immovable. It is steered by an attempt to track an emerging reformation of display cultures and to make visible the related implications of such departures for the academic discipline of performance, as well as more broadly across creative and critical engagements and institutions. This endeavour is undertaken at the ontological boundaries of the different territories across which it moves: theatre, museum, and gallery. It collects evidence by instigating dialogues between activities of display and performance, and by attending to objects and events in which their processes interact. The project of the book is to thereby reveal the practices associated with each of these settings to be based in particular and conventional arrangements of the object of attention and of the human body. It is my belief that, through engagement with different configurations of these relations, other formations and ontologies, both of display and of performance, as well as of theatre and exhibition, can be evidenced, imagined, and re-drawn.

Figure I.1 Tim Etchells and Hugo Glendinning, *Empty Stages* Maschinenhalle Zweckei, Gladbeck, Germany, 2003–present. Courtesy of Hugo Glendinning.

Beginning: Material Imaginings of Performance

The first image in this book is a photograph of an empty stage. A place for performance, this picture, and the exposed theatrical machinery it represents, could be described borrowing the terms of performance theorist Peggy Phelan, placed in preface to this introduction, and echoed already in its writing. Growing into *this* image, we are welcomed into a terrain described by its photographer as a 'photographic space that's *like* the experience of being in a live performance'.[2] This '*like*', the contested simile of Phelan's ontology, proffers knowledge in accordance with theatre. In line with recent discourses in the performance field, the image moves beyond a relation between photography and event limited to a static documentary function.[3] Rather, in its vacant seats and unrigged lights, its stony hues and steps leading elsewhere, the photograph speaks to the possibility of an encounter analogous to 'live' performance constructed through another media. Condensing something akin to performance into the photograph's arresting square, this image of an empty stage glosses the sorts of 'new modes' of performance described in Phelan's writing and with which my project is entangled, as well as those to which this book specifically attends. The premise of *Theatre, Exhibition, and Curation: Displayed & Performed* is to extend the range of forms and spaces in which performance might appear beyond the ephemeral and photographic to include the curated and, I propose, theatricalised exhibition.

This objective is approached through a focusing in on practices of performance that operate outside expressly theatrical structures and in connection with more orthodox museological thinking. The context of display provides a strong basis for reflecting on performance in terms of duration and in relation to the object. Historically, museums have given priority to the collection, conservation, communication, and display of objects. Lately, there is an increasing drive across museums and arts institutions to display performance by means of documentation and artefacts, as well as through programmes of live work and artistic re-enactments. The image of an unattended theatre which opens this book speaks to this curatorial circumstance. It is part of an on-going collaboration between photographer Hugo Glendinning and performance-maker Tim Etchells titled *Empty Stages* (2003–present). Images from this series were first shown as part of *Live Culture*, an exhibition of events exploring the evolving relation between the live and the visual arts held at Tate Modern, London, in 2003 and presented in partnership with the Live Art Development Agency (LADA), an organisation established in London by Lois Keidan and Catherine Ugwu in 1999 to support the development and contextualisation of live art practices in the UK. In Tate Modern, the photographs appeared amongst a number of visual and performance-related projects identified by curator and performance scholar Adrian Heathfield as representing a '*shift to the live.*'[4] Progressing from this *shift* and what might now be considered a seminal event in the history of live art, in this book I will argue instead for a more recent mode of exhibition practice which operates through performance and in association with the object.

Theatre, Exhibition, and Curation: Displayed & Performed is alert to a contemporary proliferation of object-centric events of display which interconnect with theatre and takes exhibition as its primary unit of discourse. My thinking towards its contents began at an event curated by Marianne Alphant and Nathalie Léger at the Pompidou Centre in Paris in 2007 and titled *Samuel Beckett*, an attempt to construct an identity of a playwright in an exhibition space from whence I recognised that an increasing number of arts institutions were engaging directly with questions of performance through the medium of display. Growing from this first encounter, in this book I hope to articulate a zeitgeist of a particular cultural and creative moment by presenting an emerging field of exhibition practice distinct from but related to increasing curatorial provision for 'live' performance. Only since the early 2000s, Head of Collection Care Research at Tate Pip Laurenson and conservation scholar Vivian van Saaze explain in their essay on 'Collecting Performance-based Art' (2014), 'have museums begun to collect live works, by acquiring the means and the rights to re-perform them.'[5] At the centre of the book is a detailed tracing of how contemporary visual arts and exhibition practices display performance and how such representations, when read collectively, suggest alternatives to epistemologies most prevalent in performance research, and in particular to paradigms premised on opposition to the object and resistance to art institutional curation.

The aim of this study is to progress a broader view of how theatricality is displayed by curators and artists. Offering revised views on what has, until recently, been often presented as a site of antagonism and exclusion, and identifying instances of reciprocal inspiration, this book addresses again the intricacy of relations between the displayed and performed. The framework of exhibition instigates a consideration of how the connotations of curation, especially those connected to conservation and preservation, operate in relation to the live and to performance's established history of ephemerality. Progressing from experiments in object-based performance emerging from the 1950s, 1960s, and 1970s, this book runs parallel to a remarkable and timely rise of interest in processes for archiving and collecting performance. Given this critical context, it is important to stress that *Theatre, Exhibition, and Curation: Displayed & Performed* does not address the theatre museum in the traditional sense epitomised, for example, by the Theatre & Performance Galleries at the Victoria and Albert (V&A) Museum in London where remnants of actual theatrical productions are displayed as evidences of something past. Nor is it concerned with the acts of live performance and re-enactment increasingly staged in gallery contexts since the 1990s. My strategy is to probe further the past moment of performance not through performance remains and collected ephemera but instead by attending to performative referents produced by visual artists working in varied media for the purpose of curation and display. It is my contention that, by looking at contemporary practices of performance operating outside structures founded on a distinctly 'live' encounter, revised and augmented models of performance come into view.

Subjecting: Performance as Curatorial Optic

My emphasis on six years of exhibiting and curating performance-related events from 2007 to 2012 might be read as a rejoinder to writer, curator, and activist Lucy Lippard's celebrated *Six Years: The Dematerialization of the Art Object from 1966 to 1972*. Itself an advanced form of archive, Lippard's annotated history convenes a particular period of practice, including work by Joseph Beuys, John Baldessari, Hans Haacke, Sol LeWitt, Bruce Nauman, and others, centred on the significant challenge to commodity and object status effected by artists working from the 1960s under a bracket sometimes termed 'conceptual'. In her preface to the 1997 edition of this text, Lippard describes her project as concerned with 'work in which the idea is paramount and the material form is secondary, lightweight, ephemeral, cheap, unpretentious and/or "dematerialized."'[6] Whereas Lippard's chronicle charts a scene in which artworks previously defined in terms of their materiality were rendered immaterial, or at least wherein material aspects associated with long-standing ideals of 'uniqueness' and 'permanence' were downplayed, my project sketches a movement occurring some forty years later wherein such forms as those once described by Lippard as 'ephemeral' are made object. That is to say, *Theatre, Exhibition, and Curation: Displayed & Performed* traces what might be thought of as a re-materialisation or other material imagining of theatre and performance played out through exhibition.

What my theory shares with Lippard's, and the works she describes, is an engagement with genres of making no longer bound by particular formal constraints but rather interested in 'intellectual distinctions in representation and relationships'.[7] For me, this includes the potential for performance to take up, occupy, and enact a material object status. If conceptual art's emphasis on ideas over materiality does, as Lippard suggests, represent a 'return to content', then my interest in the contemporary exhibitions recollected in this book stems from their taking of the 'immaterial', most often associated with theatre, performance, and other modes which fade away, as their 'content', that is as their subject, focus, or theme.[8] Addressing a number of gallery-based events in which performance interfaces with other creative and social actions, with discourses, schedules, and forms of representation that may be cast by some as peripheral, this book examines the effect of the exhibition environment on the appearance and functionality of performance, as well as the sorts of practice we might collect under that term. By investigating a new context of visual arts exhibition which draws on ideas and tropes of the theatrical event, it is my intention to profile how one mode performs in relation to the conventional ontologies of another and to propose a symbiotic relationship between theatricality and display.

Significant to this endeavour is the reformulation of exhibition as an intersection between processes which originate with display and performance. To a small extent, this project reveals how performers and theatre practitioners apply approaches usually associated with visual arts exhibition to their own work.[9] More significantly, however, the book addresses gallery-based engagements which are suggestive of the ways in which, borrowing the terms of Pip Laurenson and Vivian van Saaze, 'recent performance artworks often no longer privilege the live moment of the artist's own body.' Highlighting modes of practice wherein 'live works can exist, at least theoretically, independent of the artist and can be repeated and reactivated in the future,' the concern of Laurenson and van Saaze here is the means by which live performance might enter art collections and established systems of conservation.[10] High-profile arts institutions including, but by no means limited to, Tate Modern and the Institute of Contemporary Arts (ICA) in London, and the Solomon R. Guggenheim Museum in New York, each visited within the pages of this text, are mounting exhibitions which contribute to the display of performance not only by means of live performance and re-enactment. Rather, and of more significant interest here, such venues are engaging with the performance terrain through associations of objects, that is to say, via curation as a form of directing and conceptualising the interaction between selected works of art.

Exhibitions, like ontologies, are linked descriptions of things. My interest is in what happens to our understanding of the form and project of performance when this idiom becomes the optic or directive of a curatorial concept. Following her research project on *Performing the Curatorial* (2009–12), curator and critic Maria Lind reminds us that this mode – 'like all practices that work with defining, preserving, and mediating cultural heritage in a wider sense' – has 'clear performative sides'.[11] Within the gallery there are curated constraints on visitors' chronological experience. Through *Theatre, Exhibition, and Curation: Displayed & Performed* I want to address how our perceptions of exhibitions shift when the object is explicitly theatrical and the imperative performance. I want to question how ontologies of display affect ontologies of performance and index the possibility of presenting narratives and versions of the latter by way of collections of objects, curated in cumulative relation, and exhibited under a theatricalised title. To clarify, it is the names of the events attended to in Chapter 2, for example – *The World as a Stage* and *Renoir at the Theatre* – which first invite us to read their contents as somehow symbiotic with theatre making. My take on how the designation of performance inflects the domain of display and vice-versa will focus on the intricacies outlined above and in particular venues and events wherein it seems to me that these questions of display and performance are posed. I will pause in front of objects and in spaces where I see or feel something of performance, categorical or otherwise. To propel this project further, I will concentrate now on a specific instance which offers the opportunity to mark out some more precise distinctions between a recent plethora of exhibitions founded on the display of performance documents and the alternative forms of presentation traced in this book.

Historicising: Moving Beyond the Documentary

A Bigger Splash: Painting after Performance, staged at Tate Modern in 2012, while including some examples of contemporary practice in the later stages of its installation, engages for the most part with a precisely historicised performance art terrain. On entering this event, visitors encounter in the first gallery two related cohorts of objects which establish the premise for the exhibition, as devised by Tate's Senior Curator of International Art (Performance), Catherine Wood. These units include Jackson Pollock's *Summertime: Number 9A* (1948) plus Hans Namuth's film of the artist and

David Hockney's *A Bigger Splash* (1967) with Jack Hazan's film of the same title. Read together, these works, according to Wood's hypothesis, instigate two categories of 'painting after': one concerned with the canvas as a record of and field for action, with the painting positioned as a document residual from, and previously part of, a live performance; and another which situates the art object as a stage setting wherein latent theatrical acts might be imagined and enacted. Following Wood, these modes indicate polar positions between painting and performance, since one is 'abstract, the other figurative; one an index, shown with a film about process; the other a picture, shown with a sequence of narrative scenes.' Both suggest to Wood an 'arena to act' by associating painting and filmed documentation.[12]

In Namuth's film, returning to the phrase used by Phelan and cited as an epigraph to this introduction, it is Pollock who 'grows into the image' and it is amongst a discussion of Pollock's painting, or rather the effect of the photographer's arresting square on that act, and in direct interpretation of a statement by Walter Benjamin about the long exposures of early photographic portraiture, that Phelan's words appear. Combining histories of performance art founded in theatre, painting, and ritual, Pollock's work, and the textual, filmic, and photographic documents it has inspired, moves the emphasis in visual art away from the complete art object and towards, what Phelan calls, the 'complex drama of the act of composition.'[13] An important evolution in theatrical epistemologies, this understanding of performance as a synonym for making is now well traced. In relation to Tate's re-engagement with this conception, it is important to stress that Catherine Wood, as a key enabler of performance in art institutional contexts, will emerge as an important curator and commentator throughout my study. Indeed, a number of events for which she has been responsible will evolve as major cases in point. It is precisely for this reason that I want to pick up here on a particular core aspect of *A Bigger Splash: Painting after Performance*. It seems to me that by invoking a specific period in the development of the enduring relationship between display and performance, when, for example, artistic composition came to be thought as performative, a limitation is set on the capacity of the exhibition, or at least a central part of it, to actually display performance. By necessity of its own aspiration to historicise practice, *A Bigger Splash* can exhibit only object-remnants of past acts of making and this is the case with a number of related historical survey exhibitions which provide a cultural context to my main examples.

Prominent exhibitions – including events at the ICA in London during the 1990s, such as *Rapture* (1995) and *Totally Wired* (1996); *Out of Actions: Between Performance and the Object, 1949–1979* at the Museum of Contemporary Art (MOCA) in Los Angeles in 1998; the *A Short History of Performance* series at the Whitechapel Gallery in London from 2002 to 2006; and *Video Acts* shown at PS1 in New York and the ICA in London in 2003 – all fall precisely within the well theorised domains from which my project develops, specifically: the historical evolution of the immaterial in visual arts practice; the presence of the body and the (re-)performance of seminal live art events; the exhibition of performance-based artworks available in video format; and the display of objects and documents remaining from past performances.[14] Paul Schimmel's celebrated *Out of Actions*, to take another influential example, is concerned with a broad history of action-based and experimental art practice and covers much of the same terrain taken up by *A Bigger Splash: Painting after Performance*. Both exhibitions begin with Pollock's paintings and Namuth's documentation of that painterly process and include work by Yves Klein, Niki de St Phalle, Yayoi Kusama, Herman Nitsch and the Vienna Actionists, amongst others. Despite this shared context of practice, Wood has sought to distance her project from the former on the basis that *Out of Actions*, in her terms, positioned 'performed action and material object in a relationship that inadvertently reinforces a hierarchy of value in favour of the status of the object as an "outcome".'[15] Until recently, performance has most often entered the art museum via its documents which can more easily be accommodated within gallery and collection systems. An alternative conceptualisation of the connection between performance and object is needed.

It is no coincidence that documents of performance and their relation to histories of visual art are reassessed by a number of exhibitions during the period from 2007 to 2012. In her co-edited *Perform, Repeat, Record* (2012), art historian Amelia Jones marks the 2000s as characterised by a *'Fascination with Performance Histories and the Historicizing of Live Art'* such that a 'massive spate of exhibitions addressing various aspects of live art in history are held around Europe and North America'.[16] This 'spate' signals particular expansions in practices and understandings of performance, and their relation to the gallery, on which this book elaborates. In his foreword to the catalogue for *A Bigger Splash*, former Director of Tate Modern, and short-lived Artistic Director of the Berlin Volksbühne Theatre, Chris Dercon writes that the exhibition aims to relay a 'complex history, played back and forth between painting and performance, and between pictoriality and masquerade'.[17] Suggesting a mode alternating between figuration and enactment, Dercon's description is telling for my project. In Phelan's terms, Pollock's 'best' paintings also 'come to us as fully present objects ... in a state of almost ecstatic suspension; they resist both the pleasures and the traumas of the completed story.' Both effusively present and rapturously indeterminate, Phelan astutely registers Pollock's sense of 'painting's resistance to singularity', both identifying and enacting the ways in which the 'elision between Pollock's paintings, Namuth's photographs, and the writing about them opens up a place where a different kind of history of performance art might be written.'[18] The exhibitions explored in this book offer similar potential. I want to write about them because they present a sphere wherein an expanded mode of performance might be pursued. Recollected as an emerging field of practice, intermittent between display and performance, such events require a 'set of words and a style of address'; like action painting, they create a need for 'performance-minded criticism' within the curatorial domain.[19] It is this necessity that this book seeks to answer.

(Under)Groundwork 1: Collecting Performance

Theatre, Exhibition, and Curation: Displayed & Performed charts a particular moment in the cultural life of performance which reaches a certain crescendo with the opening of the Tate Modern Tanks in London in 2012. The development of these spaces for performance-related projects enacts a material relation between the displayed and performed, with one tank dedicated to the exhibition of contemporary art and another to performance events which speak directly to that display programme. The Tanks embed live art and performance into Tate's curatorial agenda in a way that, I hope, situates this book, and the set of evolving forces which it tracks, as valuable to the history of performance. My concern is with practices in which the exhibition form collides ideals of display and of performance in deference to the enduring relationship between these two traditions. Given that collectable objects are, as Laurenson and van Saaze remind us, 'required to be durable, collecting live performance has been considered to contradict the very nature of liveness' and in particular strategies employed by artists to defy market economies. 'When museums collected anything related to performance,' Laurenson and van Saaze encapsulate, 'they collected the material remains of the performance, never the performance itself as a live event.'[20] Only recently have specialised departments and funding frameworks come to exist for performance in art museums.

Spaces, resources, and processes for acquiring 'live' work are instigated, according to Catherine Wood's perspective, in response to the practice of artists. Wood describes the construction of Tate Modern's sublevel as a 'way of creating space for the inaccessible areas of art history that have not, until now, had an official place within the museum.'[21] This accommodating of live art and performance practices within the art museum is not without challenge given that these more 'inaccessible' histories often conceive of themselves as existing in opposition to the limitations of the commodified artwork and outside of institutional controls. In her commentary on the developments at Tate, Wood is keen to stress a contemporary climate in which a resurgence of interest in performance means that the object often 'recedes to the middle, or back' in terms of what is central to the making of and visitors' encounters with art.[22] The sort of practice to which Wood refers necessarily reverberates with strategies that have been at work in time-based projects since, at least, the 1960s and which prompted Henry M. Sayre to observe in *The Object of Performance* (1989) that, by the end of that decade, 'it was clear to virtually everyone connected with the art world that the object per se had become, arguably, dispensable' and that the museum – 'designed to house and display objects, after all – was as deeply in trouble as the object itself.'[23] While highlighting a return to action-oriented practice in her introduction to

Tate's Tanks, Wood stresses elsewhere that such modes should not be seen as an 'ultimate finality' in terms of art's progression from materiality, but rather as a means by which the 'museum's role extends beyond the point of the acquisition and display of things.'[24] In distinction to a contemporary retreat from the object, often couched in terms of the service-economy, this book, and the exhibition systems it reviews, is invested in performance-related practices wherein object status advances to the fore.

In 'Staging Meaning: Performance in the Modern Museum' (2005), Valerie Casey suggests that 'live performance in the contemporary museum has not only dispensed of the primacy of the object, but it has *become* the object.'[25] *Theatre, Exhibition, and Curation: Displayed & Performed* moves beyond the analysis of performance documentation and recent strategies for staging live performance and re-enactment in gallery and museum settings to take literally and make physical this proposition of performance becoming object. Of interest here are associations of objects which reiterate, as curator and art historian Roselee Goldberg has, and did once again during the 'Performance Year Zero: A Living History' conference held as part of the Tate Tanks inaugural *Art in Action* programme (2012), the ways in which museums always already have collections of performance; they are just called something else, be that document, film, or sculpture.[26] In this project, I am interested in rethinking the division between the live and the still arts to which, as performance scholar Rebecca Schneider describes, we have been 'habituated,' via an alternative approach.[27] It is my hope that this book will contribute to the disciplinary debates currently rewriting the performance field by taking exhibition, rather than performance or object, as its primary optic. Whereas Tate's new subterranean spaces, *A Bigger Splash*, and indeed many theoretical engagements with performance in the context of the museum, focus on the questions which live work poses for practices of curation, collection, conservation, and art making, in this book I reconsider such questions with an emphasis on performance and the potential that exhibition contexts offer to our thinking, delineation, and effecting of this form.

Over the next pages I will provide a brief contextualisation of the key conceptual terms and frameworks which this book enters into, employs, and develops. This overview is a summary necessary to all of the chapters which follow. It contains suggestions that will reverberate in different ways across the text and so, for this reason, is presented here. Where direct engagement with the particular range of events and objects addressed in the project occurs, this critique will be discussed within the respective chapter. Beyond such specific commentary, the history of relations between display and performance is complex and perspective-bound and could not be wholly represented by any précis I might provide. I include a brief outline here, however, in order to situate *Theatre, Exhibition, and Curation: Displayed & Performed* within a particular historical context and cultural moment, and to indicate something of its situation within a field otherwise articulated in terms of the relational, participational, or installational.

Uncollectable

My account focuses in majority on contemporary art historical, curatorial, and museological discourses for two reasons. First, this emphasis enables me to orientate the scene I am describing without over-rehearsing certain contexts and frameworks already only too familiar to one set of people or another. A growing number of scholarly texts articulate the multiple connections that exist between performance and its adjoining influences. Notable in this context is the *Theatre &* series edited by performance scholars Jen Harvie and Dan Rebellato, and Susan Bennett's *Theatre & Museums* (2013) published within that frame. In bringing together the terms of her title, Bennett engages with ideas of re-performance and museum-based attentions to theatrical remainders (print materials, recordings, costumes, props, etc.), as well as exhibition strategies which she finds to be theatrical, her focus being how the archive, collection, and museums more broadly fail to convey the ontology of performance. In *Theatre, Exhibition and Curation*, I want to approach the adjunction between display and performance somewhat differently. Scholars within and at the borders of the performance field, including, but by no means limited to, Amelia Jones (2011), Peggy Phelan (2004, 2005), and Rebecca Schneider (2011), have examined in detail various and ever more ubiquitous acts of live performance, re-enactment, documentation, and indeed painting as performance within and beyond gallery contexts.[28] Despite this developed scholarly engagement, to my knowledge significant attention is yet to be given to the aesthetic objects representative of theatre produced by visual artists and curated by high-profile arts institutions in recent years and what might be at stake therein.

Second, my sustained engagement with art historical and museum-oriented texts reflects the fact that these fields have been, and continue to be, so influential in terms of how we think of and define performance. Writer, artist, and curator Paul O'Neill reminds us that exhibitions are 'contemporary forms of rhetoric, complex expressions of persuasion, whose strategies aim to produce a prescribed set of values and social relations for their audiences.'[29] This book is inherently concerned with the mediation of our experiences of visual and performed objects by the text-based critical discourses which surround display practices. The challenge of exhibiting performance and what this might mean has emerged in recent years, and been articulated by museum practitioners, as complex and significant. James Fowler, formerly of London's Theatre Museum, has described this task as the museum's 'greatest challenge' since performance is, at least by definition, 'one of the great uncollectables'.[30] From the position of the art museum, and informed by *Collecting the Performative: A Research Network Examining Emerging Practice for Collecting and Conserving Performance-based Art* (2012–13), Laurenson and van Saaze echo this perspective, reiterating how 'live performances were considered uncollectable because of their intangible nature.' The assertion of performance as that which cannot be collected is indissociable from classifications of performance as ephemeral. 'Being non-material,'

Laurenson and van Saaze continue, 'performance art has long been considered at odds with well established systems and processes for managing art as a material object.'[31] It is this dichotomy, between the 'immateriality' associated with performance and its identity as 'uncollectable' versus the museum, a curated environment linked to preservation and the collection of objects, that I want to unpick. Much recent scholarship in the performance field has been concerned with, what Amelia Jones calls, 'the failure of the live to "stick" outside of its representational modes.'[32] I am interested here in moments where performance does 'stick' to and in forms that transmute the ephemeral.

Ephemeral

The complexity of the 'live' as a condition for performance, itself a thorny category, has been multiply responded to since Phelan's foundational account in 1993 and is marked by the number of recent publications attending specifically to the implications of this ontology. Addressing performance's seemingly inherent resistance to collection, Bennett in her writing on theatre in museum contexts is not unaware of the traditional distinctions between the two spaces that her book connects: theatre as directed towards the present, museums as invested in materials from the past.[33] While live art established itself in opposition to the commodified art object, the 'liveness' of performance has since come to serve to some degree the historical purpose of the museum and legitimate an underestimation and covert limitation of its potential, as well as a recent marketisation of its terms. Indeed, Rebecca Schneider in *Performing Remains: Art and War in Times of Theatrical Reenactment* (2011) suggests that, more so than in the theatre, 'it is in the context of the museum, gallery, and art market that performance appears to *primarily* offer disappearance.' The demarcation of performance as ephemeral and transitory, Schneider surmises, is a 'definition well suited to the concerns of art history and the curatorial pressure to understand performance in the museal context where performance appeared to challenge object status'.[34] The history of performance studies is inflected by expectations and agendas biased to the primacy of visual arts and gallery-based practices. Rather than resisting this legacy of influence, and some might say constraint, and by instead attending to events and objects currently occupying settings of exhibition, it is possible to identify and tease out ways in which contemporary curatorial practices now proffer alternatives to performance as disappearing.

While public museums traditionally instituted 'an order of things that was meant to last', cultural theorist Tony Bennett reminds us that temporary exhibitions, such as those addressed in this project, work to make 'the order of things dynamic, mobilizing it strategically in relation to the more immediate ideological and political exigencies of the particular moment.'[35] In contrast to the affected permanence and preservation of traditional museological display, temporary exhibitions, as well as the visitors who attend these events, occupy a gallery for only a limited time. As short-term installations, both are easy to associate with the sort of transience more usually aligned with practices of performance and the effort of gathering in a particular place at a particular time. Drawing on tropes typically allied with the event of theatre, these exhibitions initially appear, like the Great Exhibitions of the past, as 'spectacular gestures which briefly held the attention of the world before disappearing into an abrupt oblivion'. For curator Paul Greenhalgh such *Ephemeral Vistas* are 'victims of their planned temporality', their short duration limiting their efficacy.[36] Rather than thinking temporary exhibitions purely in terms of the transient or fleeting, I propose that, within the contexts examined in this project, the relation between the traditionally static order of the museum and the temporality usually definitive of performative modes is more complex. Such concepts as 'ephemerality' and the 'live' are helpfully identified as 'not so much the defining features of our objects of study as issues at the heart of our disciplinary subject' by performance scholar Barbara Kirshenblatt-Gimblett.[37] As 'issues', rather than ontologies, these models are open to debate, challenge, and revision.

This book proposes that the limits of the 'ephemeral live' might be rethought, not merely on stages, empty or otherwise, but, as Kirshenblatt-Gimblett likewise endorses, 'in relation to artifacts in a museum vitrine.' For Kirshenblatt-Gimblett, performance is 'an art form that lacks a distinctive medium' and because of this we encounter 'performance art that is expressly not theatre; and art performance that dematerializes the art object and approaches the condition of performance.'[38] It is this idea of performance as without specific medium that I want to pursue further by inhabiting the intersection between the displayed and performed so that these genre and boundary limits might be extended, through and in their interrelation, towards revised formulations. In *Theatre, Intimacy and Engagement* (2008), theatre scholar Alan Read sets out a context wherein we might acknowledge the transitory nature and 'liveliness' of human existence by engaging with theatres which work self-reflexively in relation to their 'epochal' status. He calls these spaces 'The Last Human Venue.' By taking up this location as a banner under which to work for its 2013 season, the Homo Novus International Contemporary Theatre Festival in Riga demonstrated that this concept offers a useful critical tool for thinking about theatricality and contemporary located practices. For me, its value stems in part from Read's judicious statement that the 'disappearances fleetingly thought of as the defining "being" of performance, its late twentieth-century ontology as a theatre of exits, would in the twenty-first century give way to the problem of theatre's appearance'.[39] *Theatre, Exhibition, and Curation: Displayed & Performed* is concerned specifically with alternative frames of reference through which performance might appear.

From the perspective of experienced curators and conservators it is not, following Laurenson and van Saaze, 'the problem of non-materiality that currently represents the greatest challenge for museums in collecting performance,' but rather the reality that the staging of live events requires a different set of skills to those provided by curatorial training.[40] Performances test museum systems not least, Chris Dercon agrees, because 'they are often complex to show and do not readily fit into existing frameworks'.[41] In looking for auxiliary modes of performance, we might turn to the art object and to curated exhibitions which situate live forms in an alternative relation to object status. Museums are, in the terms of Director of Tate from 1988 to 2017 Nicholas Serota, 'no longer just repositories: they are sites of experience'. According to Serota, art institutions must strive to 'generate a *condition* in which visitors can experience a sense of discovery in looking at *particular* paintings, sculptures or installations in a *particular* room at a *particular* moment, rather than find themselves standing on the conveyor belt of history.'[42] In seeking this particularity, we might say museums must adopt forms more akin with an ephemeral ontology of presence.[43] Traditionally the museum has been a 'monument', hushed, and transcendental, with collection policy driven towards, what Serota terms, the '*complete* representation of the major movements hung in chronological sequence'.[44] Moving away from principles of wholeness, succession and an experience which seeks a perfection beyond the human – we might remember with Alan Read that 'the term collective has the fortunate remainder of the *act* of collecting within it' – Serota admits that the 'encyclopaedic and dictionary functions of the museum are neither achievable nor desirable.'[45] Rather, following Serota's proposition, museums must look instead towards the sorts of singularity of experience customarily associated with performance. Displays should generate a 'condition', perhaps theatrical, which allows for subjective encounter.

(Under)Groundwork 2: Returning to Empty Stages

This is where the Tate Tanks appear and where it is useful to my current project to excavate a little further. Neither studio nor gallery in the traditional sense, these chambers offer a hybrid space for performance. 'Raw, versatile, circular and unique', Chris Dercon proposes that as 'neither white cube nor black box, they provide an entirely new type of space for Tate Modern, and museums internationally', a venue, I suggest, both displayed and performed which finds its functionality precisely in this dualism.[46] Keen to emphasise that the Tanks should not be viewed either as merely a 'fashion trend, or as an alternative to the white cube', architect Jacques Herzog promotes a reading which sees these spaces more significantly as 'the roots of something to come.'[47] Indeed the Tanks were closed following the short season of performances and events titled *Art in Action* to enable the larger-scale site development project for which they provide a supporting structure, which includes further provision for an expanded range of art forms, and which opened to the public on 17 June 2016. Neither one mode, nor the other, and indicative of something yet to appear, the Tanks, in the evocative potential of their grey and subterranean industrialism, resound with the image by Etchells and Glendinning introduced at the outset of this chapter, uniting in their shape and form the respective idealisms and complexes of the empty stage or space for performance and exhibition. Approaching such venues, questions of representation and of enactment come into play. With regards to the construction of the *Empty Stages* images, for example, the performer (Etchells) draws near to each stage with one question in mind: 'what might I *do* in this space?' The photographer, Glendinning narrates at the *Performance Studies international* (PSi) conference held at Stanford University in 2013, with another: 'what might I *see* in this space?'[48] Like the Tanks, these photographic places for performance pool two engagements: acting and observing. The possibility of each depends on a precise emptiness and apparent neutrality iconic across discourses of visual culture. Picturing a gallery, alongside a theatre, an 'image comes to mind of a white, ideal space that, more than any single picture, may be the archetypal image of twentieth century art'.[49] The 'installation shot, *sans* figures', and the associated 'eternity of display' which artist Brian O'Doherty so astutely narrates, is, however, like the emptiness of the *Empty Stages*, an aesthetic invention; the paradox of both environs is that they function, of course, as far from vacant. In both cases, the claim to emptiness and the potential for inscription works to conceal the historical specificity and institutional possession of different configurations of the theatrical stage on the one hand and the modernist construction of the white cube on the other.

There seems to be a significant correlation between the convention of the ostensibly neutral gallery or empty stage and exhibition practices which operate at a limit between display and performance; the former reappears and is revised across a number of cases both within and beyond the limits of *Theatre, Exhibition, and Curation: Displayed & Performed*. Let me focus in on a couple of examples drawn from spaces and events outside the remit of this book so as not to pre-empt its analyses. *A Bigger Splash: Painting after Performance*, for example, included Romanian artist Geta Brătescu's 1975 *Towards White*, a sequence of documentary images, framed as one, in which the artist constructs a white cube, not around her work but around herself in a space which might be her domestic studio. Along the river at the Hayward Gallery in London, American artist Doug Wheeler's *Untitled 1969*, a work labelled by the Exhibition Guide as a free floating square in an 'immaculate' environment, appears as part of *Light Show* (2013), an exhibition curated by Cliff Lauson which meditates on light as a medium for art making, drawing a parallel which one MA student working on my 'Collecting Performance' module at King's College London in 2014, Aikaterini Papadakou, articulated succinctly and eloquently as between light art and live art.

Operating between the empty stage and the white cube, the appeal to emptiness made by spaces between the displayed and the performed, following art historian Georges Didi-Huberman, draws 'from its kind of negativity the strength of a multiple deployment; it makes possible not one or two univocal significations, but entire constellations of meaning'.[50]

While evoking the sometimes 'univocal significations' delimited by certain models of visual arts and performance practices – visual arts displayed as 'permanent', performance as 'ephemeral' – the arrested square of *Empty Stages* and the spherical hybrids of the Tanks look beyond the limitations of both forms. Artists and galleries are constructing settings which disrupt the precise division of performance and display. Whereas, as Catherine Wood articulates, the 'neutral space of the white cube defined the physical frame within the ritual of art viewing in the last century – this itself superseding the importance of the literal frame around a traditional oil painting or the pedestal supporting a sculpture ... – it might be that this alternative frame is emerging as being important now.'[51] Within Tate Modern, the Tanks offer a space in which to determine alternative models and practices of curation. In their design, returning to the terms of Jacques Herzog, the air of 'rawness and immediacy holds an enormous fascination for all of us, and in many ways is in opposition to the existing galleries.'[52] The architect's words signal a broader social interest in forms not overworked and the sort of 'immediacy' most often associated with performance.

Performance Temporalities

The marketability of the kind of experiential qualities usually allied with performance is reinforced by Catherine Wood's acknowledgement, at a conference event at the University of Westminster on 'Exhibiting Performance' in 2013, that sourcing sponsorship had been relatively easier at that time for the development of Tate Modern's performance events as compared with other areas of the gallery's programme.[53] Processes of performance are, as explored in more detail later in this project, active in our engagements within gallery contexts. Beyond this, a certain kind of theatricality seems to be increasingly inherent to the construction of exhibitions and to display practices, though this sense of the dramatic, as I have already signalled, moves beyond any direct transition to the live. Museums and galleries are, as we have seen, 'not neutral containers offering a transparent, unmediated experience of art'; rather their complexity, art historian Emma Barker suggests, 'makes "spectacle" a valuable but also problematic term for considering the production and consumption of the visual arts.'[54] The notion of 'spectacle' bridges current curatorial and performance practices, uniting connotations of a specifically arranged public display with subtexts of entertainment, the summative effect of which is an exhibition of specified character, which might principally be a distinct ontology or appearance of performance.

Ephemeral modes offer to display practices the promise of contemporary resonance, of implication in a specific cultural moment. At the same time performance acknowledges, what theatre scholar P.A. Skantze calls, the 'longing for preserving the beauty of an object.' Existing in a relation between the effectiveness of the temporary and that of remaining still for a moment, the 'culture of collecting exhibits instances of the interchange between the permanent and the performed'.[55] During the aforementioned symposium in Westminster, Wood affirmed that questions of temporality are, of course, fundamental to the scheduling of performance in the museum. The persisting 'eternal' status of the neutral gallery implies a static relation to time in direct contrast with models of performance founded in disappearance. As we have seen, recent decades mark, what Jones calls, an 'obsessive interest in histories of performance or live art, ephemeral works that expose the contradiction between durationality and aesthetics – between the passage of time and the materiality that art discourse requires to substantiate the value of works of art as "unique".' Describing one mode of response in this context, Jones suggests 're-enactment actually establishes itself from the get-go as simultaneously *representational* and *live*'.[56] This book is concerned with a related intersection between depiction and enactment, characterised here as displayed and performed. It is this changeability between temporality and object status that this book investigates, progressing from the rehearsed alignment of theatricality and ephemerality within theatre and performance research in order to tease out a new temporality for performance with which contemporary curated exhibitions implicitly experiment.

Exhibiting Performance

The Tate Tanks specify a move beyond performance programming in the gallery which operates on a one-off basis. We can see here, as Kirshenblatt-Gimblett writes of other sorts of museological context, a 'critical shift from an informing museology (the exhibit as a neutral vehicle for the transmission of information) to a performing museology', or from display to performance.[57] Museums are showing increasing signs of moving towards more active and performative practices of curation, something Bennett deems to be a 'theatrical turn in museum exhibition,' and while this is very often a positive development, I would like to note here a distinct discomfort with 'theatre' being asked to stand unqualified for possibilities of accessibility, engagement, and participation.[58] Moreover, as Kirshenblatt-Gimblett goes on to state, it remains significant that the museum's role as a 'repository of objects is both very old and very resistant to change.'[59] The classic delineation of their purpose as institutions wherein things are gathered for safekeeping, preservation, and, display is something many influential museum practitioners are eager to retain. Nicholas Serota, for example, asserts that 'stasis also remains a valuable component of the museum.'[60] And, from the position of a curator with significant responsibility for performance, Catherine Wood agrees that this shift towards a greater investment in 'live' work does not mean that material objects no longer have a place in the museum.[61] Rather, we might identify an engagement with performance accommodated to or influenced by the traditional object-centric focus of the museum.

Newly developed gallery spaces, including the Tanks, as well as recently curated exhibitions, might be seen, as Kirshenblatt-Gimblett also describes, to 'extend museological values and methods (collection, documentation, preservation, presentation, evaluation and interpretation) to living persons, their knowledge, practices, artifacts, social worlds' and, I suggest, by extension to practices and processes of performance.[62] Speaking on strategies for 'Exhibiting Performance' at Westminster University (2013), Wood describes Tate's policy as directed specifically towards performance work which is strongly related to visual arts practice; it is the criteria of a more traditional museological agenda which dictates the remit for the inclusion of performance within the gallery.[63] It is this agenda which has enabled certain sectors of the performance field to discredit to some extent the value of many gallery-based engagements with live and theatricalised work. Coming from the parallel tradition of the Theatre Museum, James Fowler observes that the influence of, what he calls, 'the traditional materials-based, object-centred thinking' inherent in much museum policy means that the majority of exhibitions giving attention to performance do so primarily via archival documentation related to specific theatrical productions.[64] In contrast to the display practices described by Fowler, where there is also an attachment to the responsibility of archiving, the exhibitions examined in this project bring together associations of objects apparently referential of performance more broadly, that is to say of an ontological re-imagining of the medium rather than of any particular previous act.

By exhibiting theatrical objects not necessarily remaining from a precise 'live' event, such exhibition practices present an alternative relation between display and performance. From within a culture in which an exhibition has conventionally manifested as a static arrangement of objects, positioned according to shared characteristics and determined by curatorial aims, an increasing number of object-centric events of display are taking on the potentialities and problematics of performance. Traditionally, borrowing Bennett's terms, 'museums have housed a collection of objects arranged in particular taxonomies that determined the fundamentals of display.'[65] The question I want to investigate is what happens when the explicit organising principle is performance? We might agree with dramaturge, curator, and writer Eda Čufer that the 'advantage of the static arts is, of course, that we can contemplate at leisure a transient state of nature or daily life, and observe (and potentially intervene into) a multitude of its relationships and gradations.'[66] Making an intervention in terms of what might count as performance, and the forms in which it might be possible to identify performative action, this book builds on Čufer's belief that art forms most often conceived as static might enable more sustained contemplation of a transient state, expanding the terms of the latter to include ontologies and processes of performance itself.

Of significance here is a question of curation, a practice involving not only the presentation and display of objects but also experience, which performance studies seems particularly well equipped to answer. According to

Serota, the dilemma for modern art museums rests between the terms of *Experience or Interpretation*; in the 'best museums of the future', he proposes, some 'rooms and works will be fixed, the pole star around which others will turn'. Delivering the 1996 Walter Neurath Memorial Lecture, Serota promoted a mode of exhibition between experience and object related to that which this project traces. It is no coincidence that this lecture was reprinted in 2013, and in a climate in which principles of 'combining works by different artists to give selective readings, both of art and of the history of art,' which Serota identifies as underwriting curatorial practice, are now generating partial presentations of performance. The exhibitions restaged here combine a need, identified by Serota, for 'places of prolonged concentration and contemplation' with the avowed and ephemeral terms of performance so that the 'dialectical principle' (Serota's term) according to which exhibition practices increasingly operate, might be thought as between display and performance.[67] To impose a single discourse, historical, theoretical, or curatorial, onto an art object is to limit the range of cultural referents which inform its construction and to which it might communicate. My interest here is in interactions between individual art works, the curatorial concept of the exhibition in which they appear, and the specific ontology of performance that this arrangement implies.

Displayed & Performed: Methodology and Chapters

The book's key terms and argument, which are to do specifically with the displayed and performed, are intimately related to the exhibited and the theatrical. My concern throughout is about writing and reading performance between these two traditions and terminologies. In order to so do, I take in this book a strategic and particular position with regards to the interpretation and inscribing of events. Throughout the project, I employ a dialogical method which plays through a form of conversation complementary to, rather than conflictual with, the subject in which my enquiry is avowedly embedded. This respectful mode of writing involves a certain cohabitation and communication with its materials which reflects the fact that I sincerely wish the book to be part of a summative and on-going dialogue in a field which I value precisely for its prioritising of engagement in discussion, in support, and in mutual critique. To my mind, a loss of this kind of dialogical thinking typifies some more dogmatic and less-tolerant contemporary thinking in which a more confrontational encounter can pass too easily for critical care. My preferred approach is necessary in a project attentive to our cultural encounters being negotiated via text-based critical and curatorial discourses. It is with this focus in mind that I consider the possibility of, and put into practice, revised methodologies for investigating performance in situations of display. The expanded models of analysis I want to introduce here are realised significantly by my taking of exhibition as a primary unit of discourse for this study.

Curation Together

While I could have chosen to progress, like many recent surveys, by engaging with individual art objects or the work of specific practitioners and collectives, in this book I instead approach artworks in terms of their *curation together* and develop a position via the sustained examination of events which present a direct interaction between two fields. Alert to an exciting and original arena of work, *Theatre, Exhibition, and Curation: Displayed & Performed* restages a number of temporary exhibitions presented by high-profile arts institutions over six years. These examples are indicative of a general trend for staging intersections between performance and display, most often in gallery contexts and through the form of exhibition. My emphasis here is on large-scale art museums precisely because of the relative visibility and degree of institutionalisation of practice signified by representation within such international venues. This focus should not be read as unconscious of the wide range of related curatorial projects engaging with increasing frequency with performance in respected smaller galleries and other less formal locations.[68] It is also not my meaning to suggest that ideas of display and performance are being explored only in art galleries, indeed other types of museum are engaged with in relevant studies by Susan Bennett (2013), Valerie Casey (2005), Barbara Kirshenblatt-Gimblett (1998), James Clifford (1988), and others. Rather, the specific operations with which my study is concerned enable a theorisation of this relation not possible elsewhere. What draws me to this engagement with high-profile exhibitions in established art world contexts is precisely my experience of charting, visiting, and associating this specific history of practice over a period of six years and the consequences which provoking this particular idea of exhibition might have for performance and vice-versa.

My intention is to investigate the formal construction and conceptual premise of a necessarily limited yet illustrative number of case studies so as to develop a theory of the displayed and performed that is not only suggestive for the particular exhibitions in question but might also be applied to the interpretation, analysis, and production of a wider body of contemporary practice. So as to mark out features, including inversions in the respective situations of performer and art object, performer and visitor, and visitor and exhibit, common to these events, the chapters address each exhibition, and the workings of the objects connected therein, cumulatively. This approach represents what I hope is a strong alternative to the overtly socio-economic analyses which currently prevail in the performance field, as well as to art historical commentaries that tend to be coming more exclusively from a visual arts or allied critical theory perspective. In her study of socially and aesthetically contingent practices, performance scholar Shannon Jackson observes contemporary rejections of the 'static object conventions of visual art,' as well as the temporal conditions of dramatic theatre, and offers an astute reminder that disciplinary training necessarily inflects our readings; we encounter, for example, relational art differently if we interpret it as a revision of sculpture or of theatre.[69] Jackson's work centres on a form of response inflected by previous experience within a specific arena. My book applies performance theory to exhibition events and directs towards performance practices approaches often taken for granted in display contexts. By reframing performance within a theatricalised concept of exhibition, my hope is to reveal the reception of one art form as not so much mediated by prior encounter as via a set of expectations associated with another.

There is a question throughout the book of drawing focus between the exhibitions about which I am writing and the individual works displayed therein. In some places, single artworks may seem to become the main support for the argument being progressed, but even and especially in these instances the accumulation of these objects and the curation that has made these works the ones to which we are given to attend remains a significant unifying factor. What is indicated by my focus on certain exhibits at particular moments is an understanding that, though associated in a curated gallery, there is no expectation that the works will in themselves modify so as to speak to one other. Rather, we as visitors are invited to do the work of thinking these objects in connection under the guidance and suggestion of a curatorial regime. Some will, of course, stand out and remain with us in different ways, even as we are encouraged to consider their capacity to comment on or elucidate a certain mode of working, idea, or theme. In addition, it is not possible within a single text to attend to every object in each exhibition. The criteria for inclusion are not driven by personal judgement of artistic merit but by each work's capacity to remain in my thinking about and towards this book and to contribute in relation to those others discussed, and to an overall theory of display and performance. In this way, throughout *Theatre, Exhibition, and Curation: Displayed & Performed* certain combinations of objects, when considered as collections, come to approach questions of ontology and present particular perspectives on performance.

Collective Terminologies

Theatre and Performance

To talk about theatre and performance is to occupy a space already preoccupied with questions of exhibition, curation, and display. Performance involves activities and practices both social and artistic and refers to a specific collection and means of writing and theoretical engagement. It includes in its frame and is related to certain events of theatre, something which is particularly significant in the first and second chapters of this book, and it is as generalised concepts, experiences, or encounters taken up in arts contexts that *Theatre, Exhibition, and Curation: Displayed & Performed* engages with these terms. Emerging from a reaction against the confines of the gallery space on the one hand and traditional theatre venues on the other, performance, in the sense of performance art, is a genre easy to situate between theatre and exhibition. That said, I have found myself involved recently in a number of conversations with peers and colleagues who agree that the distinction between the relative terms 'theatre' and 'performance' may be felt and conceived less acutely, or at least differently, by the generation of scholars emerging in the 2000s and 2010s as compared with those practitioners and theorists who went before us and who needed to, and we are grateful that they did, mark the divergences between these modes more urgently and forcibly.[70] What we are witnessing is a revaluation of forms, including performance and photography, across large-scale art museum sites, which corresponds with an allied revaluation of 'theatre' by nominally 'performance' scholars and, sadly, a devaluation of the social worth of the arts more broadly in certain factions of the contemporary political sphere.

In recent years we have seen a turn away from the anti-theatrical drive most often associated with performance studies. To give a few UK-based examples, in 2005 Richard Gough and Nicholas Ridout edited a special issue of the journal *Performance Research* 'On Theatre' which incorporated a number of photographs by Tim Etchells and Hugo Glendinning from the *Empty Stages* series; scholars including Nicholas Ridout (*Passionate Amateurs: Theatre, Communism, and Love,* 2013), as well as Alan Read (*Theatre, Intimacy & Engagement: The Last Human Venue,* 2008; *Theatre in the Expanded Field: Seven Approaches to Performance,* 2013), Joe Kelleher (*The Illuminated Theatre: Studies on the Suffering of Images,* 2015), and others, have clearly associated themselves with the theatre in recent publications; and in *Drama/Theatre/Performance* (2004), Simon Shepherd and Mick Wallis admit that their book was originally conceived by the publisher in two volumes – *Drama and Theatre* and *Performance and Performativity* – but that they resisted this structure because they felt, and I agree, that this format would 'work to shore up a hierarchised binary division that needs deconstruction and is indeed beginning to crumble.' The division, they continue, 'tends to relegate "theatre" to literary models and the Aristotelian tradition; and to suggest a necessary coincidence between forms of aesthetic performance, concerns with the performativity of everyday life and the theorisation of culture through the frame of performance.'[71] While the latter might seem especially relevant to a book engaged with reading exhibitions through and in relation to performance, it seems useful here to articulate how I am thinking about and drawing on the respective terms of 'theatre' and 'performance', both of which appear in the book's title and both of which develop and unfold in different forms and associations throughout its contents.

Although Shepherd and Wallis are keen to assert that they are not offering definitions of these idioms but rather mapping how they have been interpreted and thought distinctly and together in different periods, contexts, and institutions, a statement made in their introduction is particularly resonant for me and for this study; 'performance,' they write, is now 'an inclusive term covering: performance genres such as music, dance, theatre and performance art; the specific genre of "performance art"; and a paradigm for the investigation of culture at large.'[72] It is within this definition that my own current understanding of 'performance' rests. For me too, performance is a collecting term which, even in this understanding, retains a particular relationship with visual art and theatrical experimentation. It embraces a wide variety of forms of production, including more traditional forms of theatre, and signals also a particular sort of methodology, in this case what I have called earlier, after Peggy Phelan, a 'performance-minded' approach to exhibition events and the visual artworks they associate. It is safe to say, then, that the term 'performance', as defined in these estimations, will be something primary and essential throughout *Theatre, Exhibition, and Curation*, and particularly as it comes to be connected in a symbiotic relation with 'display', the other and co-operative concept in my subtitle and theory.

Theatre and Exhibition

The word 'theatre', as connoting a particular genre of performance-making, is especially significant to my case study examples in Chapter 2 but again has a broader relevance to the project at large. It is useful to remember at this point of introduction, with Shepherd and Wallis amongst others, that the term 'theatre' derives from the Greek *theatron*, 'part of a cluster of words associated both with looking and with "theory".'[73] This primary meaning of the genealogy of 'theatre' is especially pertinent in a book which builds a 'theory' on the relation between display and performance (including theatre) by engaging with events which happen in galleries, that is to say, in sites still premised, despite the legacy of 'relational' artworks explored in Chapter 3, on a sense of heightened visual perception and as venues for 'looking'. In his preface to the interviews collected by Hans Ulrich Obrist as *A Brief History of Curating* (2008), Museum of Modern Art (MoMA) curator Christophe Cherix recalls former director of the Philadelphia Museum of Art Anne d'Harnoncourt's response to a question about advice for young curators. In her reply, d'Harnoncourt in turn cites British artists Gilbert & George's maxim: to 'look and look, and then to look again'. Curatorial practice, like that of the theatre, has at its most basic a commitment to looking. While, according to Cherix, the role, methodology, and legacy of the curator remain 'largely undefined,' what is evident, both within his narration of the evolution of the curatorial field and the exhibitions we see in galleries, is an historical shift wherein 'the majority of the most influential shows were organized by arts professionals rather than artists.'[74] In this way, the perspectives and interpretations of a particular individual or institutional curatorial team become instrumental to the available platforms in which visitors are able to view and engage with art.

At the heart of *Theatre, Exhibition, and Curation: Displayed & Performed* is a concern for the context of an artwork's presentation and the way in which, since the late nineteenth century, art has become 'deeply intertwined with the history of its exhibitions.'[75] Perhaps the most succinct expression of this interrelation between art and exhibition, and one also cited by Cherix, comes in Reesa

Greenberg, Bruce W. Ferguson, and Sandy Nairne's Introduction to *Thinking About Exhibitions* (1996) wherein these art historians, curators, and critics articulate how exhibitions 'have become *the* medium through which most art becomes known.'[76] That being the case, it seems only logical for this study to take that medium of knowing as its methodological optic. Greenberg, Ferguson, and Nairne situate exhibitions as part 'spectacle, part socio-historical event, part structuring device'.[77] Existing simultaneously as spectacular, culturally specific, and structurally determining, exhibitions form a key part of any theory correlating the displayed and the performed.

What interests me in this book, and where I think the exhibitions with which I am engaged differ from, or progress further, experiments in object-based performance dating from the 1960s, is in their taking up of theatre and performance in different ways as their subject, or as the determining factor in their curatorial conception. Productive for rethinking the connection between the displayed and the performed and the terms in which we are able to address this relation, the exhibitions examined through this book trouble models of performance founded on ephemerality. They exceed the form of the static object in perpetual display and the disappearing performance and might, therefore, be understood as expressions which operate beyond both performed modes and object-centric display practices by occupying their interstice. Resisting the division of poetic from performative analysis, W. B. Worthen reminds us that traditional forms of theatre-making have always involved an interaction between object and enactment, that is to say a 'dialectical in-betweenness' present most often in the 'encounter between writing-as-an-object (the book) and performance'. Situated between object and event, for Worthen too the 'theatre is a transitional place, not where we suspend disbelief, but where we are a visible and lively part of an event'.[78] At stake throughout my book is a concern for our position as visitors, that is to say, with our modes of attending, in the theatre and in galleries.

A Note on Attention

Describing venues for performance, Catherine Wood writes of a space within the museum which 'contradicts the institution's function to preserve and protect, allowing things to disperse, dissolve and disintegrate' by being structured from 'configurations of bodies and their attendant concentrations of minds'; a 'space that can be configured and reconfigured endlessly because it is made of people, and attention.'[79] Often throughout this study the ways in which specific art objects operate across terrains of the displayed and the performed depends on the mental concentration of gallery visitors. In the above quotation from Wood, this sort of attention creates spaces contradictory to traditional ideologies of conservation and curation wherein alternative arrangements of body and object can be imagined and repositioned. A particular focus in this study concerns how our attention is 'arrested' by particular exhibits and events and this undertone develops out of Georges Didi-Huberman's fundamental argument about a particular, long-standing version of art history and the tone of certainty traditionally so prevalent in such discourses. When *Confronting Images*, efficacy, following Didi-Huberman, depends not on the indisputable transmission of knowledge but rather on a kind of 'suspended attention, a prolonged suspension of the moment of reaching conclusions, where interpretation would have time to deploy itself in several dimensions, between the grasped visibility and the lived ordeal of relinquishment.'[80] Sustained encounters with exhibitions and objects, displayed and performed, are founded, I would suggest, in such acts of live abandon and arrested attention.

Collected Chapters

As should be clear by now, my methodology and cases are focused by this sort of more intense attendance, by the ideologies associated with specific cultural institutions and by the conventions according to which exhibitions and performances are curated. My chapters seek to illuminate specific modes of operation where one form gives way to another, where performance is arrested and reappears in exhibition, only to transition again beyond display. This programme is written by way of four chapters, each directed by a particular problematic and a pair of case studies, not easily contained either within theatrical or museological models, which generate more associatively than individually. The broad range of materials considered here thereby begins to hint at how key concepts in the performance field are linked together and how they might be associated differently. All of the examples were curated within art institutions during the same historical moment (2007–12). Each case study furthers the definition of an alternative ontology for performance emerging in symbiosis with high-profile display practice and is articulated through and alongside another event which throws it into relief. The exhibitions are partnered to accord with material connections, correspondences, and contradictions and so as to progress the development of a particular and summative argument about the ways in which ideas of display and performance might complicate, unsettle, and expand one another's ontologies.

While, for the most part, the exhibitions on which I will focus are gallery based, my first chapter addresses in addition a theatre-based example in order to establish from the outset a broader connection and interchange between practices of display and of performance. Chapter 1, 'Performer & Exhibit: Theatrical Conditions', elicits challenges to orthodox ways in which exhibition and performance are understood through attention to cases in which these spaces and practices are reversed. This section is dedicated to a detailed examination of *Drama Queens*, a play by Berlin-based artists Elmgreen & Dragset with text by Tim Etchells, performed at the Old Vic Theatre, London, in 2008. This dramatic work is addressed alongside its hitherto unrecognised inversion evident in *Marina Abramović Presents...*, an exhibition held at the Whitworth Art Gallery, Manchester, in 2009. Abramović is at the centre of what Amelia Jones calls, 'an industrial-strength institutionalization of performance histories.'[81] It is thus important to include an analysis of Abramović's work, as it appears in a form most relevant to the ambitions of this project, precisely because her recent exhibitions have drawn international attention and debate and will certainly have art historical importance. These events have also, to my mind, served as a litmus test for the inadequacy of vocabularies currently available for engaging critically with contemporary practice. These case studies give opportunity to address how aesthetic objects operate in museums and in performance and the relative repositioning of live performers as exhibits in the gallery and sculptural objects as performers before an audience.

Assuming what we might think of as a more conventional form of theatre, *Drama Queens* sheds light on the restrictions and possibilities of visual arts exhibition by mobilising six iconic sculptures on stage, while *Marina Abramović Presents...* sets a series of performances within a gallery space emptied of the art objects it usually contains. Explored together, these events raise questions about the performance of non-human objects and invert the expected play of movement and stasis within theatre and museum contexts, rethinking the relation between performer and exhibit, and exposing the physical and aesthetic conventionalities of theatre and gallery as spaces in which to view art. The paradox inherent to Abramović's recent projects is elucidated by Jones in terms of an attempt to present work within 'contradictory frameworks – both within these terms of aesthetics, presenting the work in the heart of the international contemporary art world and constructing around it the accoutrements of the typical art museum exhibition to disseminate it through the catalogue and film, *and* within discourses of live performance art, with their privileging of the live, durational, and ephemeral.'[82] Exploring a pair of case studies situated between two frameworks most often constructed, borrowing again from Jones, as 'discursively and institutionally incompatible', this chapter enables a reengagement with the traditional alignment of exhibition with the static display and accumulation of objects and theatricality with temporality and 'liveness' in performance studies through the identification and analysis of performances which work towards display rather than disappearance.

Throughout *Theatre, Exhibition, and Curation: Displayed & Performed*, there is a concern with the specificity of the contemporary moment, with historical shifts, and with anachronistic references to other related instances. In order to expand the scope of the project, in Chapter 2, 'Theatre & Gallery: Turning Away From Performance', I give attention to two 'foundational' moments in the history of performance and display. The first, *Renoir at the Theatre: Looking at La Loge*, curated by Barnaby Wright at the Courtauld Gallery, London, in 2008, is an historical example of visual arts practice in dialogue with spaces and behaviours of performance. The second, *The World as a Stage*, curated by Catherine Wood and Jessica Morgan at Tate Modern,

London, in 2007–8, acts as a contemporary reply in which artists meditate on the notion of the performed within the context of an exhibition environment. This past perspective and present response show these display practices to go beyond mere curatorial fad, though it is important to stress that the former is not introduced as a nineteenth century example in an otherwise contemporary study but rather to demonstrate how a range of high-profile arts institutions are engaging with theatre through the relative means available to them. Rethinking the relation between theatre and gallery, this chapter exhibits a less firmly oppositional relation and develops the inversion of expected models of the motionless object and mobile visitor performer, given in the first chapter, into a more nuanced interplay. Exemplary of performance as displayed within a curatorial concept, these cases present non-specific or imagined theatrical scenes and object referents of indefinite productions. Here acts of static display and fleeting performance reside within single objects so that each form is redefined as latent in the other.

This second chapter initiates a focus on the theatre-goer, the interchangeability of performer and audience, and the relative position of the gallery visitor integral to the remainder of the project. Chapter 3, 'Visitor & Performer: The Return of the Relational', picks up this emphasis, engaging with a set of comparatively new yet increasingly hegemonic vocabularies within the field of performance studies in which it has become usual to conceive of particular kinds of attention and engagement in recent years. Concerned specifically with terminologies revolving around the participatory and the spectatorial, this chapter examines two exhibitions constructed via relational referents and exemplary of what I am identifying as a contemporary 'return' to relational aesthetics. *Double Agent* was curated by prominent theorist of participatory art Claire Bishop and former Director of Exhibitions Mark Sladen at the ICA, London, in 2008 and *theanyspacewhatever* by Nancy Spector at the Solomon R. Guggenheim Museum in New York from 2008 to 2009. In this section, I engage directly with notions of activated spectatorship and the agency of gallery visitors without assuming any easy correlation between relational artworks and participation in order to develop an enhanced understanding of the relation between gallery visitor and performer. It is my contention that it is in terms of paradigms usually associated with performance practice that it is most useful to critique and re-position relational aesthetics. Revisiting practices associated with curator and art theorist Nicolas Bourriaud's designation of 'relational aesthetics' during the 1990s, within these exhibitions acts of reception are perplexed and accentuated so that the visitor appears both as displayed and performing. Within this chapter, Bourriaud's definition of the art object as an '*interstice*' between two components is expanded, such that the constituent parts of this intervention are proposed to be display and performance.[83]

The third and fourth chapters focus specifically on the agency of gallery visitors and issues of accessibility, as well as on the objects and exhibitions discussed as forms of institutional critique. Chapter 4, 'Gesture & Object:

Digital Display and Arrested Attention', develops an extended investigation of the phenomenon of visitation in order to plot around this motif further opportunities for epistemological re-categorisation and the rethinking of practice. Restaging the conceptual clashes of disappearance and documentation, this chapter investigates more specifically the transitory encounters involved in visiting and interpreting visual arts exhibitions, as well as instances of remote access, by evaluating digital approaches which function across modalities of the displayed and the performed. Technologies for digital display are particularly relevant to a project concerned with the possibility of encountering performance by means of other media. So as to explore the potential of digital tools for the curation and dissemination of performance, this chapter reunites two London-based venues also paired in Chapter 2 in order to take a digitally inflected approach to their programmes. The methodology tested within *Frank Auerbach: London Building Sites 1952–62*, an exhibition also concerned with the documentation of constructive processes and curated by Barnaby Wright at the Courtauld Gallery, London, from 2009 to 2010, enables images of visitors' engagements within gallery environments to be visualized as performative digital objects. Reviewed comparatively alongside two screen-based projects curated by Tate Modern in 2012, Tacita Dean's concluding contribution to the Unilever Series, *FILM* (2011–12), and the inauguration of Performance Room, a digitally broadcast domain for the presentation of live work programmed by Catherine Wood, this approach expands thinking on the relation between analogue and digital, and gallery and theatre. Raising questions about where performance is located in relation to arts institutions, each case study functions through a 'flickering' temporality which moves between object and performance so as to produce occurrences of the latter visible only through transformation.

Visiting Exhibitions: Returning to Performance

Theatre, Exhibition and Curation: Displayed & Performed concentrates on an emerging context of exhibition practice, and the possibilities this reformulation affords for performance. The case-study exhibitions examined throughout the book return us to theatre; they model something about processes of performance and commerce between the animated theatre, spectator, and gallery visitor and the traditionally inanimate curated collection. Working at the intersection between display and performance, and examining in specific detail ten exhibitions as cases in point, it is important in such a project to maintain the premise, foregrounded by art historian Hal Foster, that an 'understanding of an art can only be as developed as the art'.[84] There is a coeval concern here about presenting these events as more arresting, or striking, through this investigation than they appeared on first encounter, that is to say about making the exhibitions appear either too important or too radical. They are significant for rethinking how we theorise and formulate practices of exhibition and curation, theatre and performance, but, fundamentally, they are curious rather than crucial and at all times relative to other socio-political concerns.

While the book follows a fairly predictable route in some places in terms of exploring a necessarily limited cohort of situations and operating across an Anglo-American axis, the balance of the chapters is, I hope, striking for the ways in which it diversifies across tropes and media without ever straying too far from the home base of performance research. Of course the work tracks, to a certain and perhaps inevitable extent, my own cultural experience over a number of years; however, I do believe it has something significant to contribute beyond this personal foundation. Though the case study examples arose quite naturally from the way I encountered London, as well as occasionally other cities, at a specific time in my life and project, when read together they enable the identification of a developing field of arts practice and the construction of a rethought and theatricalised concept of exhibition closely related to the cultural forces of the day. While the cases in point do motion across the UK (Manchester) and internationally (New York), there is an emphasis on London perhaps not surprising given its significant place in the history of theatre making and that it is here, in 2012, that two Tanks were inaugurated as what Tate's Press Office call 'the world's first museum galleries permanently dedicated to exhibiting live art'.[85] The exhibitions with which my project is concerned, though most often located in the UK, draw together a range of international artists from countries including Austria, Canada, France, Germany, Poland, Slovakia, and the US, to name but a few. Even so, London is particularly central and a specifically rich locus for such theatre and performance-related experiments in gallery-based production and programming.

Following Jen Harvie in her recent and predominantly London-based study, *Fair Play: Art, Performance and Neoliberalism*, which also charts a period of cultural experience up to 2012, we might hypothesise a number of reasons for this emphasis concerned with specific circumstances and individuals, venues, policies, and funding structures. The close proximity of the reconstructed Globe Theatre to London's Southbank galleries, to Tate Modern in particular, does not seem insignificant here – nor does the specific context of the closure of the independent site for London's Theatre Museum in 2007 at the beginning of the period this project historicises and the opening of the Tate Modern Tanks at its end. Also influential is the practice of curators, such as Catherine Wood and Jessica Morgan, who have an established interest in the display of performance and its associated paradigms. There are also economic factors. According to Harvie, nearly fifty per cent of Arts Council England's secure National Portfolio funding was received by London-based organisations in 2012 and, in her terms, 'the majority of the UK's major exhibiting venues, producing companies and promoting agencies are in London.'[86] Feeling cautious of perpetuating a London-centric perspective and how we might determine what counts as a 'major' venue, this study is approached with an awareness that an abundance of arts institutions, does not necessarily equate to agenda-setting creative practice.

That said, I am interested in this accumulation of gallery and museum contexts and their relation to performance precisely because of their large-scale visibility and draw to national and international visitors.

Performed modes recurrently move beyond their particular, supposedly definite, paradigmatic models. It is through exchange between modes of expression traditionally associated with display practices and those most often considered definitive of performance that these exhibitions come to constitute an emerging field of practice. There are, of course, other ways of reading these events. The prevalence of a particular kind of staging of staging, which has a striking self-reflexive sense broadly sympathetic to the cultural moment, might also be seen to signal a certain quite attractive crisis in curatorial confidence in terms of what constitutes the relation between my key terms of display and performance. Art institutions are experiencing new demands levelled against them in terms of productivity in a period of intense economic instability. Perhaps such contexts might seek to demonstrate their credentials by curating what seem to be panoptic and totalising shows which encompass specific adjacent practices in order to accommodate these vistas and landscapes within their own modes of operation and thereby legitimate a continuation of models with which they are more comfortable and which are, ultimately, more profitable. Keeping this possibility in mind, I suspect rather that the exhibitions I discuss here might make manifest supplementary modes of performance which other discourses exclude.

Notes

Throughout this book, where a particular source is engaged with over a number of sentences, the full reference will be given after the final quotation.

1. Peggy Phelan, 'Shards of a History of Performance Art: Pollock and Namuth Through a Glass, Darkly,' in *A Companion to Narrative Theory*, ed. James Phelan and Peter J. Rabinowitz (Oxford: Blackwell, 2005), 501.
2. Hugo Glendinning quoted in Gabriella Giannachi, 'The Making of Empty Stages by Tim Etchells and Hugo Glendinning,' *Leonardo Electronic Almanac (Mish Mash)* 17:1 (2011), 109. My emphasis.
3. Of particular significance here is Rebecca Schneider's wide-ranging articulation of the ways in which 'theatre consistently reappears in/as photography, just as photography reappears in/as theatre.' Rebecca Schneider, *Performing Remains: Art and War in Times of Theatrical Reenactment* (London and New York: Routledge, 2011), 143.
4. Adrian Heathfield, 'Alive,' in *Live: Art and Performance*, ed. Adrian Heathfield (London: Tate Publishing, 2004), 7. Original emphasis.
5. Pip Laurenson and Vivian van Saaze, 'Collecting Performance-based Art: New Challenges and Shifting Perspectives,' in *Performativity in the Gallery: Staging Interactive Encounters*, ed. Outi Remes, Laura MacCulloch and Marika Leino (Bern: Peter Lang, 2014), 27.
6. Lucy Lippard, *Six Years: The Dematerialization of the Art Object from 1966 to 1972* (Berkeley: University of California Press, 1997 [1973]), vii.

7. Ibid.
8. Ibid., 5.
9. For recent writing on the use of objects in play-based theatre see, for example, Aoife Monks, 'Collecting Ghosts: Actors, Anecdotes and Objects at the Theatre,' *Contemporary Theatre Review* 23.2 (2012): 146–52 and Maaike Bleeker, *Visuality in the Theatre: The Locus of Looking* (Houndmills: Palgrave Macmillan, 2008).
10. Laurenson and van Saaze, 'Collecting Performance-based Art,' 33.
11. Maria Lind, 'Performing the Curatorial: An Introduction,' in *Performing the Curatorial: Within and Beyond Art*, ed. Maria Lind (Berlin: Sternberg Press, 2012), 12.
12. Catherine Wood, 'Painting in the Shape of a House,' in *A Bigger Splash: Painting after Performance* [Exhibition Catalogue], ed. Catherine Wood (London: Tate Publishing, 2012), 14.
13. Phelan, 'Shards of a History of Performance Art,' 500.
14. For an abbreviated history of events dating from the 1950s see Amelia Jones' 'Timeline of Ideas: Live Art in (Art) History, a Primarily European-US-based Trajectory of Debates and Exhibitions Relating to Performance Documentation and Re-enactments,' in *Perform, Repeat, Record: Live Art in History*, ed. Adrian Heathfield and Amelia Jones (London: Intellect, 2012), 425–34. This list includes the work of practitioners and movements such as, in the 1950s: Dadaism, the American Action Painters, John Cage, Merce Cunningham, Robert Rauschenberg, Gutai; in the 1960s: Happenings and Fluxus, Yves Klein, Niki de Saint-Phalle, Carolee Schneeman, Yoko Ono, Robert Morris, Donald Judd, Robert Smithson, Valie Export; in the 1990s: Coco Fusco and Guillermo Gómez-Peña, Barbara Visser; in the 2000s: Pierre Huyghe, Jeremy Deller, Jens Hoffman, Andrea Fraser, Tino Sehgal.
15. Catherine Wood, 'Art Meets Theatre: The Middle Zone,' in *The World as a Stage* [Exhibition Catalogue], ed. Jessica Morgan and Catherine Wood (London: Tate Publishing, 2007), 23.
16. Amelia Jones, 'Timeline of Ideas: Live Art in (Art) History, a Primarily European-US-based Trajectory of Debates and Exhibitions Relating to Performance Documentation and Re-enactments,' in *Perform, Repeat, Record: Live Art in History* ed. Adrian Heathfield and Amelia Jones (London: Intellect, 2012), 428.
17. Chris Dercon, 'Foreword' to *A Bigger Splash: Painting after Performance* [Exhibition Catalogue], ed. Catherine Wood, 6.
18. Phelan, 'Shards of a History of Performance Art,' 502, 503, and 506.
19. Ibid., 503.
20. Laurenson and van Saaze, 'Collecting Performance-based Art,' 31 and 27.
21. Catherine Wood, 'In Context: The Sublevel,' in *The Tanks Programme Notes* ed. Charles Danby (London: Pureprint Group, 2012), 38.
22. Ibid.
23. Henry M. Sayre, *The Object of Performance: The American Avant-Garde Since 1970* (Chicago and London: University of Chicago Press, 1989), 2.
24. Catherine Wood, 'People and Things in the Museum,' in *Choreographing Exhibitions*, ed. Mathieu Copeland (Dijon: les presses du réel, 2014), 121.
25. Valerie Casey, 'Staging Meaning: Performance in the Modern Museum,' *TDR: The Drama Review* 49:3 (2005), 85. Original emphasis.
26. Roselee Goldberg, 'The Next 100 Years,' keynote talk at *Performance Year Zero: A Living History*, The Tanks, Tate Modern, London, 5–6 October 2012.

27. Rebecca Schneider, *Performing Remains*, 145.
28. A selective review of critical scholarship on curation in relation to art and performance might include curatorial collections from Outi Remes et al. (2014), Maria Lind (2012), Judith Rugg and Michèle Sedgwick (2007); debates from critics such as Michael Fried (1969) on the one hand and Lucy Lippard (1973) on the other regarding the relation of visual artwork to temporality; eminent books by Roselee Goldberg (1979, 1998) documenting the history of performance art; as well as works by Amelia Jones (1997, 2011, 2012), Nick Kaye (2000), Rebecca Schneider (2011), and others emphasising and rethinking ideas of 'presence' and re-enactment. Critics and theorists have also reflected extensively on performance-related intersections at, amongst other conspicuous events, Performa's biennial visual art performances in New York (Goldberg) and the Venice Biennale (Claire Bishop, Joe Kelleher).
29. Paul O'Neill, 'The Curatorial Turn: From Practice to Discourse,' in *Issues in Curating Contemporary Art and Performance*, ed. Judith Rugg and Michèle Sedgwick (Bristol: Intellect, 2007), 16.
30. James Fowler, 'Collecting Live Performance,' in *Museums and the Future of Collecting*, ed. Simon J. Knell (Aldershot: Ashgate, 2004), 244.
31. Laurenson and van Saaze, 'Collecting Performance-based Art,' 27.
32. Amelia Jones, '"The Artist Is Present": Artistic Re-enactments and the Impossibility of Presence,' *TDR/The Drama Review*, 55:1 (2011): 19–20.
33. Susan Bennett, *Theatre & Museums* (Houndmills: Palgrave Macmillan, 2012), 5.
34. Schneider, *Performing Remains*, 98. Original emphasis.
35. Tony Bennett, 'The Exhibitionary Complex,' in *Thinking About Exhibitions*, ed. Reesa Greenberg, Bruce W. Ferguson, and Sandy Nairne (London and New York: Routledge, 1996), 102.
36. Paul Greenhalgh, *Ephemeral Vistas: The Expositions Universelles, Great Exhibitions and World's Fairs, 1851–1939* (Manchester: Manchester University Press, 1988), 1.
37. Barbara Kirshenblatt-Gimblett quoted in Richard Schechner, *Performance Studies: An Introduction*, Second ed. (London and New York: Routledge, 2002), 3.
38. Ibid.
39. Alan Read, *Theatre, Intimacy and Engagement: The Last Human Venue* (Houndmills: Palgrave Macmillan, 2009), 5.
40. Laurenson and van Saaze, 'Collecting Performance-based Art,' 39 and 34.
41. Chris Dercon, 'An Open Manifesto: 15 Weeks of Art in Action,' in *The Tanks Programme Notes*, ed. Charles Danby, 2.
42. Nicholas Serota, *Experience or Interpretation: The Dilemma of Museums of Modern Art* (London: Thames and Hudson Ltd., 2013 [1996]), back page and 55. My emphasis.
43. I am thinking here, of course, of Peggy Phelan's axiomatic chapter 'The Ontology of Performance: Representation without Reproduction,' in *Unmarked: The Politics of Performance* (London and New York: Routledge, 1993), with which Serota's terms have an uncanny resonance: 'Performance honors the idea that a limited number of people in a specific time/space frame can have an experience of value which leaves no visible trace afterward,' 149.
44. Serota, *Experience or Interpretation*, 10–14. My emphasis.
45. Read, *Theatre, Intimacy and Engagement*, 188. Original emphasis. Serota, *Experience or Interpretation*, 42.
46. Dercon, 'An Open Manifesto,' 2.

47. Jacques Herzog, 'From an Industrial Underground,' in *The Tanks Programme Notes*, ed. Charles Danby, 35.
48. Hugo Glendinning, 'Looking for Noon at Two o'Clock: Performances of Time in the Archival Trace,' panel discussion at *Performance Studies international (PSi)* Conference 19, Stanford University, 26–30 June 2013.
49. Brian O'Doherty, *Inside the White Cube: The Ideology of the Gallery Space*, Expanded Edition (Berkeley: University of California Press, 1999 [1976]), 14–15.
50. Georges Didi-Huberman, *Confronting Images: Questioning the Ends of a Certain History of Art*, trans. John Goodman (University Park: Pennsylvania State University Press, 2005), 18.
51. Wood, 'In Context: The Sublevel,' 38–39.
52. Herzog, 'From an Industrial Underground,' 35.
53. Catherine Wood, panel discussion at *Exhibiting Performance* Conference, University of Westminster, 1–3 March 2013.
54. Emma Barker, 'Introduction,' in *Contemporary Cultures of Display*, ed. Emma Barker (London: Yale University Press in association with the Open University, 1999), 17.
55. P.A. Skantze, *Stillness in Motion in the Seventeenth-Century Theatre* (London and New York: Routledge, 2003), 118 and 30.
56. Jones, '"The Artist is Present",' 27.
57. Barbara Kirshenblatt-Gimblett, 'Exhibitionary Complexes,' in *Museum Frictions: Public Cultures/ Global Transformation*, eds. Ivan Karp, Corinne A. Kratz, Lynn Szwaja, and Tomás Ybarra-Frausto (Durham and London: Duke University Press, 2006), 41.
58. Bennett, *Theatre & Museums*, 15.
59. Kirshenblatt-Gimblett, 'Exhibitionary Complexes,' 43.
60. Serota, *Experience or Interpretation*, 53.
61. Wood, 'In Context: The Sublevel,' 39.
62. Barbara Kirshenblatt-Gimblett, 'World Heritage and Cultural Economics,' in *Museum Frictions*, 161.
63. Catherine Wood, panel discussion at *Exhibiting Performance* conference, University of Westminster, 1–3 March 2013.
64. Fowler, 'Collecting Live Performance,' 244.
65. Bennett, *Theatre & Museums*, 11.
66. Eda Čufer, 'Don't!' in *A Bigger Splash: Painting after Performance* [Exhibition Catalogue], 29.
67. Serota, *Experience or Interpretation*, 9, 54–55 and 46.
68. For example, to give just a slight indication of recent events local to my own base within the University of London, *Version Control* (2013) at the Arnolfini Centre for Contemporary Arts in Bristol, curated by Axel Wieder, and *Before Performance* (2013) at Performance Space in London, curated by Bryony White.
69. Shannon Jackson, *Social Works: Performing Art, Supporting Publics* (New York and London: Routledge, 2011), 39, 2, and 18.
70. For a developed history of performance studies and its relation to theatre, see, for example, Shannon Jackson, *Professing Performance: Theatre in the Academy from Philology to Performativity* (Cambridge: Cambridge University Press, 2004) and Simon Shepherd and Mick Wallis, *Drama/Theatre/Performance* (London and New York: Routledge, 2004).

71. Simon Shepherd and Mick Wallis, *Drama/Theatre/Performance* (London and New York: Routledge, 2004), 3.
72. Ibid., 1.
73. Ibid., 2.
74. Christophe Cherix, 'Preface' to *A Brief History of Curating*, ed. Hans Ulrich Obrist (Zurich: JRP/Ringier and les presses du réel, 2008), 5 and 7.
75. Ibid., 6.
76. Reesa Greenberg, Bruce W. Ferguson, and Sandy Nairne, 'Introduction' to *Thinking About Exhibitions*, 2. Original emphasis.
77. Ibid.
78. W. B. Worthen, *Drama: Between Poetry and Performance* (Oxford: Wiley-Blackwell, 2010), xv and xi.
79. Wood, 'In Context: The Sublevel,' 38.
80. Didi-Huberman, *Confronting Images*, 16.
81. Jones, '"The Artist is Present",' 19.
82. Ibid., 33. Original emphasis.
83. Nicolas Bourriaud, *Relational Aesthetics*, trans. Simon Pleasance, Fronza Woods, and Mathieu Copeland (Dijon: les presses du réel, 2002), 16.
84. Hal Foster, *The Return of the Real: The Avant-Garde at the End of the Century* (Cambridge, Mass.: MIT Press, 1996), 28.
85. 'New Tate Modern Tanks open to the public,' Tate, last modified 16 July 2012, http://www.tate.org.uk/about/press-office/press-releases/new-tate-modern-tanks-open-public.
86. Jen Harvie, *Fair Play: Art, Performance and Neoliberalism* (Houndmills: Palgrave Macmillan, 2013), 21.

1 Performer & Exhibit
Theatrical Conditions

Imagine a world without things. It would be not so much an empty world as a blurry, frictionless one: ... there would be no resistance against which to stub a toe or test a theory. ... Nor would there be anything to describe, or to explain, remark on, interpret, or complain about. ... Without things, we would stop talking. We would become as mute as things are alleged to be. If things are "speechless" perhaps it is because they are drowned out by all the talk about them.

—Lorraine Daston[1]

Projecting the monotony of an undifferentiated territory, historian of science Lorraine Daston asks that we visualise the tedium of an objectless space, not empty but inert to the possibility of physical opposition and academic challenge. Here, there would be no matter with which to be concerned, no events to arrest our attention or to construe in speech and writing, in fact, no living 'things' to experience and encounter any other being or entity. 'Things' enact an intricate relation to the silent and the spoken, the inanimate and the animate, the non-human and the human, the displayed and the performed. They are significant to a study concerned with contemporary object-based renderings of performance and the ways in which aesthetic things perform in museums and in the theatre. In Daston's assemblage of *Things That Talk* (2004), the objects are specific, not general indescribables but particular things which convey meaning through their materiality. In her edited collection of essays, the objects are not merely spoken for by those who contribute on their behalf, rather these 'things are the dramatis personae of the book' and it is in their characterisation as actors in the drama of the text, as agents which perform and partake of action, that Daston's objects resonate with the things to which this chapter is addressed.[2]

Objects of Study

Given that debates concerning the relation between the performing and visual arts have perhaps been most polemic with regards to the specific nature of what constitutes sculpture as a category of creative production, it seems useful in this first chapter to engage with two cases wherein the sculptural condition is central to the distinctive premise of each work. The first objects of interest, or rather collection of things, with which this chapter is concerned are those brought together within the construct of *Drama Queens*, a play by Berlin-based artists Michael Elmgreen and Ingar Dragset with text by performance maker and writer Tim Etchells. Performed at the Old Vic Theatre, London, on 12 October 2008, following performances in the Münster City Theatre as part of Skulptur Projekte Münster in 2007, this first case study represents an object-based engagement with theatrical conventions. The production is essentially a play on object drama and transfers six iconic and recognisable sculptures, associated with various twentieth-century visual arts movements and philosophical schools, including conceptual art, existentialism, pop and contemporary art, and, perhaps most significantly, modernism and minimalism, from situations of storage and display onto a stage where they are mobilised on moving plinths in relation to a seated audience. In the context of the theatre, the sculptures find themselves presented in a collection unlikely to be assembled by curators in the art world and, drawing on their relative art historical expectations and receptions, attempt to make sense of their unfamiliar surroundings.

Artist and theorist David Batchelor reminds us that the 'debate over what counts as an *appropriate* context has become a drawn-out war of attrition in academic art history.'[3] In an apparent inversion of *Drama Queens*' relocation of art objects into the theatre, the second gathering of things addressed in this chapter was presented as a cluster of performances by international artists staged in the gallery spaces of the Whitworth Art Gallery, part of the University of Manchester, as they stood in 2009 and prior to their recent substantial remodelling, completed in 2015. Programmed under the leadership of former Gallery Director Maria Balshaw, Director of Tate from 2017, and the auspices of the biennial Manchester International Festival (MIF), *Marina Abramović Presents...* was curated by the title artist along with curator and critic Hans Ulrich Obrist and required that the galleries be emptied of the art objects habitually housed therein. The Whitworth's collections include historic fine art by Millais and Rossetti, Thomas Gainsborough, and J. M. W. Turner; modern and contemporary art by Degas, Gaugin, Picasso, Paul Klee, Bacon, and Frank Auerbach, as well as more recent work by Cornelia Parker and Rachel Whiteread; textiles and wallpapers; together with, following the event, a range of videos and drawings remaining from *Marina Abramović Presents...* The act of emptying the galleries of these and other existing works rendered these exhibition spaces, in one sense, objectless, and in another directed very specifically towards different categories of 'things' and their particular relations to contexts of display. This second case study represents a gallery-based engagement with performance art.

Like the things of Daston's historiographical enquiry, *Drama Queens* and *Marina Abramović Presents...* display objects and create events that 'exhibit a certain resistance to tidy classification'. In Daston's enquiry, the objects, which refuse any kind of neat cataloguing, end up generating theoretical engagements precisely situated within the confines of the respective disciplines of Daston and her collaborators from across the arts and sciences, as if, she writes, by some sort of 'process of reciprocity, our things individualized us as we picked them out of all the possibilities.'[4] My interest in the things discussed in this chapter is likewise founded on subject-specific concerns, even as the objects are categorically resistant to such delineated areas of specialism. It is through this defiance that the things come to speak to the problematics of performance in relation to spaces of exhibition so that, as in the case of Daston's study, what these 'things have in common is loquaciousness:' they communicate fluidly and significantly on the relation between theatre, exhibition, and curation, the displayed and the performed.[5]

Conditions of Theatre

In *Drama Queens* the way in which the objects talk is literal, they are given voices and actions, they move. Before looking in more detail at the mechanics of this movement, it seems only appropriate to introduce the legacy to which this motion refers, particularly, to borrow the terms of performance scholar P.A. Skantze, in relation to ideologies which value 'stillness as a higher, more refined state over the messy daily quality of those things that move'.[6] The characterisation of things in motion, that is, we might say, of performance, as something disordering and disruptive recalls something of the influence on discourses of performance studies exerted by modernist art critic Michael Fried's oft-cited proposition that '*Art degenerates as it approaches the condition of theatre.*'[7] In his seminal 1967 essay, 'Art and Objecthood,' Fried influentially cast the qualities of minimalism which make central the position of the visitor as negating and retrogressive to the category of art, aligning theatricality with temporality in his notion of the theatrical 'condition.' Remarkably for the terms of this book, Fried objected not only to the time-based emphasis, or theatricality, of such work but also to the way in which this is made manifest through the prominence or projection of 'objecthood', that is to say via its aspiration to appear as 'literal' rather than 'pictorial' and to be experienced as 'nothing more than objects' (120) through a visual proximity to everyday things traditionally outside the classification of art. In his response to Fried's argument, Batchelor laments the ways in which labels, such as 'minimalism,' work to perpetuate differences that might be superficial and wonders whether all art must be distinguished as either pictorial or theatrical; 'if this work persistently fails to stay put within either of the preferred alternative theories of modern art, might this work not lead us to consider what kind of alternatives are on offer?'[8] It is towards such 'alternative' modes of categorisation, association, and interpretation that *Drama Queens* and *Marina Abramović Presents...* motion.

For Fried, theatre is 'the common denominator that binds together a large and seemingly disparate variety of activities' (141). Employing 'theatre' as a collective term related to certain qualities and characteristics, it is important to remember with performance theorist Philip Auslander that 'Fried's prejudice is not against theatre *per se*,' that is to say not against theatre as a specific mode of production, but rather, and crucially for my project, against sculptural objects which engage with the terrain of the durational.[9] Writing ten years after Fried's critique, art theorist Rosalind Krauss makes use of 'theatricality' as a collective term under which we might assemble forms of live and performance art, as well as sculptural interventions. In her prominent study, *Passages in Modern Sculpture* (1977), Krauss follows philosopher, dramatist, and art critic Gotthold Lessing's eighteenth century aesthetic treatise, *Lacoön*, in order to investigate the possibility, inherent to Fried's position, of defining the 'unique experience' of sculpture or the 'general category of experience that sculpture occupies.' For Krauss, Lessing is still relevant to contemporary discussions because of the questions he raises about the nature of sculpture as an art form and whether or not there is an 'inherent difference between a temporal event and a static object'. According to Lessing, the 'character of the visual arts is that they are static' and, Krauss surmises that, by the 1930s, the distinction between an 'art of time and an art of space had become a basic starting point from which to assess the unique accomplishments of sculpture.'[10] The underlying premise of Krauss' study is that, in relation to analytical engagement with any medium, dimensions of space and time are inseparable and that the 'history of modern sculpture is incomplete without discussion of the temporal consequences of a particular arrangement of form.' Thus connecting minimal art to a longer history of modern sculpture, for Krauss the element of 'theatricality' associated with the work of particular artists is key to the 'reformulation of the sculptural enterprise: what the object is, how we know it, and what it means to "know it".'[11] In a direct reversal of this statement, my interest in the minimal legacies evident in the contemporary works discussed in this chapter speaks rather to a concern for what *performance* is and how we might nowadays encounter that form in relation to the object.

Drama Queens

Whereas Fried was responding to, what Krauss calls, an 'uneasy feeling that theatre had invaded the realm of sculpture', *Drama Queens* represents a specific instance wherein sculptures occupy the realm of the theatre. The interest certain post-war European and American sculptors demonstrated in theatre and an associated experience of time resulted, Krauss abbreviates, in 'sculpture to be used as props in productions of dance or theater, some to function as surrogate performers, and some to act as on-stage generators of scenic effects.'[12] In this chapter, *Drama Queens* stands as a kind of synecdoche for this direction of exchange, wherein languages of visual art have influenced the theatre, and its relation to the counterpoint practices central to the project. It is not my intention to rehearse this history here but rather to observe the ways in which an exchange between sculpture and theatricality is registering differently across arts institutions and performance venues in the early twenty-first century. *Drama Queens* takes up and makes literal the 'condition of theatre' denounced by Fried, extending this not only to a broader range of sculptural objects, including some more often associated with high modernism, but also to the context in which they operate. Playing out the potential tensions and conflicts existent between the theatrical and the sculptural in the physical conditions of a theatre, *Drama Queens* performs, what Fried called in his critique of minimalist practices, 'the theatricality of objecthood' (135). For Fried, a certain sculptural investment in the temporality and situatedness of perception, and its associated espousal of objecthood, registered as a 'plea for a new genre of theatre' (125). While I am not arguing that the singular event of *Drama Queens* constitutes any kind of 'new genre' of performance practice, the production does materialise key features of debates positing antagonistic relations between theatre and the visual arts of which Fried's essay is the epitome.

Figure 1.1 Elmgreen & Dragset, *Drama Queens*, 2007. Courtesy the artists and Victoria Miro, London. © Elmgreen & Dragset.

Transferring sculptural works representative of various aesthetic traditions into a theatrical domain, the play enacts a site-specificity unique to the animation of these objects on stage, which, borrowing from Nick Kaye's writing on performance and place, can be seen to 'begin in sculpture, yet reveal itself in performance'.[13] Situating art objects, including FOUR CUBES, inspired by conceptual artist Sol LeWitt's *Four Cubes* (1971) and voiced by actor Joseph Fiennes, and UNTITLED (GRANITE), inspired by an untitled work by sculptor Ulrich Rückriem (1984) and voiced by Alex Jennings, within a theatrical setting works to amplify the particular traits of these sorts of minimalist sculptures associated by Fried with a 'theatrical effect or quality – a kind of *stage* presence' (127, original emphasis). Within the play, relative preconceptions about traditions of display and performance come to bear on the drama as the sculptures feel the pressure of an alternative array of expectations to those experienced in the gallery. 'I wasn't born to entertain,' asserts one of the objects on stage, inviting us to consider how the interest derived from looking at artworks in art museums differs from that which we experience at the theatre.[14] Drawing on conventions of minimalist work in order, following Peter Bürger, to dispute 'the possibility of positing aesthetic norms as valid ones', *Drama Queens* plays with traditional boundaries in artistic and critical practice and what art historian Hal Foster invokes as minimalism's move to initiate a '*redefinition* of such aesthetic categories' and 'transgress its institutional limits' by removing sculptural works from conventional contexts of display and presenting them on stage and in performance.[15] Articulated through a script founded in a multiplicity of perspectives on, and proclamations about, art, *Drama Queens* is precisely engaged with the ontological expectations associated with theatre and museum-going.

Dedicating a chapter of her 2011 book *Social Works* to the practice of these artists, Shannon Jackson addresses how performance has developed Elmgreen & Dragset's critique of institutional regulation and their liminal position between 'criticizing an institutional world and announcing their absorption by it'. Concentrating for the most part on gallery-based projects, including the concurrent *Too Late* (2008) at the Victoria Miro Gallery in London, Jackson's references to *Drama Queens* focus less on the specifics of the production, which, by virtue of its location, is presented as 'play' rather than 'performance art', as on the financial mechanisms of the project and its 'artist-to-artist artist-to-theatre network of economic reciprocity.'[16] This is a play situated at the periphery between theatre and visual arts display and in this chapter a sustained examination of its text and imagery makes possible a detailed exploration of some of the ways in which objects emergent from one tradition of making might perform in a context more usually associated with the other. According to the preface to the script, distributed for free, in place of an often costly and elaborate West End programme, at the performance in October 2008, the 'drama unfolds through a series of clashes and crossovers between the various "isms" and aesthetics which these sculptures represent' (5). Traditionally, critiques of art have held to a number of contested and differentiated movements. Since the 1950s, art history has been 'strewn with new classifications', writes Batchelor, and 'work listed under one heading has been isolated – in criticism, exhibitions, art history and journalism – ... from work held under any other heading.'[17]

By situating FOUR CUBES and UNTITLED (GRANITE) amongst other objects inspired by modern sculpture by Barbara Hepworth, existential work by Alberto Giacometti, and pop art by Andy Warhol and Jeff Koons, *Drama*

Queens plays out the tensions between different artistic traditions on two levels: first, via the transferral of visual art objects out of the museum and into the theatre; and second between the various aesthetic categories represented on stage. In this way, the play generates, what the Koons-inspired sculpture calls, a 'moment for the paparazzi or at least the art historians' (52) as onstage relationships are forged between the different aesthetic traditions, most notably in a romance between minimalist FOUR CUBES and ELEGY III, inspired by Barbara Hepworth's *Elegy III* (1966) and voiced by Lesley Manville. Despite, or perhaps because of, Fried's belief that it is the 'overcoming of theatre that modernist sensibility finds most exalting' (140), Etchells scripts ELEGY III as concerned about how to behave on stage and 'that problem – expectation again' (24). While ELEGY III aspires to meet the expectations of a theatre audience, her character flouts those articulated elsewhere, and not least in Fried's essay, concerning autonomy, medium specificity, and the relation between minimal and modernist artistic practices. *Drama Queens* suggests that viewing one artistic tradition through the optic of another might enable a rethinking, or here a restaging, of certain aesthetic assumptions. In galleries, mobile visitors approach static objects exhibited in association. In the theatre, portable objects further and support the onstage action.[18] Through its interconnection of a variety of sculptural objects and conventions of theatre and exhibition, *Drama Queens* expresses, by means of material 'things', a sort of tongue-in-cheek approach to the conceptual clashes addressed in this book. Presented as a 'Gala' in aid of the Old Vic Theatre Trust, the play was framed by then Artistic Director Kevin Spacey, in his address at the end of the performance on 12 October 2008, as part of a 'new initiative to bring theatre practitioners and visual artists together to create work for the stage'. It is such recent collaborations between performance and display which this chapter highlights.

Marina Abramović Presents...

Also engaged with the boundaries of aesthetic conventionality, through *Marina Abramović Presents...* Manchester International Festival (MIF) returned, in its second iteration and according to its own online publicity, 'to the crossroads of visual art and performance.'[19] In an inversion of Elmgreen & Dragset's staging of a performance of objects, between 3 and 19 July 2009 long-established performance artist Marina Abramović and curator Hans Ulrich Obrist presented an exhibition of performers. In her essay 'On Duration and Multiplicity' (2012), performance scholar Lara Shalson suggests that 'durational performance enters the museum as that which solves the very difficulty of ephemerality (and theatricality) that live art presents,' not least since it can be performed throughout the period of gallery opening hours and therefore appear within a seemingly enduring time frame most often the reserve of objects. Installing a performance artist in each room of the Whitworth Art Gallery, this event, while claiming to extend the framework of such 'durational' work, in fact, as

Shalson argues, limits our capacity to focus on any individual performance since our attention is split between the multiple and separately instated artists.[20] Therefore, although *Marina Abramović Presents...* is marketed by MIF as 'unlike anything staged before in the UK', certain conditions limit the affectivity of the event which is 'like', or at least related to, the recent plethora of international exhibitions operating in dialogue with performance practices by means of live and re-performed actions and stands within this project as the only case in point of this kind with which I will engage.[21]

Such exhibitions run the risk of diminishing performance to its most stereotypical forms in order to install something 'live' within the confines and preservatory ideology of gallery and museum institutions. Having worked closely with Catherine Wood on Tate's performance programme, former Curator of Interdisciplinary Projects at Tate Modern, Kathy Noble, has expressed concern for this sort of negative potential, noting that, while the 'format of a live exhibition of performance is of course a valid curatorial choice, albeit one that has been experimented with in various ways recently', *Marina Abramović Presents...* 'verged on a parody and risked reducing the medium of performance to a series of clichés.' At stake here for Noble is the perpetuation of what she calls a 'reductive stereotype' of performance as something conveyed through 'bodies, possibly naked, doing something extreme or absurd' and concerned with themes including 'control to anarchy, movement to stasis, sexuality to suffering'.[22] To debate whether the work of any or all of the performers participating in *Marina Abramović Presents...* has this effect is not the purpose of my reviewing the exhibition here. Rather, what does concern me are the ways in which such attempts to present, and perhaps thereby generalise, something of performance within gallery spaces might in turn reveal something intrinsic to that particular genre and how we can define its terms. An exchange, signalled by Noble, between the animate and inanimate, is integral to that project. Invested in the place of performance in history, Abramović's recent exhibitions function via, what theatre scholar Susan Bennett describes as, an 'oscillation between ephemerality and preservation' particularly pertinent to this book.[23]

I have chosen to align *Marina Abramović Presents...* with *Drama Queens* in this first chapter because of the extreme and explicit nature of the reversals which both events enact in their relative repositioning of performance 'things' (live artists) within the gallery and 'things' of exhibition (art objects) on stage. Commenting on the credit given to *Drama Queens* as a play by Elmgreen & Dragset with text by Tim Etchells, Jackson observes that this 'collaboration reproduced visual art conventions of authorship in lieu of theatre's distributed conventions of artistic crediting'; given the theatrical context of the performance, we might assume the play to be 'written' by Etchells and 'devised' or 'directed' by Elmgreen & Dragset.[24] A similar confusion of the creative roles customary in the theatre and in exhibition is instigated by art critic Adrian Searle in a video report on *Marina Abramović Presents...* produced for the website of *The Guardian* newspaper. Referring to the exhibition in his concluding remarks as '*Marina Abramović Curates...*' Searle's misnaming invites a consideration of the recurring proximity between concepts of the displayed and the performed and what difference it would make to the framing of this event if it were titled as 'curated' rather than 'presented'.[25] It seems to me that the concept of 'curation' situates us more emphatically in the realm of the museum, connoting an element of care, of selection, and also of conservation. 'Presents', on the other hand, is broader, maintaining a certain ambiguity between the exhibited and the enacted and focussing on an idea of presence that is temporally constructed. The intentionality of the ellipsis, evident both in Abramović's selected title and Searle's misnomer, signifies not the trailing off of an unfinished formulation but rather a promise, like that proffered by the Tate Modern Tanks, addressed in this book's introduction, and the motif of the empty space more broadly, of something yet to come.

Maintaining a sense of expectation, the ellipsis connotes an absence related to the illusory promise of the empty space for performance. Presenting the event as something 'unmissable', a quality reserved for those occasions which it is perfectly possible to miss, former Gallery Director Maria Balshaw established *Marina Abramović Presents...* within the Whitworth's Exhibitions and Events Leaflet for May to August 2009 as dependent on a context in which 'all of the public spaces of the Whitworth have been emptied of their art and design' so that, with no thing or object of the collection on display, the gallery might be given over to the 'making and experiencing of performance art.'[26] It remains unclear to me why an encounter with live performance within a gallery might require the removal of the more permanent collection of art objects from that space, as if it might not be possible to focus on one mode of production in the presence of the other. This important feature of the exhibition is something addressed only by way of slight introduction in other accounts of the event. In art historian Amelia Jones' critique, for example, the empty galleries are mentioned only briefly as a bracketed aside within a footnote: 'The entire event felt coercive, though some of the performances were powerful and among the most inspiring interventions into a specific gallery setting (the Whitworth was completely cleared of all permanent collection items) that I have seen.'[27] According to the MIF website, this preparation is necessary in order to 'create room for this unique work to develop and breathe.'[28] The poetics of this rhetoric, and the suggestion that seminal objects from the Whitworth's collection might somehow make claustrophobic the performers' breath, reveals the complexity of creating space in which to traverse across practices of performance and display. Within the Whitworth Gallery, the art objects must be removed to make room for performance.

The Empty Space and the Expanded Gallery

Representing a previous exchange between concepts of theatricality and display, Krauss reminds us that the 'very term minimalism itself points to this idea of a reduction of art to a point of emptiness.'[29] In *Six Years: The*

Dematerialization of the Art Object from 1966 to 1972, Lucy Lippard too casts minimal art as involved in a 'cult of "neutrality"' and thereby implicated in the false promise of the tabula rasa.[30] In keeping with this association, for *Drama Queens* the stage is correspondingly emptied of human performers and notably without scenery or set. This may, of course, to some degree, be to do with the show being a gala event playing on a Sunday evening, rather than a fully installed production running for a number of months. That said, I suspect rather that the lack of elaborate scenery has to do with the established legacy in the performance field of the 'empty stage,' as well as certain claims to 'neutrality' perpetuated by minimalism. The image centrefold in the playtext also evokes this history. Showing three of the character-sculptures on stage, ELEGY III, FOUR CUBES, and RABBIT, inspired by American artist Jeff Koon's *Rabbit* (1986) and voiced by Kevin Spacey, the image pictures the auditorium unoccupied; it is the empty installation shot transferred to the theatre. The sculptures are still, or at least there is no impression of motion in their rendering. In their respective venues of performance and display, *Drama Queens* and *Marina Abramović Presents...* both reverberate through initial elliptical gestures towards the idealism of the empty space for performance.

Figure 1.2 Marie Cool Fabio Balducci, *Untitled*, 2006. 4 sheets of paper, table (180 × 100 cm). Video: 2 min 11. ed 3 + 1. Courtesy Marcelle Alix, Paris.

The exquisite sculptural actions of Marie Cool Fabio Balducci, which come to be the exhibit from *Marina Abramović Presents...* with which I will engage most substantially and at multiple points throughout this chapter, also 'speak of the empty space' and begin in what critic Laurent Goumarre calls in his evocative writing on this work, a 'whiteness activated by Marie Cool, dressed in black.'[31] In the Whitworth Gallery, as in other spaces of exhibition before, Cool makes momentary sculptures from string, paper, and sugar, which she shapes and reshapes through movement. Manipulating and transforming objects, this white is the shade of the sugar she pours, the paper she folds, the string she plucks, all of which display what Goumarre calls this 'whiteness worked into a state of transparency', made visible to visitors through Cool's physical affinity with the objects and the sensitivity of her handling.[32] While Cool/Balducci work at the intersection of sculpture and performance, elsewhere in the gallery Mumbai-based performance artist Nikhil Chopra acts at the crossroads of performance and drawing. So as to create a space in which to enact the fictional persona of a landscape painter, loosely based on his grandfather, Chopra covers every surface of a room centrally located within the Whitworth Gallery with brown paper on which he sketches. In amongst his scribbled lines, the artist leaves untouched a flawless white rectangle. This could perhaps represent a window but to me it reads rather as a space in which a painting might hang, or has once hung, the vestige of a fictional object. Nearby, we find the trace of the string and screw, action-props which might have kept this pretended image in place. Experimenting with the inscriptive promise of the blank page, scrawled everywhere but within this canvas space, Chopra's etchings literally 'draw' our attention to the materiality of the gallery as a space for display, for art making, and for performance, a space emptied, in this case, so as to make room for the imaginary object.

Much of the work of Elmgreen & Dragset employs, in a related way, the structures of the now long-established tabula rasa. In many of their projects, in the words of writer and curator Marcus Verhagen, 'the gallery is transformed from a container into a sculptural form, so that the discreet effects of the white cube are both laid bare and short-circuited.'[33] Whereas Cool/Balducci make transparent the beauty and simplicity evident in the behaviours of material objects, Elmgreen & Dragset seek to make visible the faux-neutrality of gallery operations. *Drama Queens* does not render the Old Vic Theatre itself 'sculptural' in the way that other works have, such as *Powerless Structures* (1998) and *Elevated Gallery/Powerless Structures* (2001). Rather, the play reifies theatrical action, subjecting gallery operations to the conventions of the theatre and working to expose the effects and customs of both forms of venue. For Fried, art that relies on its presence within an arts institution for its status as such is inherently problematic. From the opposite standpoint, Lippard describes how, from at least the 1960s, the 'overlay of an art context, an art framework, or simply an art awareness, that is, the imposition of a foreign pattern or substance on existing situations of information. ... led away from marking the object into remarking direct experience.'[34] By applying, in the case of *Drama Queens*, a theatrical context, framework, and awareness to a collection of objects usually presented in the gallery, Elmgreen & Dragset reveal the constructed nature of these 'patterns' of viewing and encounter.

Through their respective engagements with material conceptualisations of the 'white cube' and the 'empty space,' both *Drama Queens* and *Marina Abramović Presents*... expose the physical conditions and engrained expectations of the theatre and the gallery as spaces in which to view art. Outside the contained four-hour duration of *Marina Abramović Presents*..., the Whitworth Gallery invited visitors to explore parts of the building and the collection not normally on display, promising, in its Exhibitions and Events Leaflet for May to August 2009, 'behind-the-scenes' tours, a concept immediately evoking the inherent theatricality and staging of the gallery space. Offering a 'unique view' of the Whitworth and its absent, or rather stored, collections, this is the first time according to that leaflet, that the gallery has been visible 'empty' since its reconfiguration during the 1960s. This action of 'emptying' is presented by Balshaw as 'radical' yet 'appropriate', framed by the news that a grant from the Heritage Lottery Fund will enable the subsequent expansion of the gallery into the surrounding parkland. This means, paradoxically, that curators will in future be able to display more of the Whitworth's collections and, with this in mind, Balshaw invites 'everyone to explore the Gallery in a different way while it is empty' so that, when the art objects are returned, 'it will feel like a different Gallery'.[35] Seeking to make new a familiar exhibition context, *Marina Abramović Presents*... invites visitors to rethink how we conceptualise the gallery, while *Drama Queens* invites a related re-evaluation of the theatre and the engagements and operations conceivable within these spaces.

Durations of Encounter and Alternative Perspectives

Alternative possibilities of encounter are integral to the conception of *Marina Abramović Presents*..., an event which designates, like many live performances, a prompt start time (7 p.m. with no admittance for late-comers) and begins with an hour-long performance-initiation, led by *Abramović* and titled 'The Drill.' Here, participation in several acts designed to bring awareness to the body and sensitivity to the gallery surroundings, including drinking slowly a small amount of water, holding the gaze of a stranger, and travelling across the room in a gradual cooperative motion, typifies a number of conditional terms of engagement. Like the timed entrances of high-profile temporary exhibitions, the restricted time frame of *Marina Abramović Presents*... differs from usual gallery opening hours which provide, at least the potential for, lengthier periods of engagement. While exhibiting a running time perhaps more akin to theatrical production than gallery exhibition, or indeed durational performance, the way in which visitors encounter live acts within the Whitworth parallels conventional modes for exploring displays of objects. Each visitor's mobility facilitates a series of meetings with often-static performers who seem, in striking correspondence with Fried's description of minimalist practices, to have been 'waiting' for our arrival (140). This sense of expectancy is exemplified by the contribution of Irish artist Amanda Coogan, who stands outside the banister of the Gallery's central staircase, occasionally leaping onto a cushioned heap below. In between her intermittent flights, Coogan appears to be on the verge of activity; something about her posture suggests that she is about to act, so that we, as visitors to the gallery, stop and wait to see performed the promise of this impending motion.

Theatre, Fried reminds us, '*has* an audience – it *exists for* one – in a way that the other arts do not' (140, original emphasis). Also experimenting with controlled interactions between visitor and performer, and expressing an interest in the 'audience coming in and actually sitting down, spending time with one's work', Elmgreen & Dragset, in an artists' publication titled *The Incidental Self* and accompanying a 2008 edition of *Art Review,* foreground the probability that the duration of visitors' engagements with a single work in the theatre, when compared to an encounter with a specific object in a gallery, are likely to be much more sustained.[36] Performing to a seated audience, the sculptures on stage at the Old Vic Theatre present, during *Drama Queens*, an alternative engagement between visitor and artwork to that experienced in exhibition environments where, most usually, the visitor is mobile and the object static. Inverting this relation so that the object is in motion and the audience seated, still in the sense of remaining within a single perspective throughout the performance, the production begins with the stage unlit as the sculptural actors attempt to make their way from backstage in the dim light. Emulating the theatrical convention of sitting in the dark and waiting for something to happen, the objects, as they enter the stage, sound like audience members arriving late to a show and trying to find their seats, whispering 'excuse me, pardon me' to facilitate their arrival.

For Fried, minimalist sculpture is a fundamentally theatrical form because it demands a 'special complicity' (127) from the viewer. From the moment the Jeff Koons–inspired RABBIT appears on stage, this character attempts to exploit the presence of the spectator necessary to both minimalist and theatrical encounter: 'I could really use a bit more reaction here' (21). Acknowledging the ways in which actors might build on and respond to the feedback and energy of the audience in their performance, RABBIT seeks to elicit this kind of more heightened, or more overt, audience participation throughout *Drama Queens*. By contrast ELEGY III, emergent from and representative of a more modernist tradition of art-making, finds the situation of being on stage 'rather intimidating'; she is 'just not used to this kind of attention' (18) which, it seems, manifests differently in gallery and theatre-based settings. Associable with paradigms of performance in motion, WALKING MAN, an object inspired by Alberto Giacometti's *Walking Man* (1947) and voiced by Jeremy Irons for *Drama Queens* at the Old Vic, indicates in response to the attendance of the theatre audience, 'I don't mind the staring so much. I'm used to it' (19). It is not so much the intensity of attention on the object that has shifted in the transference of artworks to the theatre, but rather the physical position of the visitor in relation to these objects.

Performance scholar Rebecca Schneider usefully recalls that in historic theatrical practices, 'many living stills were encountered *in passing*', either because the performance remained still and the visitor passed by, as in *Marina Abramović Presents...*, or, because, as in a formation such as *Drama Queens*, the audience stay put and the 'live actors, standing as surrogate statues, passed by' on movable platforms.[37] In contrast to the itinerancy of the gallery-goer, in traditional theatre venues spectators are, as WALKING MAN highlights, 'all seated. No one walks around' (17). Through a reversal which sees habitually inanimate art objects mobilised on stage, *Drama Queens* plays out the sculptures' responses as they inspect the seated audience from multiple standpoints, mirroring acts of viewing enacted by gallery-visitors in relation to art objects on display. Presented as 'a group of people with a shared attention' – 'One claps, they all clap' – the audience are characterised as limited and conventional in the responses available to us (16–17). In the theatre, reception theorist Susan Bennett reminds us, practitioners traditionally 'rely on the active decoding, but passive behaviour of the audience'.[38] The theatricality of minimal art is, in Fried's rendering, connected to a related experience of distance between the artwork and spectator, so that spatial detachment comes to be associated with an experience of temporality. In *Drama Queens*, this distance is doubled: rendered first by the distinct spaces for audience and player maintained in the Old Vic and second through the literal presentation of the sculptures' material qualities, associated by Fried with minimalism, objecthood, and theatricality.

Obdurate Objecthood and Untitled Performance

On stage and off, 'we look *through* objects (to see what they disclose about history, society, nature, or culture – above all, what they disclose about *us*), but we only catch a glimpse of things'; according to cultural theorist Bill Brown, it is difficult to focus intently on the things around us because, rather than responding to the tangible qualities of objects, we employ codes 'by which our interpretive attention makes them meaningful'.[39] Transposing Brown's theory to realms of the aesthetic, these elucidatory strategies differ in the theatre and the gallery, where we look for and expect different types and modes of meaning. Rather than missing their materiality in the application of analytic strategies, according to Brown, we might begin to face the 'thingness,' that is to say the materiality, of objects only when they break down and their usual functionality is disrupted, however fleetingly. Encountering sculptural objects in the theatre rather than in the gallery, and therefore in a 'changed relation to the human subject', in *Drama Queens* we can, following Brown, perceive more directly their specific physical attributes precisely because they are operating outside their usual modes of action. The theatrical context emphasises the 'kind of directness in the use and presentation of materials' most often considered characteristic of minimalism and foregrounded by Batchelor, and means that we are able to focus more specifically on the particular materiality of the artworks on stage.[40]

Krauss reiterates how minimalist artists were reacting against a mode of 'sculptural illusionism which converts one material into the signifier for another: stone, for example, into flesh – an illusionism that withdraws the sculptural object from literal space and places it in a metaphorical one.'[41] Taking up minimalism's archetypal literalism in its text, many of the jokes and puns within *Drama Queens* play on the physical appearance of the objects. At one point, for instance, the shining figure of RABBIT pleads of the rectilinear and angular forms of FOUR CUBES and UNTITLED (GRANITE): 'don't act like squares!' (47). At another, and infuriated by the impoliteness of the ostensibly solid UNTITLED (GRANITE), FOUR CUBES threatens, 'I'll take that blockhead outside and knock a few corners off him,' meanwhile UNTITLED (GRANITE) laments, 'If I must suffer this I at least want to get stoned' (39). In distinct yet related ways, both *Drama Queen* and *Marina Abramović Presents...* invest in what Daston calls the 'obdurate objecthood' of the things they display and enact, exploring how objects communicate through their physical shapes and attributes, and manifesting such things as 'simultaneously material and meaningful.'[42] Working through physical rather than linguistic play, Marie Cool Fabio Balducci also bring focus to the physical nature and affordances of objects through the terms of performance within the context of the Whitworth Art Gallery.

Celebrating the materiality of objects, Cool's silently eloquent sculptures 'prove the specificity of their mediums' – the artist gives, in Goumarre's terms, her 'action the specific quality of the manipulated object,' working to reveal something of the peculiarities of each substance by accommodating her gestures to the terms of their formal characteristics and possibilities.[43] Through Cool's animation of these materials, the salt appears palpably more granular, the tape stickier, the page more expectant, because the action that articulates the object is specific to that thing. The substances do not come to be representative of anything further than the particularities of their respective forms; as in Fried's summation of minimal work, 'they are what they are and nothing more' (143). These are not actors, symbolic of other bodies within the theatre, nor objects token of something else in the museum and this focus on the specific sculptural qualities of the things Cool manipulates is heightened through a lack of verbal description. The actions are performed silently; they are unspoken and unnamed, suggested only as *Untitled (Prayers)*. Reaffirming the performative nature of the prayer as an utterance constructing the act which it denotes, Goumarre reads this absence of designation as 'less a refusal of naming than a resistance to theatricality.' Defining theatricality as an 'artificial construction that cannot exist without an audience,' Goumarre distances the work of Cool/Balducci from affected acts of representation and simulation, suggesting instead that Cool, 'absorbed in her action to the point of ignoring the spectator's presence,' thereby signals that her performance is not dependent on the latter and less akin to theatricality than pictoriality.[44] In this way, these *Untitled (Prayers)* diverge from Fried's association of literalism and temporality. They share with the minimal an investment in objecthood but, even as they occur in time, deny, or at least do not acknowledge or seem to promote, the necessity of the presence of the spectator.

In keeping with Fried's identification of minimalism as a category committed to objecthood, in *Drama Queens* an emphasis on materiality is also played out in close relation to acts of naming. Throughout the play the sculptures voice assumptions about each other's titles based on their physical features. Near the beginning of the play, for example, UNTITLED (GRANITE) deduces, on hearing the name of WALKING MAN, that this object 'doesn't realize he's a sculpture' (14) because his title connotes the figure represented by his form rather than the specific materials from which he is constructed. This exchange plays out in microcosm Fried's argument; UNTITLED (GRANITE) makes a case for foregrounding the literal qualities of the art object while WALKING MAN projects a title which explicates his pictorial meaning. As WALKING MAN and ELEGY III politely exchange introductions, UNTITLED (GRANITE) comments derisively on their 'Poetic namen' (14). In contrast, the latter has 'no name. Ich bin Untitled. Ohne Titel. Ohne Titel. Ganz concrete' (14); his status as untitled emphasises the literalism of his form. In his research on radical inclusion and the expansion of the collective, theatre and performance scholar Alan Read reflects, in a vignette about the animacy of quick-drying cement, on the ambivalent nature of concrete, stating that the 'ontology of performance cannot be this thing because of the thing's performance, under this ontological necessity, *excludes.*'[45] Performance has been more comfortable with what Read calls a 'teleological presentness' and unaccommodating to stone-like things or to existing in unyielding forms.

Accumulated Instances and Loquacious Structures

While many visual qualities associated with minimalism are accentuated by the theatrical context of the Old Vic, others are challenged or compromised. Some of Batchelor's generalisations – that such works are not complicated by 'dynamic or unstable arrangement' or separated from the space of the viewer by frame or plinth, for example – are conceded to the set-up on stage.[46] A few scenes into *Drama Queens,* when FOUR CUBES enters in '*systematic movements*' appropriate to his minimalist construction, ELEGY III bases her initial impression of this figure on his external concreteness and structural resemblance to UNTITLED (GRANITE): 'Not another nameless rectilinear structure please. … Let's hope he's not as rude as the other square one' (19–20, original emphasis). These assumptions, made according to art historical classifications and comparisons of physical appearance, prove, in the case of FOUR CUBES, and perhaps the interpretation of artworks more broadly, to be misleading. Presented as polite and attentive, FOUR CUBES does have a name, which, Fiennes articulates on behalf of the object, 'comes from the number and kind of geometric forms of which I'm comprised' (26). While ELEGY III ridicules this as, '*Very* inventive', RABBIT asks, 'Why not "Two Cubes and One Big Vertical Rectangle?" It's sexier. Better Box Office' (26). This question reveals something specific about the legibility of this object and indeed of minimalism as a broader category, so far as such a thing can be abstracted. Like others of his contemporaries, LeWitt sought to distinguish his objects from the tradition of sculpture, referring instead to his works as 'structures.' The name of FOUR CUBES follows a pattern of construction archetypal of minimalism wherein 'one basic regular unit or module is repeated ... to form an overall regular shape'.[47] In this case, the reiterated unit is a white cube which appears on stage as a visual reminder of the object's relocation outside the gallery.

RABBIT's flippant reading of FOUR CUBES' composition as a combination of different shapes reveals that, as Batchelor states of LeWitt's work more broadly, the 'system is really very simple, and relatively easily *stated*; but it is very difficult to *see*. ... because the sheer accumulation of lines and planes tends to mesh together the formally distinct elements'.[48] Looking at FOUR CUBES in this context, the audience, like RABBIT, observe an accumulation of interconnected poles. Describing an encounter with such structures, art historian Douglas Crimp suggests in his 1977 essay on 'Pictures' that, 'we generally think of perspective as an illusionistic device by which we represent a three-dimensional object with a two-dimensional image, but when we look at a LeWitt, what we see is perspective. LeWitt points to the process of converting the complex data of sensory experience into the schematic representation of it ... but he does so not by making the image of a cube but by making a *cube* itself.'[49] In his analysis, Crimp expands Fried's critique of minimalist works as objects which avoid pictorial illusion by casting LeWitt's structures as experimenting with perspective. In line with Fried's argument, Crimp's reading agrees that objects, such as FOUR CUBES, reveal an interest in the relative position and distance of the viewer, but explore this not only via attention to the sited position of the object but also with reference to pictorial techniques that appear to extend space.

Marie Cool Fabio Balducci seem also to be interested in ideas of perspective and distance. In one action performed within *Marina Abramović Presents...* Cool makes vivid the materiality of an oil painting resting on her knee. Scratching a fingernail along the lines of its surface, she renders visible the illusion of its three-dimensionality, teasing out distinctions of plane and colour. Through this act of impressing, the performance – in Goumarre's reading too – 'contradicts those discourses that unidimensionalize the figurative elements of a painting under the pretext that they inhabit same surface.'[50] Invested in the physicality of the image as object, as well as the representational qualities of its visual imagery, this work, while in many ways worlds away, shares with LeWitt's a combination of pictoriality and literalism. Through its investment in the latter, Cool/Balducci's performance exerts, following Goumarre, the 'forceful expression of a tautology: ask it about its own meaning, it will merely repeat its own self-utterance'.[51] In their work, signification is encoded in expression. The actions operate through a quiet repetition of gestural phrases and a persistent rearticulation of materiality across different objects and media. Emphasising the form of the things she handles, Cool's motion is inseparable from the transitioning shapes it produces. At stake here is a self-reinforcing enactment of objecthood, a rule of inference or transformation which takes a material, analyses its form, and concludes with that entity's specific objectness. The paradigm for this work is a rhetorical formula premised on repetitive speech, a proposition invested with exactitude because of its logical form.

In her 1978 essay, 'LeWitt in Progress,' Rosalind Krauss critiques customary interpretations of the work of this artist which foreground logic, formal reasoning, and an idea, such as that held by art critic Donald Kuspit, that, since the viewer might complete the structure of LeWitt's white cubes by imagining lines concealed from view, the 'artist is depicting the cognitive moment as such.'[52] Intercutting her essay with extracts from Samuel Beckett's 1965 novel *Molloy*, Krauss suggests instead that LeWitt's 'outpouring of example' and 'piling up of instance' finds a model in an episode of the former wherein the character devises a system for distributing stones between his pockets and sucking them in turn through reliance on an empty compartment. This circulation of stones, themselves rudimentary sculptures, is, like the actions of Cool within the Whitworth Art Gallery, both systematic and compulsive. Comparable to 'music-hall performers doing a spectacular turn, switching hats from one head to the other at lightning speed', Molloy's co-ordination shares with LeWitt's structures a premise wherein what is represented is not 'an idea', or process of thought itself, but rather a 'pretext for a display of skill'.[53] For Goumarre, the actions of Marie Cool Fabio Balducci are a performed analogy of cyclical discourse. For Krauss, LeWitt's work is a sculptural correlative of 'uninflected repetitious speech', a more systematic version of the 'loquaciousness of the speech of children or of the very old, in that its refusal to summarize, to use the single example that would imply the whole, is like those feverish accounts of events composed of a string of almost identical details, connected by "and."'[54] In both *Marina Abramović Presents…* and *Drama Queens* intersections occur between performance and objecthood via a sort of excess of expression. Interconnective and verbose, for Krauss, the logic of LeWitt's work is akin to speech and performative writing, even before FOUR CUBES is transferred to the Old Vic and ascribed words by Tim Etchells.

Theatre: What Is the Point of That?

The opening exchange in *Drama Queens* takes theatre as its subject. 'Soll das ein Joke sein? Wer bin Ich? Where am I?' asks UNTITLED (GRANITE) of his unfamiliar surroundings before calling out into the wings for company and assistance (11). 'Keep the noise down', ELEGY III responds as she enters, that's 'really not the kind of atmosphere we need here' (12). Hearing these lines, it is unclear whether ELEGY III's instruction is founded on the object's usual status as a 'silent' work of art or on the basis of the hushed reverence conventionally expected within a theatre, and most often, a gallery. Existing between concepts of exhibition and of performance, the play functions within what Fried thinks of as an indeterminate and pervasive theatricality which reveals not necessarily the breaking down of established aesthetic categories, but rather a specific concern for the 'conventions that constitute their respective essences' (142). Unequipped to identify the stage setting, UNTITLED (GRANITE) demands, in not particularly polite terms, to know where the sculptures are. 'My dear, it's a theatre', a superior ELEGY III replies, her condescension trumped immediately by the quick retort of UNTITLED (GRANITE): 'Scheisse, was ist the point of that?' (12). At varying moments throughout the play the art objects attempt to answer this question. That is to say, performing out of context and by means of proxy, the artworks attempt to understand and express the purpose of theatre. Despite her physical allusion to the autonomous traditions of modernism, it is ELEGY III who tests a first definition of the theatre as a 'place where people come to see things' (13). As referenced in this book's introduction, derived from the Greek *theatron*, the etymology of 'theatre' situates it first as a place for viewing. With a marked emphasis on the visitation of objects, this art object's designation could just as easily be applied to the function of a gallery as to that of a theatre.

A few lines later ELEGY III tries again. This time the theatre becomes not only a context in which to view certain entities, but rather, a 'place where people come to watch and listen to things' (13). This incorporation of the aural into a definition of theatre draws attention to the fact that, though *Drama Queens* is described in the preface to the script as 'a play without actors' (5), the things on stage do not themselves speak. Articulated by play, or rather by *a* play, in the context of the Old Vic, each of the sculptures is characterised by an actor. Voiced by human performers, including Joseph Fiennes, Alex Jennings, Lesley Manville, Jeremy Irons, and Kevin Spacey, already mentioned, who, like the audience, are seated, the art objects onstage physically displace these celebrities into boxes to the right of the stage where they are lit, their presence illuminated, throughout the performance.[55] This is the sort of theatre Alan Read might enjoy, wherein performance enables us to 'place things in the centre and us at the periphery,' to 'reorientate the privilege of humanist space' and promote modes of attending which require 'performance to give up what it considers its decidedly human ontology'. Following Bruno Latour, Read is interested in the 'myriad ways non-human objects are implicated in ways of speaking', from the laboratory, and as and in performance, as well as the spectrum of infidelity to the object that any sort of critical speaking on behalf of performance and its objects encodes.[56]

Their own positions restricted, the human actors in *Drama Queens* perform by proxy or as if ventriloquists, producing sounds which we associate with the mobile art objects, rather than with the speaker. By reading the lines of the script on behalf of each object, these performers extend art historical discourses which figure visual art objects as 'peculiar kinds of things that need other kinds of things to function. We might even say that together the artwork and its interpreter form one talking thing'.[57] For art curator and theorist Caroline A. Jones, talking is connected to visibility; without critics speaking about and in place of art objects, these things might not enter a realm where they can be seen by public visitors. Whether on display within the gallery or in performance on stage, art objects are depicted as requiring external expression, as being compound 'things' constructed and animated by others. Both exhibitions and theatrical performances are subject to criticism, to being spoken for. In *Drama Queens*, the objects are allocated accents and traits founded on the gender and nationality of their artist-maker. This association takes to a certain extremity ideas of intentionality and the act of substitution evident in the 'personifying of objects as the representations of their makers'.[58] Parodying ideas of talking in place of artworks, Irons repeats, as the voice of WALKING MAN, stereotypical reviews which appeal to the object's character: 'They said that I ... symbolized eternal aspects of human experience, the walk of the thinker' (41). In this way, the human actors take on the role, previously reserved for the art curator, or critic, of speaking on behalf of and about objects.

Concerned with the ways in which objects are articulated by external agents and how this speech is both culturally and physically constructed, Lorraine Daston divides 'things that talk' into two categories: 'idols', whose speech acts are designed to 'manipulate and deceive'; and the 'thing that speaks for itself', as in the 'self-evidence' of geometry and the Christian miracles performed in things 'without the distorting filter of human interpretation.'[59] Despite the loquaciousness of their relative materialities, the art objects of *Drama Queens* are, in these terms, idolatrous, revered as epitomising their respective 'isms' and, given the articulations of the actors, voiced through a type of idolatrous utterance, which is deceptive, at least when we give into the illusion. What, according to Daston, such objects share with the self-evidently speaking thing is that both function through 'mechanisms of reversal and replacement' which contribute to the 'enduring ambivalence of idols', making them 'more real (and therefore more efficacious) than the worldly things they seem to be.'[60] Speaking both through their apparently self-evident geometry and their understudy performers, the objects on stage in *Drama Queens* are precisely ambivalent, seeming not only 'more real' and more affecting than the art objects they represent but actually to be the iconic works which they replace on stage. In the cast list at the beginning of the playtext, each character is introduced as 'inspired by' an artwork: 'FOUR CUBES inspired by Sol LeWitt's *Four Cubes* (1971),' for example. Resembling those distinguished works rather than being the actual masterpieces, the objects are citations of sculptures, props standing in for the artworks they falsely pretend to be. As representations, these objects flout yet again, at least in the case of FOUR CUBES, minimalism's stated denial of the pictorial. A key feature of minimal structures, Batchelor reminds us, is that the 'materials are not disguised or manipulated to resemble something they are not.'[61] In *Drama Queens* this statement is inverted so that objecthood becomes precisely representational, forged and made up to simulate certain well-known artworks.

No More Masterpieces

By their very nature equivocal, objects appear even more ambivalent when assumed into the language of the theatrical. Writing about objects in the context of naturalism, theatre scholar Aoife Monks, in her 2010 work on stage costume, develops further this sense of the ambiguous object in performance. Written in relation to a specifically modernist theatre, Monks' words find further resonance in *Drama Queens* where, too, the 'observable qualities of objects invariably become "untrue" when put onstage'. Within the construction of this play, this is the case not only because by entering a space of performance the objects are, as Monks suggests, 'rendered theatrical', but also because, before the action even begins, they are not the artworks they outwardly appear to be. Just as 'the notion that real objects could preserve their reality when in performance was unsustainable on the Naturalist stage' in Monks' analysis, so the idea that iconic artworks could occupy the stage is unsupportable in the contemporary theatre. Of course, Monks is quick to remind us that the 'untruth' of objects onstage might well provide alternative insights into 'truths that can only be found in theatre and art more generally' but, in terms of materiality, there is a clear transition 'from the metonymical to the metaphorical.'[62] 'Can we dress up?' requests RABBIT in *Drama Queens* (24), but the objects on stage are already costumed, 'dressed up' and attired to appear as the artworks they represent and parody onstage.

Performance, Alan Read suggests, is always 'performance by proxy; there is always someone speaking for performance, in the name of performance' and elsewhere, as in the case of *Drama Queens*, the 'spokesperson simply extends the *doubt* about the fidelity of the representation to non-humans'.[63] Presumably concerns of value and care make necessary the proxy sculptures produced for Elmgreen & Dragset's play. Secondary depictions of other artistic representations, the object-performers of *Drama Queens* are doubly 'objects' rather than 'things,' according to Daston's tracking of philosopher Martin Heidegger's insistence that the 'thing', something 'self-sufficient', be set apart from the Kantian 'object' as the 'product of ideas and representations of the thing.'[64] As models rather than iconic artworks, the objects in *Drama Queens* might be dissociated from the 'masterpieces' modernist theatre practitioner Antonin Artaud sought to eradicate. Describing such art as 'formal, moreover always dead exhibits', Artaud casts canonical works in language which aligns them with the traditionally static and preservatory ideologies of the museum. According to Artaud, reverence for such master-pieces manifests as, and this returns us to a term shared with Daston, a 'new form of idolatry,' which Artaud aligns with a certain kind of 'middle-class conformity' by which our aesthetic approaches are 'affected'. Masterpieces, he writes 'are fit for the past, they are no good to us', and perhaps particu-larly to those us of engaged in theatre. Perpetuating an ephemeral ontology of performance, Artaud aligns the decline of form with the dissipation of the spoken utterance: 'all speech is dead and is only active as it is spoken. Once a form is used up it has no more use, bidding man find another form'.[65] For Artaud, the theatre offers a domain in which to challenge aesthetic conven-tions and introduce new practices and modes of transformation.

Not the iconic works, but rather symbolic of these, rendered in mate-rials appropriate to the theatre where their 'stage life diverges from their real-life equivalents', the objects are 'drawn into action rather than merely displayed, exchanged, or used as furniture'.[66] In the theory of drama scholar Andrew Sofer, an object becomes a property through involvement in theatri-cal action; while inanimate stage objects are 'basic to theatrical commerce', by contrast, 'props are elusive' and involved in 'material trajectories in concrete stage space'.[67] Casting props as evasive, mobile, and evanescent objects, Sofer thinks these very much in line with ontologies of performance usually defined by ephemerality and an exclusion from economies of reproduction. On the other hand, following philosopher and cultural critic Walter Benjamin, actions of 'reproduction can put the copy of the original into situations which would be out of reach for the original itself.' Bringing the economy of reproduction into the theatre, *Drama Queens* substitutes works of art, associated by Benjamin with 'uniqueness and permanence', for replicas characterised instead by a certain quality of 'transitoriness'.[68] In contrast to the ubiquity of the autonomous art object, these reproductions operate on stage in terms more conventional to the transience of performance. They are ephemeral representations and, in the context of the Old Vic, these objects are mobilised on plinths which, after Fried, simultaneously 'reinforce the statue-like quality' of the props while, at the same time, signalling their presence as 'something like a surrogate person' (128). For Fried minimalist work is 'blatantly anthropomorphic' (129) and, functioning between prop and performer, these representations of art objects, when transferred to the stage, come to resemble and reference the human. The prop-objects are, like others who populate Read's *Last Human Venue*, 'peculiarly human' and peculiarly theatrical precisely 'not for their potential to act, but for their impotential to be realised', for the impossibility, within this theatre setting, that they might be the artworks to which they pretend.[69]

With this idea of a 'peculiar humanity' in mind, it is useful to consider now the foundational tableau of the play wherein the lights come up on the lone form of UNTITLED (GRANITE). This first image, of a single col-umn on stage, recalls a performance created by minimalist artist and writer

Robert Morris with the Judson Living Theatre in 1961. For this seven-minute stage performance, Morris constructed a 'hollow column which appeared alone on stage. Standing vertical for three and a half minutes, the column was made to topple, where it rested, horizontal, for the remaining amount of time.'[70] In her *Passages in Modern Sculpture*, Krauss narrates how the quality of the object changes when it is upright, and apparently 'light' and 'thin', and when it is prone, and seemingly 'constricted' and 'heavy' so as to reveal something about how meaning is constructed according to an object's orientation in space. Marked into four seemingly perforated horizontal sections, the tall vertical form of UNTITLED (GRANITE) appears onstage at the opening of *Drama Queens*, apparently solid and stony. We know now, however, that it is not a minimalist masterpiece but rather a theatrical prop, most likely made of a lighter and cheaper material than its namesake. Krauss' description of Morris' column is also applicable to UNTITLED (GRANITE): 'being an actor, it is anthropomorphized ... at the same time that, being an object, ... it strikes out at the viewer's conventional assumptions about how his experience is formed.'[71] In each case the object is altered and ascribed human attributes through the onstage action and exists, like Sofer's prop, between object and anthropomorphic actor.

Stasis and Motion

Artworks, Daston reminds us, have frequently been afforded a 'special status as midway between the objective and the subjective, things that purportedly incarnate selves (both individuals and collectives) as objects'.[72] In *Drama Queens*, the distinction between these agents becomes increasingly difficult to maintain. Here, borrowing from Daston, the mobile objects operate as 'active agents that engage with viewers as if *they* (the artworks) were the persons and their viewers were mere things'.[73] The play works to highlight the animacy of the objects and the lifelessness of the seated spectators and throughout, the '*sculptures' attention is on the audience*' (15, original emphasis), as the objects return the gaze of those for whom they perform. Restricted to a stasis that, even to a bronze sculpture frozen in an attempt to move, seems inexplicable, the audience are represented as a collective and a thing by WALKING MAN who finds us to be 'strange though, so still like that' (17). At the same time, this object paradoxically seeks to align himself with the static human audience, asserting: 'I love the crowd. I love meeting fellow men' (43). 'You're not really one of them', RABBIT replies unsympathetically, 'You're no man of the people. Too thin, too thoughtful' (43). Expressing a distinction in terms of physical form and mental aptitude which casts the stage object as more thinking than the subdued theatre audience, RABBIT's assessment is countered by WALKING MAN in terms of the face. In contrast to the evident nose, the pursed mouth and shaded eyes clearly marked in the texture of WALKING MAN, RABBIT's head is a featureless, reflective sphere. 'You aren't a real rabbit', WALKING MAN retorts, 'You don't even have a face' (43). While *Drama Queens* is staged so that one surface of each object always looks in the direction of its attention, the sculpture's words reference, what Read calls, a 'rash of theorizing of theatre as a "face-to-face" encounter' and a 'certain clichéd presumption of humanness that foregrounds the face' which these cases contest.[74] Even in the example of WALKING MAN, the exchange here is face-to-object.

Also conveying something of the performance and agency of non-human objects, within the confines of *Marina Abramović Presents...* Marie Cool 'evacuates all personal expression' so that we might watch the objects that her actions, as Goumarre describes, 'activate but do not interpret.'[75] Her head lowered, Cool is like a surrogate puppeteer, plainly visible and yet invisible somehow as facilitator of where and to what visitors are drawn to look. The sculptures created by Cool in her manipulation of everyday materials work to conceal her presence as performer, directing our attention elsewhere. In this way, visitors experience, what Goumarre calls, the 'exact movement of disappearance', as Cool's figure fades from our attention by 'being one with the action.'[76] In this performance, the human agent subjugates herself to the material object. Cool makes her own body sympathetic to the 'intimate vitality of "inanimate" things, which are led to revelation' by her gestures and by her breath.[77] As Cool walks along a line of A4 white pages folded in half on the floor of the gallery, for example, her motion is transferred to these sheets which ripple with the flow of her movement. This action and the momentary sculptures visible in the instantaneous positionings of the paper occur in and remain for a specific duration before the pages still and require Cool to repeat her steps. In another instant, Cool holds a length of string at one end and lights the other, gradually lowering her body so as to keep the flame ablaze at a constant height until it burns out. Here, the length of the string and speed of the flame determine the period of the action. Watching the cord rather than Cool, visitors witness a disappearance that is threefold: first of the performer, second of the thread, and third of the fire. In order to make expressive these objects, Cool/Balducci must, Goumarre notes, adhere to an apposite duration.[78] In the case of the burning thread, there is a particular interval inherent to the action.

Elsewhere in *Marina Abramović Presents...* the expected duration of a movement is resisted and prolonged. Whereas minimalist work confused what Fried called the 'continuous and perpetual *present*' in which painted, sculptural, and other modes of the visual arts are traditionally imagined, with the durational 'presence' of things encountered in time (146), the live performers in the Whitworth Art Gallery most often protract everyday temporalities. Attendant to the 'slower truths' associated by Alan Read with performance, UK-based artist Kira O'Reilly takes the time of the four-hour event to fall naked down a curved stone staircase.[79] Her tumble is not undertaken in any sort of hurtling or naturalistic motion, rather the period over which a fall of this description might occur is stretched and extended. In her analysis of the performance, Lara Shalson reads *Stair Falling* in relation to a traumatic history of concealed domestic violence, while Branislava Kuburović in her study thinks O'Reilly's work in relation to feminist strategies for blurring distinctions between subject and object and explores the 'treatment of movement as a means of introducing a highly specific temporality to the work'.[80] In Kuburović's terms, *Stair Falling* enacts a '*complex negotiation of the anatomy of the artist's body and the anatomy of the architecture ..., each posture establishing the middle ground between two frames*'.[81] Investigating relations between structures of the human and non-human, O'Reilly resists the gravitational pull and her body's corresponding impulse towards to the floor.

By slowing down the act of falling, and making this controlled and deliberate in a sustained act of enduring physical labour, O'Reilly makes visible this usually fleeting and accidental, or at least unsolicited, moment. With awareness that such a reference might risk '"disciplining" the live work back into the canon of art history,' Kuburović thinks *Stair Falling* as a 're-interpretation' of Marcel Duchamp's *Nude Descending a Staircase, No. 2* (1912), highlighting how, unlike in the painting, in performance the nude is also the artist. Kuburović reminds us that Duchamp's image was once considered an 'equally scandalous descent of the canonical object of the nude static reclining position' and suggests that these works share a 'particular intervention into sexuality in the field of vision through a relation between stasis and motion'.[82] Duchamp's modernist masterpiece reveals, in its neutral colours, a certain dynamism; the nude is no longer still and reclining but mobile and descending. Within the frame of the painting, consecutive abstract shapes convey an articulated motion via a series of interconnected and overlapping representations. Putting Duchamp's artwork into practice in the gallery, *Stair Falling* shares with this image a sense of rotation and twisting, as the artist falls so gradually that sometimes it is as if she is ascending, rather than descending, the stairway, or remaining still. Preparing for her performance, O'Reilly describes how the 'movement needs to be so very slow, allowing for gradual progression, but there needs to be rest points, still points'.[83] While the performers in *Marina Abramović Presents...* inhabit the possibility of stillness in the galley, within *Drama Queens* the objects engage with a related discourse of performance in motion.

Still Movement

Aligning sculptural work with the historical development of phenomenology and structural linguistics, Krauss defines the 'condition' of sculpture as involved in a mode of meaning making wherein 'any form of being contains the latent experience of its opposite'.[84] This classification is particularly useful for thinking about the relation between display and performance. Sculpture is, Krauss writes, a 'medium peculiarly located at the juncture between stillness and motion, time arrested and time passing' and while historically this form has limited itself to the 'lifelike but static representation of human or animal figures, there have been ... attempts to break out of the limits of this immobility.' Relating kinetic sculpture to the theatre, Krauss notes that, if such a work did not function by transforming its space of presentation into a 'theatrical or dramatic context,' it might instead 'internalize a sense of theatricality – by projecting, as its *raison d'être*, a sense of itself as an actor, as an agent of movement.'[85] Within *Drama Queens* the existence of WALKING MAN is figured as dependent on the necessity of motion: 'I need to keep moving. I love to walk – you know, perambulate, contemplate. That's my thing' (14–15). This action is definitive of his character, established in his name, and key to his potential to function on stage.

Associated by Fried with theatricality, Giacometti's lean bronze figure is sculpted as if still in transit, one foot in front of the other, weight thrust forward into his step.[86] Whereas earlier works by Giacometti, including *Suspended Ball* (1930–31), engage in what Krauss calls 'real movement and literal time', in WALKING MAN the movement is illusory; it is performed through a form of stasis.[87] Though the mobility of the remote-controlled plinth alters his position in relation to the audience, the object does not walk; it is simultaneously still and in motion. In this way, *Drama Queens* speaks to Sofer's articulation of the 'performance life of theatrical objects' and adheres to his rendering of the 'double life' of props which function multiply 'as stubborn playhouse stuff, mere things, and as evanescent stage performers'.[88] Simultaneously an object and yet somehow ephemeral, this character of acting between two modes, as both 'thing' and 'performer,' is integral to these cases and my tracing of the displayed and the performed throughout this book.

Both in *Drama Queens* and *Marina Abramović Presents...* the two modes of display and of performance are mutually co-dependent and intricately melded in combinations of sculpture and action. In relation to the work of Cool/Balducci, art theorist Luciana Rogozinski has written that 'the message contained in the Matter must be revealed and allowed to act' and that this 'enables the evolution into drama of a scene which would otherwise be static.'[89] Interrupting, what Rogozinski calls, the 'false eternity of appearance', the intensity of Cool's attention makes visible momentary and transitioning sculptures, held only for a second before they become another form. Each configuration, like the images of Joe Kelleher's *Illuminated Theatre*, appears as a 'fluid thing,' not 'the fixed contents of a stage picture ... but as a sort of impression ... taken from what the spectator sees and hears'.[90] These shapes are distanced both from the atrophy and deceptive perpetuity of the art object, and from the oft-cited ephemerality of performance. Enabling a 'transformation of passive objects in the inanimate world, turning them into subjects for a common, as yet unnamed action', through Cool's performance, borrowing again from Rogozinski, the 'most common materials are abstracted from their destiny of insignificance, from the degradation through consumption, and their unnamed and immemorial disappearance.'[91] In contrast to pervasive discourses and accepted ontologies of performance, and the specific instance of the burning thread, in the broader range of work by

Marie Cool Fabio Balducci, the performance of the objects prevents, rather than instigates, disappearance.

In an aside to his essay, which seems to be a quotation from Balducci, Goumarre cites a priority for 'static actions' and a 'pictorial quality' essential in the practice which Cool enacts, so that the work, instead of being wholly performed, becomes about the possibility of 'translating Marie's presence and physicality into a painting.' In this concern to produce display rather than performance, Goumarre locates a danger vitally linked to strategies which 'systematically erase the idea of theatricality, searching instead for traces of the pictorial' and that is the 'risk of banishing the sculptural and visual dimension of Cool/Balducci's performance work.'[92] This idea of eradicating the theatrical in favour of the pictorial returns us again to the terms of Fried's argument. In the work of Cool/Balducci there is both the theatrical and the pictorial and the progression is not from one to the other, rather, they coexist. The sculptural elements of their practice are inextricable from and ultimately reliant on the performance through which they emerge and become visible. It is a performance of shapes and stillnesses, of moments arrested and suspended in the stretching of a piece of string, until Cool's motion changes and another form occurs. It is not possible to have one aspect without the other; by ignoring the theatrical we lose the pictorial and vice-versa. For Goumarre, and for me too, the 'action is the image' and Cool's handling of the materials is directed towards the 'action/image that is floating in the space, the emptiness and the "slow motion" of time; in a word, to the medium of performance.'[93]

Non-Sequential Depiction

Invested in the latent activity inherent in the make-up of apparently stable objects, within *Marina Abramović Presents...* Cool's performance plays with forms and modes of making which do not invite a progressive interpretation but rather reveal a capacity to 'go from presentation (action) to vision (image) without the latter being the result of the former' – the objective of this work, again following Goumarre, is to make performance and object coincide.[94] In the potential of their quiescent excess, their situation as simultaneously action and object, Cool's performances, and the sculptures these instigate and eradicate, work ambiguously across terrains of the displayed and the performed, susceptible to more than one meaning and conceptualisation. They are, however, not wavering or uncertain in their formation, but precisely determined as equivocal. 'Depicting a thing is not quite the same as making one,' prompts art historian Joseph Leo Koerner.[95] We might consider the sculptures which become visible, still for a second amongst the movements of Cool's performance, in this way, as 'depicted' rather than made or built. Between manipulating a piece of string and moving to disturb sheets of paper, Cool enacts a pause, a withdrawal which signals a 'refusal to witness the development of a sequence'; here, in Goumarre's terms, 'truth rests in each action, rather than in their tallied sum.'[96] In this way, this exhibit differs to models both of performance and exhibition in seeking to maintain individual acts rather than generate a cumulative experience of additive scenes or exhibits.

Both *Marina Abramović Presents...* and *Drama Queens* engage in modes of presentation which operate between the static object and temporal acts of performance. Towards the end of the latter, music plays and the objects dance. FOUR CUBES says at this moment, 'I haven't moved like that in my whole life' (48) and, of course, he has not. Though art objects are transferred between galleries in crates, through spaces of exhibition in boxes and on plinths, never before has this object, or rather what the object represents, Sol LeWitt's *Four Cubes* (1971), appeared mobile in relation to a static audience, the still sculptural form made itinerant on a moving platform. Earlier in the play, FOUR CUBES invests in the summative mode of most art curation, the invitation, which this book takes up, to read the objects within exhibitions in association, and the related progressive narrative of traditional theatre production. His first impulse is to interpret the component parts of the play cumulatively so as to 'know how this whole structure adds up' (26). Sol LeWitt's sculptures are invested too with a 'serial methodology', a mode of construction involving systems and instructions in which each step is determined by the previous action.[97] Alongside this sequential practice, in 1967 LeWitt coined the term "Conceptual Art". It is a label, Batchelor reminds us, 'usually associated with forms of textual or "dematerialised" work, but LeWitt's structures are no less an art of conception'; they emphasise process over appearance. To encounter this work, Batchelor writes, is to become 'overwhelmed by a proliferation of relations-between-parts' which appear 'not balanced so much as catalogued, not intuitive so much as logical, and in some cases not seen so much as implied' such that an intersection between the 'known and the experienced' comes to be important for LeWitt's practice.[98] In his work, the excess of connections and accumulations is overpowering and this is played out in *Drama Queens*. Drawing on LeWitt's 'Statements on Conceptual Art', first published in 1969, FOUR CUBES determines 'since we've got a captive audience and a lot of expectations, I propose we each make a series of numbered statements about art' (24).

As the play continues, the chronological numbering that is attached to FOUR CUBES' declarations begins to break down. The phrasing exactly replicates LeWitt's original manifesto but the order is disrupted: '34. When an artist learns his craft too well he makes slick art. 17. The artist's will is secondary to the process he initiates. 8. ...' (36). *Drama Queens* is not, then, constructed according to paradigms founded in progressive and cumulative processes either of art making or performance. Fried describes the theatrical preoccupation with temporality and the specific duration of experience as revelatory 'of time both passing and to come, *simultaneously approaching and receding*, as if apprehended in an infinite perspective' (145, original emphasis). As in the experience of watching Cool's performance in which action and sculpture simultaneously come into and withdraw from view, time in these case studies is not merely progressive and ephemeral, rather it looms and recoils. Writing in the 1990s, Hal Foster described emerging engagements with minimalist practices in similar terms, so that this tradition 'recedes from us as an archival object' and, at the same time, 'rushes toward us' as artists seek alternative modes of practice.[99] Minimalism returns in *Drama Queens* in similarly mixed terms, the expectations it connotes intermittently celebrated, critiqued, parodied, and extended.

Within the play any investment in seriality breaks down to make way for a more intricate exchange between performance in motion and stilled revelations of display. In Fried's argument there is, Batchelor reminds us, 'no transcendence from the literal into the pictorial, and in the absence of the pictorial there was only the theatrical.'[100] Making symbiotic the pictorial and the literal, the displayed and the performed, *Drama Queens* and *Marina Abramović Presents...* reveal, borrowing again from Batchelor, the 'possibility of an art which is *neither* pictorial *nor* theatrical, or which is *both* literal *and* allusive. That is to say, the evidence of the work both shows and occupies a space for which there was no logical room in Fried's argument'.[101] The works presented in this chapter exist between sculpture and performance, gallery and theatre, autonomy and accumulation: they are equivocal.

Equivocal

Working comparatively across two relatively traditional venues for performance and exhibition, this chapter has examined a pairing of recent intersections between practices usually associated with these respective forms. Addressing the reciprocal acts of exchange between object, audience, and performer enacted by Elmgreen & Dragset's *Drama Queens* and *Marina Abramović Presents...* the chapter has suggested ways in which these events draw on and play with references to conventions of minimalist practice in order to dispute boundaries of institutional and aesthetic traditions. Playing out the performative potential of sculptural objects in the physical conditions of a theatre, *Drama Queens* makes dramatic particular aesthetic characteristics deemed by Fried to be already theatrical even before this relocation from gallery to stage, while *Marina Abramović Presents...* reveals, too, the complexity of making space in which to traverse across practices of display and of performance. Both events draw on the twinning of the tabula rasa – the idealism of the empty space for performance and the 'white cube' for exhibition – in order to experiment with this inscriptive promise and examine the established expectations of the theatre and the gallery as spaces in which to view art. Read in combination, they approach questions about the temporal frameworks in which we experience objects, presenting alternatives to conventional formations and resisting the cumulative productions of art-making and performance, as well as any static endurance of the object.

Resembling iconic art objects rather than being actual 'masterpieces', the characters of *Drama Queens* make explicit the equivocal nature of objects on stage. At the climax of the play a new character enters; BRILLO BOX inspired by Andy Warhol's *Brillo Box* (1964) falls from a black cube hidden in the lighting rig onto the stage. Based on recognisable packaging from the domestic environment of everyday life, BRILLO BOX is, within the theatre, doubly outside its conventional frame of reference, being both removed from a gallery situation, in which a number of similar objects, in contrast to this singular appearance, are usually displayed together, and from the context of daily household tasks from which its form is appropriated. Writing of art objects such as this one, art historian Henry M. Sayre asserts that Warhol 'addressed the question of the materialization of the art experience directly. He refused to mask the question either by valorizing the immediacy of the art experience or by aestheticizing art's object. He consistently forced us to ask ourselves just what the object of performance might be.'[102] In contrast to the autonomous art object presented in lasting display, in *Drama Queens* these objects function as props, made mobile and ephemeral in one sense but enduring and seemingly stable in another.

Making visible the performative nature of objects, on stage and in the gallery, here performance works towards visibility and display rather than disappearance. Returning to Daston's theory at the conclusion of this chapter, such 'talkative things' bring into being 'novel, previously unthinkable combinations' via their 'thingness,' thereby advancing 'new constellations of experience that break the old molds', in these cases, and in the context of this project, in relation to ontologies of display and performance.[103] Appearing intermittently as object, the work produced is not solely ephemeral. Fading and transitioning in performance, neither is it purely static and object based. Sometimes displayed, sometimes performed, neither 'exhibition' nor 'performance' can singularly describe these events. In relation to the performances of Marie Cool Fabio Balducci, which have come to be so significant to my thinking in this chapter, art theorist Luciana Rogozinski defines ephemerality as 'faithful to that reality which, in its dream, moves in excess of itself. Only by going beyond its own limits can it be reborn'.[104] Operating equivocally as both material object and ephemeral performance, the actions of Cool, and the overall formations enacted by *Marina Abramović Presents...* and *Drama Queens*, exceed the boundaries of usual paradigms of performance and exhibition practices.

Engaging with notions of performance and exhibition, of human actor and of object-thing, in order to create something 'concrete yet ambiguous,' these art events, like other 'things' in Brown's formation, 'index a certain limit or liminality'; they 'hover over the threshold between the nameable and the unnameable, the figurable and the unfigurable, the identifiable and unidentifiable.'[105] Easier left untitled, like many of the works they contain, *Marina Abramović Presents...* and *Drama Queens* evade any straightforward act of designation or categorisation. Rather we might consider them for now as 'things' that stand in for the loss of other words, as a 'place holder for some future specifying operations', for further examples of events operating within gallery spaces which figure equivocally across domains of the displayed and the performed and thereby exceed persistent models founded either on static arrangement or temporal ephemerality.[106] It is with forms such as these that this book is concerned.

Notes

1. Lorraine Daston, 'Introduction: Speechless,' in *Things That Talk: Object Lessons from Art and Science*, ed. Lorraine Daston (New York: Zone, 2004), 9.
2. Ibid., 10.
3. David Batchelor, *Minimalism* (London: Tate Gallery Publishing Ltd, 1997), 64. Original emphasis.
4. Daston, 'Introduction: Speechless,' 10–11.
5. Ibid.
6. P.A. Skantze, *Stillness in Motion in the Seventeenth-Century Theatre* (London and New York: Routledge, 2003), 6.
7. Michael Fried, 'Art and Objecthood' [1967], in *Minimal Art: A Critical Anthology*, ed. Gregory Battcock (London: Studio Vista, 1969), 141. Original emphasis. Since this chapter engages in detail with Fried's polemic essay, further citations to this work are given in the text.
8. Batchelor, *Minimalism*, 66.
9. Philip Auslander, *From Acting to Performance: Essays in Modernism and Postmodernism* (London and New York: Routledge, 1997), 51. Original emphasis.
10. Rosalind Krauss, *Passages in Modern Sculpture* (Cambridge, Mass., and London: MIT Press, 1981 [1977]), 1–3 and 204.
11. Ibid., 4 and 242.
12. Ibid., 203–4. Krauss gives an example of the first category of theatricalised sculpture, that is sculpture as prop, through a visual reference to the Martha Graham Company and specifically to a stage set for a production of *Phaedra* by Isamu Noguchi from 1960. The second form, related to a kind of theatrical surrogacy, is illustrated through László Moholy-Nagy's *Light Prop* (1930), which Krauss describes as a 'surrogate person, an actor in technological disguise' (207).
13. Nick Kaye, *Site-Specific Art: Performance, Place and Documentation* (London and New York: Routledge, 2000), 3.
14. Michael Elmgreen, Ingar Dragset, and Tim Etchells, *Drama Queens: A Play by Elmgreen & Dragset with Text by Tim Etchells* (London: The Old Vic, 2008), 17. Further citations to this script are given in the text.
15. Hal Foster, *The Return of the Real: The Avant-Garde at the End of the Century* (Cambridge, Mass.: MIT Press, 1996), 51 and 57–58. Original emphasis.
16. Shannon Jackson, *Social Works: Performing Art, Supporting Publics* (New York and London: Routledge, 2011), 182 and 206–7.
17. Batchelor, *Minimalism*, 7.
18. For a related discussion of the supportive qualities of props see chapter 3 of Shannon Jackson, *Social Works: Performing Art, Supporting Publics* and particularly pages 78–80.

19. 'Marina Abramović Presents...,' Manchester International Festival 2009, accessed 16 July 2009, http://mif.co.uk/event/marina-abramovic-presents/.

20. Lara Shalson, 'On Duration and Multiplicity,' *Performance Research* 17:5 (2012), 98–99 and 104.

21. Oft-cited exhibitions of live performance and re-enactment in recent years regularly have a relation to *Abramović* and her work. High-profile examples include *Marina Abramović: Seven Easy Pieces* organised by Artistic Director and Chief Curator, Nancy Spector, at the Solomon R. Guggenheim Museum, New York, in 2005; *Marina Abramović: The Artist Is Present* organised by Klaus Biesenbach, then Chief Curator at Large at the Museum of Modern Art (MoMA), New York in 2010; and *Marina Abramović: 512 Hours* curated by Abramović and then Co-Directors Julia Peyton-Jones and Hans Ulrich Obrist at the Serpentine Gallery, London, in 2014. In the context of this discussion of *Marina Abramović Presents...* it is also relevant to note here *11 Rooms* curated by Hans-Ulrich Obrist and Klaus Biesenbach at the Manchester Art Gallery as part of the subsequent Manchester International Festival in 2011.

22. Kathy Noble, '*Marina Abramović Presents,*' *Frieze*, last modified 21 August 2009, http://blog.frieze.com/marina_abramovic_presents/.

23. Susan Bennett, *Theatre & Museums* (Houndmills: Palgrave Macmillan, 2012), 26.

24. Jackson, *Social Works*, 206.

25. Adrian Searle, 'Marina Abramović Presents the "Unnerving and Unforgettable" at Manchester International Festival,' last modified 7 July 2009, http://www.theguardian.com/culture/video/2009/jul/06/marina-abramovic-manchester-festival-adrian-searle.

26. Maria Balshaw, 'Welcome' to *Exhibitions and Events May–August 2009* [Gallery Brochure], Whitworth Art Gallery.

27. Amelia Jones, '"The Artist is Present": Artistic Re-enactments and the Impossibility of Presence,' *TDR/The Drama Review*, 55:1 (2011), 38.

28. 'Marina Abramović Presents...'

29. Krauss, *Passages in Modern Sculpture*, 254.

30. Lucy Lippard, *Six Years: The Dematerialization of the Art Object from 1966 to 1972* (Berkeley: University of California Press, 1997 [1973]), xiv.

31. Laurent Goumarre in *Marie Cool Fabio Balducci: Untitled (Prayers) 1996–2005*, ed. Marie Cool and Fabio Balducci, trans. Julien Bismuth, Charles Penwarden and Simon Turner (London: South London Gallery, 2005), 7.

32. Ibid., 11.

33. Marcus Verhagen, 'Elmgreen & Dragset: Inconvenient Truths,' *Art Review* 26 (2008), 74.

34. Lippard, *Six Years*, 5.

35. Balshaw, 'Welcome' to *Exhibitions and Events May–August 2009* [Gallery Brochure].

36. Michael Elmgreen and Ingar Dragset, 'The Incidental Self' [Art Review Artist Publication], *Art Review* 26 (2008).

37. Rebecca Schneider, *Performing Remains: Art and War in Times of Theatrical Reenactment* (London and New York: Routledge, 2011), 146.

38. Susan Bennett, *Theatre Audiences: A Theory of Production and Reception* (London and New York: Routledge, 1990), 206.

39. Bill Brown, 'Thing Theory,' in *Things*, ed. Bill Brown (Chicago and London: University of Chicago Press, 2004), 4. Original emphasis. Subsequent references in this paragraph refer to the same page of this work.
40. Batchelor, *Minimalism*, 13.
41. Krauss, *Passages in Modern Sculpture*, 266.
42. Daston, 'Introduction: Speechless,' 11, 20, and 17.
43. Goumarre in *Marie Cool Fabio Balducci: Untitled (Prayers)*, 13 and 11.
44. Ibid., 7 and 10.
45. Alan Read, *Theatre, Intimacy and Engagement: The Last Human Venue* (Houndmills: Palgrave Macmillan, 2009), 192. Original emphasis.
46. Batchelor, *Minimalism*, 11.
47. Ibid., 15 and 11.
48. Ibid., 46. Original emphasis.
49. Douglas Crimp, 'Pictures' [1977], *X-tra Contemporary Art Quarterly* 8 (2005), 19.
50. Goumarre in *Marie Cool Fabio Balducci: Untitled (Prayers)*, 11.
51. Ibid., 9.
52. Rosalind Krauss, 'LeWitt in Progress,' *October*, Vol. 6 (1978), 51.
53. Ibid., 58–60.
54. Ibid., 60 and 55–56.
55. The concept of the theatre box or *loge* is engaged with more substantially in Chapter 2 of this book.
56. Read, *Theatre, Intimacy and Engagement*, 189, 192, and 195.
57. Caroline A. Jones, 'Talking Pictures: Clement Greenberg's Pollock,' in *Things That Talk: Object Lessons from Art and Science*, ed. Lorraine Daston, 329.
58. Donald Preziosi and Claire J. Farago, 'General Introduction: What Are Museums For?' in *Grasping the World: The Idea of the Museum*, ed. Donald Preziosi and Claire J. Farago (Aldershot: Ashgate, 2004), 5.
59. Daston, 'Introduction: Speechless,' 12–13.
60. Ibid., 13.
61. Batchelor, *Minimalism*, 11.
62. Aoife Monks, *The Actor in Costume* (Houndmills: Palgrave Macmillan, 2010), 63.
63. Read, *Theatre, Intimacy and Engagement*, 227 and 196. Original emphasis.
64. Daston, 'Introduction: Speechless,' 15.
65. Antonin Artaud, *The Theatre and Its Double*, trans. Victor Corti (London: Alma Classics, 2013 [1964]), 54, 56, 55, 57, and 26.
66. Andrew Sofer, 'Properties,' in *The Oxford Handbook of Early Modern Theatre*, ed. Richard Dutton (Oxford: Oxford University Press, 2009), 562 and 568.
67. Ibid., 568 and 560.
68. Walter Benjamin, 'The Work of Art in the Age of Mechanical Reproduction' [1936], in *Illuminations*, ed. Hannah Arendt, trans. Harry Zohn (London: Jonathan Cape Ltd, 1970), 222 and 225.
69. Read, *Theatre, Intimacy and Engagement*, 4.
70. Krauss, *Passages in Modern Sculpture*, 236. References in the following sentence refer to pages 238–39.
71. Ibid., 236–37.
72. Daston, 'Introduction: Speechless,' 13.
73. Ibid., 22.

74. Read, *Theatre, Intimacy and Engagement*, 227. Original emphasis.
75. Goumarre in *Marie Cool Fabio Balducci: Untitled (Prayers)*, 7.
76. Ibid., 10.
77. Luciana Rogozinski, 'Winter Peacock,' in *Marie Cool Fabio Balducci: Untitled (Prayers) 1996–2005*, 24.
78. Goumarre in *Marie Cool Fabio Balducci: Untitled (Prayers)*, 9.
79. Read, *Theatre, Intimacy and Engagement*, 97.
80. Shalson, 'On Duration and Multiplicity,' 105; Branislava Kuburović, 'Sta(i)r Falling,' *Performance Research* 16:1 (2011), 96.
81. Kuburović, 'Sta(i)r Falling,' 93. Original emphasis.
82. Ibid., 94–95.
83. Kira O'Reilly, 'Notes for Whitworth Art Gallery Staircase (North),' accessed 10 November 2011, http://www.kiraoreilly.com/blog/?p=216.
84. Krauss, *Passages in Modern Sculpture*, 4–5.
85. Ibid., 209 and 204. Original emphasis.
86. Fried, 'Art and Objecthood,' 145.
87. Krauss, *Passages in Modern Sculpture*, 114.
88. Sofer, 'Properties,' 560–61.
89. Rogozinski, 'Winter Peacock,' 24. The reference in the following sentence refers to the same page.
90. Joe Kelleher, *The Illuminated Theatre: Studies on the Suffering of Images* (London and New York: Routledge, 2015), 5.
91. Rogozinski, 'Winter Peacock,' 25 and 28.
92. Goumarre in *Marie Cool Fabio Balducci: Untitled (Prayers)*, 13 and 10–11.
93. Ibid., 7 and 5.
94. Ibid., 5.
95. Joseph Leo Koerner, 'Bosch's Equipment,' in *Things That Talk: Object Lessons from Art and Science*, ed. Lorraine Daston, 57.
96. Goumarre in *Marie Cool Fabio Balducci: Untitled (Prayers)*, 14.
97. Mel Bochner, 'Serial Art, Systems, Solipsism' [1967], in *Minimal Art: A Critical Anthology*, ed. Gregory Battcock, 100.
98. Batchelor, *Minimalism*, 47
99. Foster, *The Return of the Real*, 59.
100. Batchelor, *Minimalism*, 65.
101. Ibid. Original emphasis.
102. Henry M. Sayre, *The Object of Performance: The American Avant-Garde Since 1970* (Chicago and London: University of Chicago Press, 1989), 34.
103. Daston, 'Introduction: Speechless,' 24.
104. Rogozinski, 'Winter Peacock,' 29.
105. Brown, 'Thing Theory,' 4–5.
106. Ibid., 5.

2 Theatre & Gallery
Turning Away from Performance

Visiting Tate Modern, London, as it was in November 2007 visitors encounter an exhibition called *The World as a Stage* and within this event an opening exhibit by Slovakian artist Roman Ondák. Titled *I'm just acting in it* (2007) and displayed on three walls of the foremost gallery, each drawing in this series of images is produced by a non-professional maker. The sequence, in contrast, is constructed by the artist, Ondák, whose name is appended to the piece, and whose figure the images attempt to represent. The artist's labour here is not pictorial but curatorial. It signals a certain intricacy of arrangement and composition significant to the schematics of exhibition as well as to my work in this book as concerned with drawing focus between the events about which I am writing and the individual artworks as related therein. This exhibit speaks too of commissions, substitutions, and acts of standing in. Based on verbal accounts given to each of the participants by the exhibition curators, Catherine Wood and Jessica Morgan, the pictures show Ondák moving alone through the empty spaces of Tate Modern prior to the installation of *The World as a Stage*. Displaying the physical limitations of artistic ability and based upon oral descriptions of an unfamiliar figure in a familiar environment, *I'm just acting in it* is a compound record based on multiple events which begin with an artist in a gallery space.

Represented in a variety of perspectives, colourations, and stances, the figure of the artist becomes in these images not performer, as the title of the work *I'm just acting in it* might suggest, but rather, I would propose, art object, observed and displayed through collaborative acts of delegated remembrance. Amateur impressions of a now absent artist, the drawings recall Peggy Phelan's influential discussion of photographs by conceptual artist Sophie Calle. Showing galleries in the Isabella Stewart Gardner Museum in Boston from whence valuable paintings were stolen, Calle's images, as well as Phelen's prominent engagement with this project, also display something misplaced. These photographs of empty galleries, the installation shot not, this time, *sans figures* but rather, in this case, *sans objets d'art*, were displayed alongside interviews with museum staff and visitors also recalling the lost works. Each of these descriptions, or documents as they come to be through Calle's attention and transcription, becomes an affecting and 'unstatic' object, or, more significantly, an articulation celebrated by Phelan as a 'performative expression,' when placed within the representational field of the gallery.[1]

Affording to museological objects the possibility of performative status, in Ondák's work, as in Calle's, the act of display is the means which renders the object-document performative. These actions of 'substituting the subject's memory of the object for the object itself' initiate a process by which it might be possible, following Phelan, to 'redesign the order of the museum'.[2] Presenting what the gallery first seems unable to contain, the object lost or the performance past, exhibition events which operate in dialogue with performance, or take on motifs and conceptions of the theatrical event, are explicitly concerned with reimagining how the latter might function within contexts of display. The question then becomes about the prospect of reconciling the stipulation of ephemerality, until recently endemic and still appropriately persistent in performance studies, with exhibitions such as *The World as a Stage* which present an expanded view of what might count as performance, as well as within which institutional, exhibitory, and formal frames it might be possible to look for and indeed locate this practice.

A Rich Terrain to Be Plundered

Recollecting an accumulation of exhibits which, in their curation together, both reflect and impact on recent dialogues between display and theatrical encounter, this chapter restages particular elements from two concurrent visual arts exhibitions which took on the potentialities and problematics of performance and its associated paradigms. It would be obvious to say that two major cultural institutions were at the same moment, or, in quick succession, engaging with similar concerns. It is not surprising that such spaces share narrative connections, especially given the recent plethora of interest internationally in gallery-based explorations of performance and the questions of liveness, ephemerality, and documentation connected with performative modes. There are, however, certain contours and dynamics which are useful to tease out from these specific operations and, by putting two distinct events in conversation, I want to use the happenstance of parallel programming to discuss conceptual and theoretical implications which exceed the coincidental and speak to the complexities of theatre and the gallery.

The events addressed in this section are founded on, and titled as explicitly concerned with, concepts of performance but take the form of exhibitions of curated physical objects. The first, *Renoir at the Theatre: Looking at La Loge*, was curated by Barnaby Wright in a single room on the second floor of the Courtauld Gallery in London from 21 February to 25 May 2008. Centred on Pierre-Auguste Renoir's iconic painting *La Loge* (1874), a work showing two figures in the auditorium of a performance venue and significant in terms of visual arts' historical investment in images of the theatre, this exhibition brings together pictures from a previous period of artistic practice. It combines a number of artworks with popular fashion images and caricatures, all of which reveal a fascination with the loge, or theatre box, as a place for social display. Looking again at works produced during the nineteenth century, *Renoir at the Theatre* finds its significance through a kind of double return: first, in its focus on documenting, or at least representing, fleeting moments in the theatre; and, second, by its re-collection of images illustrative of this depiction in a present-day context, in an arrested again or another illumination.

Also invested in possibilities of performance not made manifest through a transitory 'live' encounter, but rather in more object-centric formulations, *The World as a Stage* occupied a large exhibition space on the fourth floor of Tate Modern in London one month earlier, from 24 October 2007 to 1 January 2008. Appropriating a Shakespearean title, this exhibition takes simile as a means of conceptualising the interaction between selected works and genres and casts one form as another, life as art and display as performance. Director of Tate Modern at the time, Vicente Todolí, proposed in his Foreword to the exhibition catalogue that, the 'idea of "theatre" is treated by artists within *The World as a Stage* as both an analytic tool and a rich terrain to be explored, experimented with, and plundered.'[3] Thinking theatre both as a means of production and as a distinct field with specific ontological and epistemological conventions, this exhibition, at least conceptually, models exactly my concern in this book, specifically how imagining performance through the optic of another mode of production and public display might allow us to extend our formulations of what constitutes performance as occasion and as practice.

While not uniformly successful in terms of affective experience, these exhibitions are curious for their investment in the presentation of performative referents. Given this attribute, and the emergence of both cases in a specific moment in the history of the display of theatricality in London, that is, in the aftermath of the 2007 dissolution of London's Theatre Museum, it seems productive to formulate the implications of these exhibitions for performance. Todolí's terminology in his Foreword is troubling. To 'plunder' recalls a museological history which includes appropriated objects and contemporary calls for repatriation. It speaks too about the ways in which performance has most commonly come to enter art institutions by according or being assumed into the systems of the latter. *The World as a Stage* and *Renoir at the Theatre* address precisely the possibility of displaying performance in gallery settings and the ways in which, according to the exhibition leaflet accompanying the event at Tate, 'ideas of performance and staging inflect our understanding of art' and, I would propose, vice-versa.[4] It is noteworthy that in these case studies the terrain of engagement is specifically theatrical. Read in association, these events take forward the discussion in different but related ways from the previous chapter of this book and those, like Michael Fried, for whom theatricality was an indecorous subject and mode in twentieth-century art practice. The exhibitions progress from the coincident rejection of the temporal qualities linked with theatricality by modernist art critics, and, along with ideals of the autonomous art object, the theatrical properties of illusion by artists claiming a distinct domain for performance. As in the examples addressed in Chapter 1, this expansion is approached via works that, in Wood's terms, 'deliberately muddle literal presence with the possibilities offered by the aesthetic imagination, mixing direct experience and representation.'[5]

Ambitious Antecedents

Recollecting works from a previous period of artistic practice, *Renoir at the Theatre* necessarily relates the contemporary moment to an historical creative one, while the works assembled for *The World as a Stage*, according to their textual curatorial framing, are 'brought together in an attempt to consider the renewed appeal of the notion of "theatre" for a significant number of artists working today.'[6] These exhibitions respond to and redraw the allure and possibilities of theatricality for artists presenting their work in gallery-contexts and offer the opportunity to rethink the points of connection between theatre and gallery, exhibition and performance. In this chapter, I want to reconfigure these events in a cross-temporally inflected contemporary relation in order to explore in detail this rekindled interest in performance, specifically theatre, and the shared narrative and conceptual concerns to which these events are addressed and on which their curation expands. Both exhibitions are constructed through the association of objects not artist or medium-specific but rather collected thematically and concerned with theatre and performance and the relation between the displayed and the performed even, and perhaps especially, before their revelations are applied here. The theatre offers a useful space through which to imagine contemporary relations between performance and exhibition not least because, following Wood, in its bringing together of actor and audience, scenery and prop, it is already a 'territory that links image, object and embodied perception' prior to its evocation in the gallery.[7] I turn to the two specific cases presented in this chapter in order to illustrate the ways in which these topical debates of performance and display are currently being communicated and what aspects of their present intersection and exchange the revival of a former creative climate might work to clarify.

Addressing a pair of examples, one in which a traditional gallery context, renowned for its impressionist and post-impressionist collections, draws together historic works which depict the theatre, and another which constitutes an exhibition-based engagement with performance founded in contemporary practice, establishes the scene in which these events occur as difficult to dismiss as a mere curatorial fad. Rather, *The World as a Stage*, and *Renoir at the Theatre*, form within each gallery space an intertwining of exhibition and performance, and, across London, construct a cumulative and interwoven series of events. Nineteenth-century images of popular culture reinstalled by the Courtauld resonate in subject and approach with newer works curated by Tate Modern, mutually engaging with and inflecting contemporary dialogues between exhibition and the theatrical event. Brought into contact with another curatorial project similarly attuned to the performance field and engaged with the display of performance-related objects, the resonance of older artistic productions exceeds the cultural context of their making. That is to say, the historical moment of composition of the works within *Renoir at the Theatre* cannot be read as straightforwardly indicative of their chronological imperative. Considered alongside *The World as a Stage,* the art reframed by and displayed within *Renoir at the Theatre* can be reviewed in relation to current gallery-based intersections with practices of performance. There are implications in this re-association for the later works too. When looked at in combination, these exhibitions reveal the ways in which creative practices employ, what art historian Hal Foster might call, 'ambitious antecedents' in order to respond to and advance present preoccupations and possibilities, as well as generate prospects and scenarios through which to consider further, in this case, the complexities of theatre and performance in and as exhibition.[8]

Striking similarities between these two distinct events emerge if we take seriously and relatively their curatorial conceptions and the language in which these framings are conveyed to visitors. Renoir was, according to the Courtauld Gallery website, 'the first artist to make the theatre box a subject for modern painting'.[9] Transposing theatrical situations into painted forms and moving the dramatic into the world of visual arts, and by implication into institutionalised art galleries, the works collected for *Renoir at the Theatre* are presented as primary correlations between the displayed and the performed within a specific period of creative practice. While the Courtauld Gallery positions their exhibition as founded on an original artistic engagement with a particular theatrical space, *The World as a Stage* is correspondingly marketed as a novel connection with a specifically theatrical subject and introduced as the 'first exhibition at Tate Modern to bring the realm of performance into dialogue with gallery-based work.'[10] The paintings collected for *Renoir at the Theatre* recall a significant departure from convention, an initiation of original figurations and, according to curator Catherine Wood, the artists in *The World as a Stage* mean also to construct a 'different kind of space that lies between two representational modes,' colliding the four walls of the white cube and the proscenium theatre.[11]

Grouping the exhibitions initially through this shared agenda of originality focused through performance, as in the case of *The World as a Stage*, so it is 'precisely a rejection of medium-specificity that unites the artists here; a willingness to reintroduce elements of narrative, figuration, theatre and a refusal to exclude the possibilities inherent in other disciplines.'[12] Impressionist painters, via their engagement with theatrical spaces, developed, in the first instance, a new form of expression, attending within the canvas to the coeval panoramas of their social milieu. Not only figuring scenes of 'profound change in French society', theatre boxes also provided, drawing text from a wall plaque on display within the Courtauld's exhibition, a 'stage for the expression of a radical new language of painting' and, I want to suggest, performance. All of the images collected together for *Renoir at the Theatre* focus invariably on the theatregoer, rather than the performer, particular details of an historic production, or specific acts of performance. In this way, the theatre comes to represent a space wherein, following historian of fashion Aileen Ribeiro, 'people acquire social status through display' in an intriguing affiliation of theatre, exhibition, and public stature.[13] What is significant about this refocusing of and on the auditorium, and the stress on visitation and pageantry which results from this emphasis, as well as its curatorial narration, is the emergence of a principle of exhibition founded in the theatre – itself a material space where actions of display and performance combine.

Turning Away from Performance

Involved in an intricate exchange with a range of other media and modes of expression, the theatrical context which drew the attention of Renoir, as well as other impressionist painters, was realised through and in association with practitioners working across adjoining art forms. 'That there was a highly permeable interface and multifarious two-way traffic between art and the stage is hardly an unfamiliar aspect of the cultural history of this period,' write Sarah Hibberd and Richard Wrigley of the early nineteenth century in their study of *Art, Theatre, and Opera in Paris, 1750–1850*, however, following their perspective, 'what has been too little explored and focused on is precisely which ideas and images were crossing over'.[14] One such impression or motif which emerges as significant in *Renoir at the Theatre* and elsewhere, for example within Marcel Proust's great literary work *À la recherche du temps perdu* (*In Search of Lost Time* 1913–27), is the loge. In a section of the latter depicting a gala evening at the Paris Opéra, the narrator renders each of these spaces as a 'cube of semi-darkness,' a black box wherein spectral occupants, alike to a 'theatrical apparition,' have 'taken refuge against their shadowy walls and remained invisible' until the onstage performance begins and draws these figures outwards to the periphery of that zone.[15] Proust's words take us beyond the bounds of *Renoir at the Theatre* and into the world which the particular collection of images presented within the latter seek to evoke.

Back in the Courtauld Gallery, the exhibition unfolds exactly as its full title suggests. The artist, Renoir, positioned as metonymic for a number of image-makers, takes the art world to the theatre. His attention, and by implication that of the gallery visitors, is not, however, directed to the confines of any specific or delineated theatrical performance; none of the images constituting *Renoir at the Theatre* depict a stage or any action of performers at work. Rather, the exhibition, and the paintings which comprise it, are constricted by a particular field of encounter: the subject of the theatre box and the theatre-goer on display within that frame. As visitors to this event, we are *Looking at La Loge* and this space is characterised recurrently as a place for social agency and encounter. In Proust's imagining, stalls seats are purchased by those wishing to 'study the appearance of people whom they might not have another opportunity of seeing at close quarters. And it was indeed a fragment of their true social life, ordinarily concealed, that one could examine here in public,' at the theatre, paraded and on show.[16] In *Renoir at the Theatre* too, the theatre box is presented in the texts accompanying the exhibition as a particular and alternative kind of 'stage where status and relationships were on public display', exhibited precisely through actions of 'turning away from the performance'.[17] Broadening the remit of the theatrical experience to acknowledge acts of attendance, of watching, and of being watched, the paintings displayed within this exhibition look away, I would suggest, not from performance, as the gallery texts support, but rather from the limitations of the stage and towards supplementary modes of performance which function through display.

Figure 2.1 Mary Stevenson Cassatt, *Woman with a Pearl Necklace in a Loge*, 1879. Courtesy of the Philadelphia Museum of Art.

At the Opéra, 'the society people sat in their boxes (behind the tiered circle) as in so many little suspended drawing-rooms, the fourth walls of which had been removed,' writes Proust in a striking turn of phrase which translates the terms of the fourth wall of the proscenium box set to the situation of the loge. Within these little theatres, the occupants of each loge sit, bordered by 'mirrors in gilt frames or the red plush seats, in the Neapolitan style, of the establishment.'[18] Investing in the social world of the playhouse as, what history of dress scholar Aileen Ribeiro calls within the exhibition catalogue for *Renoir at the Theatre*, a 'theatre of display,' the absence of any rendition of a stage or designated performance area is particularly notable in American painter and printmaker Mary Stevenson Cassatt's painting *Femme dans une loge* or *Woman with a Pearl Necklace in a Loge* (1879).[19] Looking beyond the factions of any particular ensemble and towards the auditorium and other sorts of drama founded in social spectacle, the image depicts a woman reclining in a theatre box. The background of the scene is constructed through a mirror which reflects the theatre setting as it might appear to the figure from her position within the loge. Rather than representing a stage production or the presence of professional actors, the reflected scene reveals only further loges and audience members. Visible neither in the primary plane nor the reflected surfaces of the image, the stage is not the object of interest either for Cassatt or, it would seem, for the theatre-goer on display within her work. The focus for both women is on other actions and models of performative encounter occurring in the vicinity of and in relation to the stage, and thus on an expanded notion of the occasion and event of theatre.

In Cassatt's painting, as in Proust's transcription of a comparable theatrical scene, such figures 'emerge into the chiaroscuro of the surface where their gleaming faces appeared behind the playful, frothy undulations of their ostrich-feather fans,' the detail of the descriptions, both painterly and written, drawing focus to accessories of costume such as to imply that the wearers, as well as those observing these fashions, 'paid no attention to what was being played.'[20] Throughout *Renoir at the Theatre*, in the caricature 'Le Folies-Garnier-Nouvel Opèra' and the engraving 'Loges et Types de Grand Théatre', both originally published in *Le Vie Parisienne* in 1875, the painted spectators persistently look, and are narrated by the wall plaques within the exhibition as looking, 'everywhere apart from the stage.' The artists of these engravings, like the audiences they present, make no attempt to observe or envision a particular theatrical production. Rather, as is the case throughout *Renoir at the Theatre* and *The World as a Stage* more broadly, these represented theatregoers engage with performance obliquely, through other optics of interest and encounter. The inhabitants of these loges, though present in the theatre, are not attentive to any implied stage play but rather drawn to other types of social experience offered by their surroundings, and it is to such scenes that the attention of gallery visitors is also directed.

Performing the Object

Despite, or perhaps because of, its title, *The World as a Stage*, like *Renoir at the Theatre*, contains no exhibit which explicitly represents a stage setting. Instead, as visitors move into the gallery, prior even to discovering the installation by Ondák, with which I began my narrative and thereby marked my account as a reconstruction of the event and its curation towards a further end, we are addressed by a staff member who speaks according to the directions of Berlin-based artist Tino Sehgal. Following the instructions of the artist, each entry to the exhibition initiates, what co-curator Jessica Morgan calls, an 'unexpected announcement'.[21] Surprising only to one participant in what is, in fact, a pre-scripted exchange, the caption voiced on my first visit to *The World as a Stage* was spoken tentatively: 'Tread lightly and make a difference'. This phrase, and others which different attendants might choose, is repeated, I discover later, from a headline in a daily newspaper selected each day by the gallery assistant on duty. The expression transcribed here represents the only occasion on which I experienced this act without understanding the source and motivation behind its utterance. Mistaking the phrase for an invitation, recognition of the possibility that my visit to the exhibition might somehow alter what happens therein, it is only afterwards that I appreciate the implications and loaded nature of this encounter.

Transliterating newspaper headlines into the curatorial framework of a gallery exhibition inflects the attention these phrases and notices receive, changing their character from the domain of everyday exchange into another sort of cultural encounter. Inserting what Wood describes as 'scripted episodes' into what is made to appear, at least, as an 'apparently "neutral" staffing structure,' these attendant-nominated headlines shift the potential for natural dialogue between visitor and gallery employee.[22] Performed under the paradoxical title *This is new* (2003), and considered as 'episodes', a term deeply rooted in the interlocutory, the interpolated, and the incidental, these artist-directed phrases, despite their spoken form, do not remain in the domain of the intangible. 'Motivated by a desire to resist his works being replaced by a photograph or video,' Sehgal's creative projects evade the complications of performance documentation via a 'complete disavowal of material remains' while at the same time, as Head of Collection Care Research at Tate Pip Laurenson, and conservation scholar Vivian van Saaze note, 'his practice shows a more complex relation towards material objecthood.' Enacted throughout gallery opening hours and issued as a limited edition with a minimum display period, instead of 'going against the traditional way of dealing with artefacts within a museum structure, Sehgal's works take on many of the forms of a material object', these conservators suggest, so as to become profitable, procurable, and collectable.[23]

From the perspective of preservation management, Laurenson and van Saaze are keen to stress the influence of models such as Sehgal's for the development of practices of collection. By thinking performance in an altered relation to commodity status, situational work, such as *This is new*, offers an approach through which, in the terms of Laurenson and van Saaze, 'artists, both contemporary and from an earlier context, can frame their works in ways in which they might be collected and ... integrated into existing systems.'[24] What is perhaps troubling here is an implicit suggestion that live work ought to aspire to, be structured so as to promote, museological accommodation and inclusion. While, as Wood observes in her writing on 'People and Things in the Museum' (2014), Sehgal's high-profile installations have, in recent years, 'played a major part in forcing the question of liveness in the museum,' these actions have 'had to perform a kind of sophisticated "drag" as objects in order to find firm footing in its permanent collection.' Impersonating the object-centric formulations of traditional museology, Sehgal's work, Wood writes, 'invariably possesses limits that give it a sculptural singularity, meaning that as a total entity on display, it somehow "behaves" very much like a Rodin or a Mondrian.'[25] In this case, the spoken interactions of *This is new* are sculptural and inscriptive, such that their forms speak to visual masterpieces well instated in the canon. While presented live within exhibition contexts and therefore, at least in some aspects, akin to performance, such strategies, which allow Sehgal's work to be accommodated within the terrain of art institutions, require a different kind of engagement to that necessitated in relation to live performance and in the realm of the theatre.

When we speak to those interpreting Sehgal's instructions, Wood suggests, 'we experience it without dissolving ourselves into the suspended disbelief that we'd take to a play. Rather, we are self-conscious of being next to and "in" an art work, and we feel ourselves somehow solidify into an object too within this exchange.'[26] Making interactions within the gallery artefactual, these interactions implicate the visitor in the domain of the objectified. In the experience of theatre scholar Nicholas Ridout, we also encounter visitors' contributions to Sehgal's works as 'already pinned up on the wall for inspection.'[27] These are experiences always already designed, collected, and exhibited. Employing a museological image which situates enactments of pre-scripted dialogue as objects on display, both Ridout's evocative phrasing and Wood's engagement with Sehgal's practice capture the constructed and deliberate nature of this initial exchange. Within the confines of Tate Modern, visitors' first initiation into *The World as a Stage* is not an invitation to interpret the gallery in terms of theatrical performance. Gallery-goers do not discover familiar theatrical spaces or stagings but rather are presented with an inversion in which the temporality of speech and the performance of the spoken word are assimilated into and re-focused according to the patterns of viewing more conventional to the object-centric materiality of the museum. It is not, however, safe to assume that this relation between performance and display will remain consistent throughout the exhibition. Rather, other exhibits challenge the ways in which it might be possible to encounter the museological object.

Substitutional Curation

Invested in exploring the object-status of performative referents, American artist Trisha Donnelly contributes to *The World as a Stage* a work encountered by visitors as a still and indeterminate instant related to the promise of performance. Emerging from what art historian Henry M. Sayre might call 'a curatorial taste for documentation,' *The Redwood and the Raven* (2004) contradicts the designation of stillness often associated with performance photography and brings into question the modes of knowing possible and anticipated within exhibition contexts.[28] Appearing to visitors as a single, relatively small, black and white image, this work might show, as it did when I encountered it in November 2007, and as it is does here within the pages of this book, a dancer in front of a large tree trunk with her gaze lowered, her right hand raised above her head. Presented in this way, Donnelly's *The Redwood and the Raven* stages, in Wood's terms, the 'dilemma of representation as a moment of stasis straining against life's mobility.'[29] Pinned to the wall of a central gallery without explanation and almost unnoticeable, this understated image seems initially to be a solitary photograph portraying a dance enacted well beyond the confines of the Tate Modern galleries. In short, it appears as a performance document.[30] Despite its apparently simple veneer, *The Redwood and the Raven* is in fact composed not merely in one picture but as a sequence of thirty-one photographs. These stills, which, visitors are told, record a dance choreographed to a poem by Edgar Allen Poe, struggle not only against the momentum of dancer Frances Flannery, and her performance, but also the itinerancy of gallery visitors, since each day a different image from the series is displayed within the context of the exhibition.[31]

Figure 2.2 Trisha Donnelly, *The Redwood and the Raven*, 2004. 31 C-Prints changed each day.

Inciting visitors, as Rebecca Schneider does also, to 'look differently at the photos we pass by,' *The Redwood and the Raven* hails gallery-goers to return to *The World as a Stage* multiple times.[32] The images thereby raise a not immaterial question about the conventional temporal frames in which we view art and how many times a visitor might reasonably be expected to attend a temporary, and I should add, ticketed, exhibition event. In contrast to its initial appearance as static object, *The Redwood and the Raven*, what visitors see of this work, and the acts of re-visitation this might prompt, position the exhibit as precisely time specific. The images function in a space between the seeming endurance of the photograph and the presumed transience of performance. With other parts of the routine concealed from view, the dancer's steps can be inferred only by the imaginative recombination of elements which continually and cyclically evade us, both within the frame of each image and their sequential display. In this way, *The Redwood and the Raven* counters interpretations which locate photography as still and develops instead, what Sayre calls, photography's 'double stance – its ability to be read in terms of *both* presence and absence.'[33] Playing with the position of the photograph as simultaneously present as an art object and at the same time rendering an absent experience, in Donnelly's sequence of images this framework is inverted. Here, the objects disappear, or at least change, while a dance of a different sort appears through acts of circulatory and substitutional curation.

Working against the ubiquity of the autonomous art object, these images operate in terms more conventional to performance, so that, looking towards the return to relational aesthetics on which I will focus in the next chapter of this book, the artwork is presented here not to be 'consumed within a "monumental" time frame' but rather 'elapses within a factual time, for an audience *summoned* by the artist.'[34] In addition to the shifting images which are replaced and re-displayed over the course of the exhibition, motion comes also to *The Redwood and the Raven* via the performance of hailing inherent in this interplay. Attendance, how many times a visitor comes to *The World as a Stage* and our inclination to come to the gallery again or not, impacts literally on what can be seen of the exhibit. So too do aesthetic and institutional expectations. Prompting a series of errors in terms of visual interpretation, we assume the image on first appearance to be singular, we assume its installation to be enduring, we assume that it documents a previous act of performance; in short, visitors, or at least I, make the reasonable, given the gallery context, mistake of thinking about *The Redwood and the Raven* in terms of paradigms of display rather than those of performance. While Sehgal's *This is new* converts a scripted exchange into the terms of the traditionally object-centric museum, Donnelly's *The Redwood and the Raven* reveals objects as in performance, signalling the reception of a specific art form as something often mediated according to the set of expectations associated with another.

Creating photographs that 'both document theatricality (the posing subject) and *are* theatrical (the photograph *is* the performance)', *The Redwood and the Raven* creates an experience, which Schneider might call, 'disturbingly ongoing, even "live," in the global space of the encountered photograph.' Thinking photography as 'another among a great many technologies of the live,' Schneider has, amongst others, been extensively engaged in a reconfiguration of discourses which adhere to the disappearance of performance and the exclusion of qualities of liveness from other documents and objects.[35] On discovering that Donnelly's exhibit is constructed as a sequence of photographs, our engagement with the installation inevitably alters. Whether the photographs document a past event and what sense of this previous performance they might enable visitors to perceive is perhaps not important. What becomes significant, rather, is the performance these images play out within the context of exhibition and the ways in which this performance is displayed through a mode of expression that is object-centric. Both Schneider and performance scholar Philip Auslander have made a case for the document as a site of performance but, from within the context of display, *The Redwood and the Raven* thinks this relation somewhat differently. Donnelly's installation appears to me to be distinct from the interrelated categories of performance documentation observed by Auslander as the *documentary*, that is to say the object as record, evidence, and supplement of the event, and the *theatrical,* wherein the document becomes 'the only space in which the performance occurs.'[36] Rather than transpiring within the frame of the photographic document, the performance of *The Redwood and the Raven* occurs through the space of exhibition.

Referents of Performance

Reaching spatially and temporally both across and beyond the confines of the gallery, many of the objects collected for *The World as a Stage*, including *The Redwood and the Raven,* are positioned, by co-curator of the exhibition Jessica Morgan, as making 'reference to arts and performances previously staged'.[37] Though perhaps at times misleading, it is not surprising that Morgan positions the exhibits as referential of past acts given that documentation can be identified in recent discourses of performance research, borrowing Matthew's Reason's succinct précis, as a 'strong though contradictory thread running through the live arts.'[38] Some of the works collected for *The World as a Stage* have appeared before as facets of exhibitions on other themes and in other places, but as referents of performance, I want to suggest, these objects, as is the case with *The Redwood and the Raven,* as well as others of its compatriots, need only *appear* to be remains of performance, rather than being actual material detritus from specific theatrical productions, in order to conjure this terrain. The relation of document to performance pans out differently here to that categorised by Auslander as *theatrical* by relying on curatorial practice and the space of exhibition, as in the case of *The Redwood and the Raven*, or, as in the following example, because the action invoked by the document is not specific or easily identifiable.

Frequently included in appraisals of participatory art, such as those with which Chapter 3 of this book engages, the work of Polish artist Pawel Althamer often involves delegation or collaboration with participants, including those with personal experience of homelessness, immigration, and disability. Within Tate Modern, Althamer's *Self-Portrait as a Businessman* (2002–4) conveys a sense, also evident in Ondák's work, that others have been here in the gallery before us. There is a suggestion that what remains here, in terms borrowed from Joe Kelleher, are 'signs of life that are both fleeting *and* remaining, signs of others who were there and who almost *seem* to be there still, but who have left us'.[39] Ephemeral and residual, Althamer's installation appears as a heap of discarded clothes and other personal belongings which rest on the floor of the gallery, crumpled and unattended. Occupying positions which feel temporary and suggest a sort of casting off, these trappings shift and materialise in alternative associations and formations each time I visit *The World as a Stage*. Suggestive of a former act of presentation and portrayal, this stuff, what Morgan calls 'props or costumes from an earlier performance', is narrated by the exhibition texts as 'abandoned in a swift change of role and left as evidence of the "act"'.[40] Morgan's terms are precisely indefinite here, suggesting an indeterminate action taking place at some time past. In fact, this accumulation remains from a performance through which Althamer deposited these belongings within an exhibition in Berlin wherein *Self-Portrait as a Businessman* was first exhibited in 2002. These object-documents, and their curatorial framing within Tate Modern, do not make clear whether an equivalent performance took place prior to *The World as a Stage* or whether their referent is the preceding sequence of events.

Documentation has a complex relation not only to the ontology of performance but also to art. Writing in 2008, art theorist and curator Boris Groys observed that, in recent decades, 'it has become increasingly evident that the art world has shifted its interest away from the artwork and towards art documentation.'[41] For Groys, the latter is displacing traditional expectations about what we might encounter within exhibition environments since, according to his theory, 'documentation is by definition *not* art; it merely refers to art, and in precisely this way it makes clear that art, in this case, is no longer present and immediately visible but rather absent and hidden.'[42] Art has, in short, taken on certain qualities more often associated with the after-effects of performance. What interests me about Groys' argument, particularly in relation to Althamer's installation, is his elucidation of the document as referent. In his rendering, documentation cannot be an artwork but rather refers to that structure. In this chapter, the art document comes to reference not a specific art event but rather performance in more general terms. Within the case studies presented here, as in Groys' analysis, 'more and more art documentation is being produced and exhibited that does not claim to make present any past art event.'[43] While Groys is referencing artworks which involve interventionist actions into everyday life, rather than art encounters more explicitly identified as such, through this chapter this statement becomes applicable to the workings of a different kind of referent that engages with performance.

Installed in the Tate Modern galleries, the objects which make up *Self-Portrait as a Businessman* come to insinuate not a distinct antecedent but rather, borrowing from Schneider's related study, 'something that might have been, as the precise reference is intimated but not immediately apparent.'[44] Resisting any drive to convey the particularities of a specific event, Althamer's installation functions so that, rather than revealing the disappearance of a performance, as documents in other contexts might, this accumulation, by presenting a less distinct experience, makes visible some sense of performance more broadly. As in the case of *The Redwood and the Raven*, so *Self-Portrait as a Businessman* seems to function differently to Auslander's entanglement of documentary and theatrical categorisations. The precise referent of the document is unclear and so cannot be easily identified as imagined or otherwise, even though these are quite definitely objects related to an 'ostensible' performance.[45] The range of referents is not clearly stated but rather obscured and obliquely professed by the exhibition curators and the discourses they construct around this work as it appears within *The World as a Stage*. This framing seems to me to make the objects all the more compelling and suggestive of the interconnections between performance, document, and display and the potential of this relation.

Reconstructing Narratives

In Donnelly's *The Redwood and the Raven*, performance documentation, often conceived, as in Groys' analysis, as 'images and texts that are reproducible, acquires through the installation an aura of the original, the living,' and, I would add, the performed.[46] Within the same exhibition, Althamer's *Self-Portrait as a Businessman* shifts the place of the apparent performance-document from an act of preservation to something which, within projects in other times and in other places, might initiate remaking. The objects from which the installation is constructed which seemed, as Schneider describes of comparable performing documents and remains, to 'indicate only the past, are now pitched toward the possibility of a future reenactment as much as toward the event apparently recorded.'[47] Within Tate Modern, the garments belonging to *Self-Portrait as a Businessman* have already started to move and migrate gradually in their relation; the clothes and collectables call forth motion and action. At first, a tie sits on top of a jacket, below this, a white shirt, to the left, a belt and trousers, to the right, a pair of spectacles. Certain changes indicate a fragility, or mobility, inherent to the installation of these apparently forgotten items so that, by the time of my second visit, the glasses have wandered onto the shirt, a mobile phone touches the collar of this garment, and an open wallet of tickets and cards, which I had not noticed before, sits centrally. Limited only by the distance visitors are instructed to maintain, these objects might come to be costume and props for future acts of making and performance.

Pursuing this line of thought through a further example so that the accumulative force of these artworks in their curation together might be appreciated, Canadian artist Geoffrey Farmer's *Hunchback Kit* (2000) is also poised towards the potential of this interface between exhibition and inferred performance. Resonant with the material form of Althamer's installation, this *Kit* appears as an 'accumulation of objects or props', this time for use in what co-curator Morgan cites as 'conventional adaptations' of Victor Hugo's novel *Notre-Dame of Paris*.[48] Looking towards coming acts of traditional theatrical production, this work, spread throughout a large room in Tate Modern, like Ondák's, Donnelly's and indeed Althamer's, though perhaps more explicitly, embeds an artistic concept of curation in its installation, becoming a kind of micro-exhibition within the larger frame of *The World as a Stage*. *Hunchback Kit* shares with *Self-Portrait as Businessman* a feeling of instantaneous abandon characteristic of the style of display found throughout the surrounding exhibition. Adopting a deconstructive approach to objects, and thinking conceptually about the material space in which Hugo's narrative is set, this collection of prop-objects maps the notion of a bell across the gallery. Looking broadly, we see the large bell wheel which provides a reference point for understanding what is contained within the multiple display cabinets as a set of connected concepts. Employing a range of scales, varying from the substantial to the intricate, from videos and books to tuning forks, the installation must be viewed laterally by visitors in order for the potential of this specific assemblage to be seen.

Thinking about this collection, and the different layers of its curation, cumulatively, visitors might add together its exploded parts according to multiple associations and in different formations. Revealing and exploiting what Wood calls theatre's 'extreme capacity for dispersal and portability,' within Farmer's installation visitors discover a beige luggage tag with a black printed address which reads, 'WHITECHAPEL BELL FOUNDRY LTD. 32 & 34 Whitechapel Road, London, E1 1DY.'[49] In this temporary context, this location appears as a forwarding address, a future or past venue, or a context which lends veracity to the accumulation of objects. The kind of formal and official text in which this label, as well as the display information printed onto the gallery walls, is inscribed contrasts to descriptions in pencil which supplement this, extending the feeling of provisionality within the installation and suggesting more personal, informal clues to its possibilities. By framing the installation as a 'kit', Wood suggests, Farmer invites the 'viewer to imaginatively reconstruct a well-known narrative.'[50] Of course, this elucidation of Farmer's titling refers to Hugo's novel. I would suggest, however, that installations such as Farmer's, and *The World as a Stage* more broadly, also offer the opportunity to rebuild, or at least stage anew, a different sort of narrative, founded in relationships between visual art and theatricality, ephemerality and documentation, and performance and object.

Offering a variety of constructions and assemblages, the objects within Farmer's *Kit*, Morgan suggests, 'can be displayed – that is, staged – in radically different ways with each presentation.'[51] The intersection of ideas of staging and display is telling here. This opportunity for re-staging and revised presentation looks to future existences and imaginings of the work, and of the relation between concepts of performance and those of exhibition. *The World as a Stage* is one in a number of exhibitions in which, in Wood's words, rather than 'championing performance as a form of "authentic" opposition to gallery-based art,' it might now be more productive to 'understand relations between performance and the object in terms of a theatrical situation.'[52] Rethinking the interconnection between performance and art object as a combination of circumstances inherently theatrical, *Hunchback Kit* invites performance through object-display. What links the works exhibited within *The World as a Stage*, including Farmer's *Hunchback Kit*, Donnelly's *The Redwood and the Raven*, and Althamer's *Self-Portrait as a Businessman*, is a curatorial concept which describes the state of relations between performance and display, taking up Wood's suggestion, as a 'co-dependent situation of reciprocity that fears neither the "achieving of objecthood" for live work, nor the art object as prop or "stage setting".'[53] Having engaged with two events in Chapter 1 which exemplify the possibility of the human body occupying positions usually held by curated objects and vice-versa, *The World as a Stage*, at least theoretically, develops this transposition into a more nuanced interplay. Applying Wood's conception literally and specifically to the works her exhibition connects, it is possible, as my last examples show, to support this correlation of art objects with places for performance and props, and, further, to identify these as already intermediate sites between theatre and visual art. As in Chapter 1, performance is associated here with object-status, not least in Donnelly's location of liveness within a displayed photographic series. In order to concretise these reflections, it is this idea of a sort of 'live objecthood' which I would now like to pursue further.

Objecthood for Live Work

Having lingered in Tate Modern, and offered some readings of certain exhibits presented therein, as well as of their interconnections, let me continue by taking this condition of interdependence between objecthood and performance back to *Renoir at the Theatre* and pursuing some of the works which this exhibition contains with this thesis in mind. The exhibits presented within the Courtauld Gallery can comparably be seen to operate across terrains of object and action, this time in order to arrest and depict something of the theatrical encounter of spectatorship. As in the case of *Self-Portrait as Businessman*, the artworks here often speak to performance in general. Many of the canvases reveal, this time on the behalf of the artists, rather perhaps than the curators, what catalogue-contributor and curator Nancy

Ireson reads as, a 'reluctance to indicate precise theatre interiors', with many of the canvases from the 1870s and 1880s representing instead auditoria that are 'non-specific and timeless'.[54] The point I want to make through this citation has two elements: first, that the theatrical experience presented within *Renoir at the Theatre* is again extrapolated beyond any specific encounter; and second, that the relation to time in which this experience is described is twofold. Presented in one interpretation as concerned with 'timeless' display, the paintings receive a different narration in other exhibition texts. Elsewhere, the intention of these images is presented as concerned with conveying a broader sense of theatricality tied to the ephemeral. The paintings exist between the specific transient and the non-specific timeless.

Let me track that through. *Étude de loge au théâtre* (1880), for example, shares a feeling of temporary arrest with many of the paintings which make up *Renoir at the Theatre*. In this pastel image Edgar Degas, an artist well known for his preoccupation with rendering movement, particularly in relation to practices of dance, urgently sketches an isolated pale face peering out from the black interior of a lavish golden theatre box. Through what Head of the Courtauld Gallery Ernst Vegelin van Claerbergen terms a 'dramatically steep perspective, bold cropping and blurred effects Degas here aims to replicate for the viewer a momentary experience in the theatre.'[55] The tight focus and vertical view of the depicted scene is directed towards the experiential and the theatrical. Turning to another painter whose work is on display within the Courtauld Gallery in order to apply this accumulative approach to the objects and artists connected therein, visitors are introduced to the sketchy and energetic style of French illustrator Constantin Guys once more in terms of the arrest of something transient. Guys' work is framed by the curator of *Renoir at the Theatre*, and situated within the exhibition concept, as an attempt 'to capture fleeting moments observed in the theatre'.[56] Looking at one such theatrical instant more specifically, the brown washed and watercoloured image of *A L'Opéra* (1860) shows a female figure glancing out from the secluded corner of a loge in the upper section of the picture. This part of the representation is differentiated, both in style and by the spatial barrier of the theatre box, from the more fluidly represented male characters beneath. In contrast to these more freely depicted male figures, the woman, I agree with exhibition curator Barnaby Wright, 'takes on the form of a sculptured torso on a pedestal', tellingly associated in this position not with another human companion but rather with a bouquet of flowers, a rudimentary art object.[57]

In Proust's representation of the 'vaguely human forms' inhabiting each loge, the occupants are also associated with floral displays since the theatre boxes '(even those in the highest tier, which from below seemed like great hampers studded with human flowers and attached to the ceiling of the auditorium by the red cords of their plush-covered partitions) composed an ephemeral panorama which deaths, scandals, illnesses, quarrels would soon alter, but which this evening was held motionless by attentiveness'.[58] Framed in a play of transient appearance and petrification, within Proust's text,

Renoir at the Theatre, and Guys' painting in particular, the theatrical experience is represented as sculptural and statuesque. The live moment made object and immobile allows us to perceive an experience of performance. An impression of stasis is integral to the vitality of the fleeting perceptions rendered visible in Guys' work and, in symmetry with the writings of Schneider, *A L'Opéra* presents an experience of performance in which the 'moving and stilled, are not in this sense diametrically opposed'.[59] Rendering theatrical scenes as they may or may not have appeared in actual physical venues, Guys' paintings, like others in *Renoir at the Theatre*, as well as the referents of theatre practice produced by artists including Donnelly, Althamer, and Farmer and on display within *The World as a Stage*, convey something of the experience of theatre-going in object form, that is to say, they exhibit a co-dependence between object and live encounter or display and performance which makes these exhibitions formally and theoretically significant to the project of the latter.

In Hibberd and Wrigley's writing about exchanges between *Art, Theatre, and Opera in Paris, 1750–1850*, a complex relation to time is also observed. According to their account, the 'different temporal and spatial constructions of art, drama and music sometimes led to confusion – and interest – when translations were effected between one medium and another, or when attempts were made to bring them together in a single work.'[60] Evoking theatrical experiences in pictorial media necessarily has implications for the temporal imaginings of these forms. Further consequences of Guys' creative practice arise when we take seriously descriptions of the artist written by his contemporaries. It is precisely his 'quest of the ephemeral, the fleeting forms of beauty', invented and represented, which prompted Charles Baudelaire to champion Guys in 1863 as 'The Painter of Modern Life.'[61] Commenting on the intense dynamism of Baudelaire's narrative depiction, French literature and philosophy scholar Patrick Ffrench, in his inaugural lecture at King's College London, noted the ways in which Baudelaire 'pictures Guys at work frenetically and spasmodically.' In Baudelaire's portrayal of the labouring artist, Ffrench explicates, a 'degree of violence and of bodily innervation is required for the fixing of the transient impression.'[62] As in the statuesque appearance of the female figure in *A L'Opéra*, a combination of energy and inertia is integral to Baudelaire's illustration of Guys' creative practice. The process of painting performance is described in terms of interruption and discontinuity; to render visible theatrical experience requires not only a form of representation but also a mode of production intermittent and characterised by the immobilisation of bodies.

Oblique Observations

Within Baudelaire's representation of Guys' painterly process, as interpreted by Ffrench, the object-centric representation of a theatrical experience is produced by means discontinuous and distracted, that is to say, via a mode of production which might be thought itself as existent between moving performance and the body rendered motionless. This kind of erratic production of object-based performance is evident too within *The World as a Stage,* first in a work produced by Paris-based artist Ulla von Brandenburg and second in the contribution of Austrian artist Markus Schinwald. In *Kugel* (2007), as in much of Brandenburg's practice, according to Wood's introduction, 'live presence is frequently figured as stillness in a protracted moment of ending.'[63] Related to her other work on display within *The World as a Stage,* titled *Curtain* (2007) and reproducing a patchwork textile designed by Walpole Champneys for the Royal Shakespeare Theatre in 1932, in terms of an investment in a persistently delayed and expanded sense of conclusion, *Kugel* also resonates with the images of Guys and of Degas exhibited as part of *Renoir at the Theatre* by rendering liveness in and through an object. The title of this black and white silent 16mm film, two minutes in duration, refers to a metallic ball central to the work. Lying in grass, this mirrored sphere captures a reflected scene which, in turn, is recorded by the camera. Within this construction, a sense of motionlessness is exaggerated by a blurring or shaking in the production wherein costumed figures, perhaps mannequin, perhaps human, hold postures throughout a framework of shuddering stillness.

Not pretending to any illusion of continuous movement, in *Kugel,* borrowing once again from Patrick Ffrench, 'the intermittence and contractions of the film image produce bodies whose movement is itself intermittent and spasmodic.'[64] This condition of indeterminacy between animation and inanimation, and between different temporal moments, points to the interplay between the still and the moving inherent to film production. Through what feminist film theorist Laura Mulvey calls, the 'introduction of staging and manipulation' it becomes possible to appreciate film's 'apotheosis as frozen movement.'[65] It is the theatricality of Brandenburg's work which makes visible the arrested motion contained therein. In its juddering stillness, *Kugel* is exemplary of the kind of theatre proposed by Wood as 'performed stasis', a motionlessness that shifts and is enacted, in this case, through the medium of film.[66] Recalling the debt owed by photography and film to what Schneider calls other 'technologies of the live, such as tableaux-vivants', *Kugel* regenerates this form of 'living picture', founded in customs of the dramatic.[67] Established in a past period of practice and staging motionless performers in a pictorial scene, the tableau vivant, and its resurrection in the formation of *Kugel,* speaks specifically to the interrelation of performance and display. 'I like replayed things', Brandenburg asserts, 'roles, movements, patterns, repeated words and sentences, reanimated feelings.'[68] Drawing on the form of the tableaux vivant, popular simultaneously with Renoir and his contemporaries during the nineteenth century, within *The World as a* Stage, Brandenburg shows an investment in a replayed and reanimated form. Limiting performance to a transient and moving present, Schneider warns, is to deny the ways in which, 'the live is not only vulnerable to suspension, but the very material of arrest.'[69] In *Kugel,* the communicative force of the work exists in a perplexed containment of motion and an inference of performance arrested in a lingering visual stasis, stuttering through the projector's whirring resonance.

Despite being the site and mode of the works' expressive dynamism, the shuddering inherent to Brandenburg's filmic picture makes it difficult to watch for any extended period of time. Prioritising those images, those sights, like *Kugel,* on which it is difficult to focus directly, *The World as a Stage* reveals the greatest resonance between acts of display and of performance through those objects which must be observed strangely, intermittently, and obliquely. In his writings on mobile observers characterised as flâneurs, Walter Benjamin cites English writer G. K. Chesterton's belief that the 'underlying scenes we can all see when we shut our eyes are not the scenes that we have stared at under the direction of guide-books; the scenes we see are the scenes at which we did not look at all.'[70] It is the temporary and provisional aspects of this exhibition, those works partly obscured and apparently neglected, which remain unforgettable. Within Tate Modern, Markus Schinwald's puppet, *Bob* (2007), does not appear in the position indicated numerically on the exhibition map. Instead, in accordance with the style of makeshift curation evident in *Hunchback Kit, Self-Portrait as Businessman,* and across the event more broadly, the marionette occupies a sort of functional space near to the exhibition exit. Positioned behind a barrier which makes it impossible to stand in front of this unnerving puppet, it is only possible to view the configuration of *Bob,* his suit-clad form and wood-cut face, around a corner, from a position that is indirect and askance. Looking from this angle, visitors might perceive that the title of Schinwald's work, *Bob,* seems to not only denote a name, a character, and a persona for the costumed marionette, but also to describe the motion ascribed to this figure, the moving up and down his shape sporadically enacts.

Resonant with the sorts of painterly and poetic originality described by Ffrench, *Bob* appears as an object in which artistic practice is figured as an 'interruptive, stuttering or shuddering movement.'[71] Invested in the potential of motional and creative experiences that are disruptive and erratic, if the exhibit was an attempt to represent a working puppet we might expect to see string attached to both of the doll's feet, but *Bob* operates and moves not as a fully functioning marionette and rather as an idea out of context. Not all of the puppet's limbs are workable and strings are only connected to the moving parts, only to one foot, which taps intermittently, waiting for something, perhaps, and not to both. In part time-sensitive, *Bob* brings together the temporal and the static, the displayed and the performed, within one object, questioning the ways in which it might be possible for the artwork and exhibition to perform. Encountered both in and out of time, the puppet stirs, and so exceeds the usual functionality of the art object stilled in perpetual display, then pauses and restarts, moving out of time with any performance which fades away. Thinking through the terms of

French philosopher Henri Bergson helps here to pursue the significance of *Bob*'s refusal of the position of still-life object. The significance of the work lies in the fact that 'in its very depths it lives and vibrates' so that 'in every perception there is a disturbance'. In line with Bergson's definition of 'real' movement, each shifting in *Bob*'s posture, and each observation of that discontinuous motion or spasmodic immobility, corresponds to '*the transference of a state*', an exchange which shifts intermittently, I want to argue, from performance to exhibit and back again.[72]

Another Identity Which Is Theatre

Within *The World as a Stage*, the exhibits do not follow the linear progression either of the finished object on display or the simultaneously created and observed performance. Exemplary of an alternative mode of expression, *Bob* operates rather between the performed and the displayed. His structure materialises a reflection made succinctly elsewhere by P.A. Skantze with regard to the interplay of forms which makes up our cultural encounters; that is, that we 'lose much when we treat one as an *experience* and the other as an *object*.'[73] Exceeding formal distinctions, *Bob* operates outside the remit of the static exhibited object, because this installation can be experienced in motion, in an instantaneous spasm, and therefore in time. Simultaneously, the puppet functions beyond ephemeral models of performance, because visitors might encounter this work arrested, still, and out of time. Interrupting and disturbing any advancement towards stasis, Schinwald's marionette halts movement and sets it going again and thereby enacts a return between the static and the temporal which differs both to transient paradigms of performance and discourses of exhibition invested in the eternity of object status. The performance of this work occurs not in a progression towards stillness and the endurance of the object-document but rather flickers in relation to this immobility, in an interplay and symbiosis of features and forms.

For Schinwald, the main difference 'between an exhibition and a performance is the immediacy. In a performance, the audience agrees to watch something together while it is being made. In an exhibition, usually the work is already done when the audience gets to see it.'[74] Of course, Schinwald admits, there are exceptions, not least in the increasing provision for live performance in museums, and, retaining an object-centric focus, *Bob* for one exceeds this rule. Another departure comes in the form of Rita McBride's *Arena* (1997), a work which, while invoking, in line with other exhibits within *The World as a Stage,* the notion of the gallery as a place for performance, like *Bob,* both appeals to and exceeds the sort of immediacy usually associated with the latter. *Arena* appears within the exhibition as a large-scale raked seating structure which partitions off a substantial region of the gallery as if delineating a specific stage. Resting on the rising seats of this construction, visitors might watch the performance of other gallery-goers as we move through *The World as a Stage* and engage with other exhibits, as well as each other. On the other hand, mobile visitors might perceive the seated participants as part of the work to which our attention is drawn. Working to make us aware of our relative positions within the gallery, McBride reflects on this structure in terms of a dialectic, quoted in an event leaflet produced by Tate: 'When the *Arena* is full of people its role is fulfilled and emptied at the same time. It loses one identity, as a sculpture, and gains another identity which is theatre.'[75]

Shifting from theatre to exhibit according to viewing patterns, *Arena* is resistant to singular designation and McBride's description of her work seems to exclude any simultaneous existence as both object and performance. Rather, as with *Bob*, there is a transition, a return which recalls to some degree an earlier school of animate art objects, such as those narrated by Rosalind Krauss in her *Passages in Modern Sculpture*. In her analysis, Krauss describes a range of works, including Alexander Calder's *Hanging Mobile* (1936), Len Lye's *The Loop* (1963), and the 'subliminal animation' of Pol Bury's *18 Superimposed Balls* (1967), in terms of theatricalised sculpture. Talking about Calder's mobiles, employed as 'plastic interludes' during certain dance performances of the Martha Graham Company, Krauss observes that because the motion of each of these objects is 'intermittent rather than mechanically continuous' viewers are 'impelled to set it in motion' so that it might perform and in this way the 'mobile locates its sculptural meaning as a kind of actor.'[76] Such objects enact their significances through and in performance. It is a certain intermittency which invites visitors to convey motion to these works and to interpret their capacities in relation to performed modes of presentation. As art object, there is promise for the work in performance and vice-versa; each form is inherent in the other. And in the cases of *Bob* and *Arena*, the subject as well as the potential is performance.

Exceeding categorisation either as performance or object, *Arena* demonstrates the ways in which, borrowing Alan Read's terms, the 'arrested life of performance is one such form of suspension in which the singular does not so much appear, as desist at a certain limit.'[77] The performance of the work is arrested and exists multiply according to the perspectives and approaches of gallery visitors. Here, and resonant with a particular history of previous sculptural works, as described by Krauss, it is the individual movements as each gallery visitor 'walks around the sculptural diorama, or takes time to interpret the narrative meaning of the various details of the tableau, that endows these works with dramatic time.'[78] It is the versions of these object-based exhibits played out through gallery visits which implicate the works in temporalities associated with performance. Picking up on terminologies examined in detail in the previous chapter of this book, and not least art critic Michael Fried's lexicon, *The World as a Stage* reveals how, as Wood asserts, a 'sense of "theatricality" has, in recent practice, become invested in the perception of the art viewer over and above a quality of the object itself' such, we might say, that it has implications for the project, parameters, and participants of performance.[79]

An Attentive Exit

Viewing artworks in their curation together makes it possible to observe and tease out not only commonalities and certain shared characteristics and potentials but also different modes of operation. In contrast to Schinwald's *Bob*, the status of McBride's *Arena* as intermittently displayed and performed is dependent on the actions of gallery visitors. Without our presence, the object exists singularly as sculpture; it is only when occupied that this work becomes theatrical. In this way McBride's installation, as the curators had hoped of the exhibition more broadly, works by 'turning the institutional space into a changeable and constantly staged arena in which the audience is as central as player or performer.'[80] Despite this figuring of an intensified direction of attention onto the constructed nature of the gallery as something transformational, this context is always already a curatorially and institutionally regulated frame. It is noteworthy, however, that, within this curatorial rendering, the visitor is *as* central as an actor but not an actor, distinct as another agent in relation to performers, artists, and curators. By different means, both *The World as a Stage* and *Renoir at the Theatre* enact, as Wood describes in relation to the former, a 'genuine transferral of attention towards inter-subjective relations'.[81] Attending to social and experiential connections, these exhibitions reveal this focus not only in the subject matter of the art works on display but also through the positions these objects prompt visitors to perform and occupy.

Within *Renoir at the Theatre*, many of the paintings directly address the relative positioning of the gallery visitor in relation to the imagined theatrical spaces they depict. Renoir's renowned painting from which the exhibition takes its subtitle, for example, shows a female figure dressed in a black-and-white striped gown looking out from the canvas towards the viewer of the painting, while her male companion studies another area of the implied auditorium through a pair of lorgnettes. Viewing this work, catalogue-contributor John House observes, it is as if the gallery visitor occupies the same level as the loge contained within the painting, 'implicitly viewing the figures from another box'. If, however, this is the implication, House continues, the figures then 'seem very large in relation to the format of the canvas, perhaps hinting that we, too, might be using binoculars to scrutinise the woman.'[82] In relation to this painting, the gallery visitor is assigned a role through a manipulation of scale which works to bring the action and situation of the theatre-goer into focus. In this way, the gallery visitor, borrowing from art historian Michael Baxandall, 'colludes in the project of exhibition'.[83] By *Looking at La Loge*, each visitor adopts perspectives assigned by an artist. The positions and operations available to the gallery visitor in relation to the art object are manipulated and predetermined and, in this case, the designated role is troubling and voyeuristic, suggesting observation from the concealment of a nearby theatre box.

Implying some sort of augmentation of the theatrical scene, *La Loge* plays with perspective and the constructed nature of cultural encounters.

'In early nineteenth-century galleries,' theatre historian David Wiles interprets, 'the viewer used the frame in order to isolate one canvas amidst a crowded wall, in much the same way as the theatre spectator used the frame and opera glasses to isolate images within a bustling, fully illuminated environment.'[84] In this rendering, the mounting of an artwork within a space of exhibition is conflated with the proscenium of traditional theatre venues, as well as the lens of the binoculars and beyond that, we might add in this context, the structure of the theatre box. Sitting in a lit auditorium, audience members employ lorgnettes to mark out distinct areas of visual interest on and beyond the stage. Focusing on this public setting, the perspective provided by the painters in each image, appropriating the terms of Krauss and directing them towards another context, 'theatricalizes the room to the point where it is the *viewer* who is the actor in question.'[85] The spectators, and their performance within the context of the theatre, are the subjects of Renoir and his contemporaries, who also implicate viewers of each painting in this network of observation. This investment in attending to the relations and receptive strategies of gallery visitors, and their situation as akin to performers within the exhibition frame, anticipates the relational practices which I will review in Chapter 3 and is materialized explicitly within the confines of Tate Modern through the final exhibit of *The World as a Stage*.

Following the shape of that exhibition further and moving to leave the event, we journey into a blue room which contains French artist Dominique Gonzalez-Foerster's *Séance de Shadow II (bleu)* (1998). Entering a space clearly configured for visitors to move through unimpeded, the traffic of each body activates a sequence of lights positioned along one side of the gallery. These beams cast visitors' shadows onto the not white but blue walls. Poised towards movement, Gonzalez-Foerster's project happens, is performed in time, through each visitor's steps and breath. Rendering visitors' reactive and interactive motions in shades of light and dark, *Séance de Shadow II (bleu)* makes live action into a sort of painterly project. On my first visit to *The World as a Stage*, all of the lights in the installation were set in motion by visitors walking ahead of me. Choosing not to exit the exhibition immediately, I waited instead for darkness and then moved through the space once again so that I might experience a triggering prompted by my own motion and affected through the enactment of my own trajectory. Deciding to pause in this blue scene until my stride might be effectual, with every step I observe the scale of my shadow cast onto the blue-painted walls. This same colour tints the carpeted floor, breaking the boundary between horizontal and vertical planes so as to maintain focus on the cast silhouettes. Enacting pathways and positions, the formation of the exhibit we see, its shadows and shapes, reveals quite directly the ways in which, following Bergson, the '*actuality* of our perception thus lies in its *activity*, in the movements which prolong it'.[86] Accepting the installation's summons to action, or at least the reality that to exit the exhibition we must pass through the space which this work inhabits, each visitor sees their figure translated onto the canvas of the blue-toned gallery.

Performance in General

Within *The World as a Stage*, visitors cannot expect to experience a static engagement with the objects displayed, just as we cannot expect these still objects to remain as such, unmoving. Rather, we find here a conception of the art object as something subjective, intermediate, and transitioning which enables a re-engagement with the conventional alignment of exhibition with the static display of objects in gallery contexts and theatricality with ephemerality in performance studies. This exhibition, following Wood, is founded on a kind of 'dynamic tension between movement and fixity' which we find in an accumulation of objects throughout its curatorial arrangement: in Donnelly's *The Redwood and the Raven*, for example, Brandenburg's *Kugel,* and Schinwald's *Bob*.[87] Were it not for the situation of these objects within *this* exhibition, that is, alongside other exhibits which share a certain topicality and theatricality accented through a curatorial mode stylistically impermanent, other aspects of their composition and character might come to the fore. It is the context and concept of the overall event which makes these particular attributes visible, even as our perspective of them is at times skewed. Interfacing 'live-ness with stasis, subject with object, entrenched convention with unpredictability', *The World as a Stage,* and *Renoir at the Theatre*, function in exchange between the seemingly fleeting and the apparently permanent.[88] Situated between disappearance and the ostensibly eternal object, these exhibitions implicitly experiment with a new temporality for performance.

Contemporaneously with the composition of the impressionist loge paintings displayed in *Renoir at the Theatre*, Baudelaire, in his writings on the arresting power of Guys' painterly strokes, asserted 'the transient, the fleeting, the contingent' as 'one half of art, the other being the eternal and the immovable.'[89] Locating art as the space in which the transitive and the timeless meet, Baudelaire's words are evocative of what is modeled in both *Renoir at the Theatre* and *The World as a Stage*. Reflecting on *The World as a Stage*, to which he is a contributing artist, Tino Sehgal suggests that theatre 'belongs to antiquity in the way that exhibitions belong to our times.'[90] Positing a contemporary re-articulation of the ways in which exhibitions which discourse with performance might unite practices associated with a specific time into a larger temporal frame, this interface between the displayed and the performed, like the comparative analysis of *Renoir at the Theatre* and *The World as a Stage* in this chapter, combines elements of the distant past, of a long-standing and contested relation between performance and visual arts exhibition, with contemporary concerns and experiences. This shift in dominant form, from the theatrical to the displayed, is, for Sehgal, 'one of the many indicators that the process of individualisation, or rather a consciousness of oneself as an individual, has accelerated.'[91] The conversion from performance to exhibition, while contestable, transfers focus from audience to individual visitor.

Imaginatively reconstructing apparently still assemblages of objects and moving in and out of time with the installations, visitors' movements and perceptions enable re-imaginings, both of the provisional collections of objects on display and of recognised ontologies of performance. Bergson writes that the 'nascent generality of the idea consists, then, in a certain activity of the mind, in a movement between action and representation.'[92] Moving between acted performance and representational exhibit, the works reviewed and associated in this chapter, as well as visitors' engagements with these, are promising in their suggestion of a paradigm which exceeds both static object and fleeting performance. *Renoir at the Theatre* and *The World as a Stage* think about indefinite conceptions of theatre, of performance in general rather than particular productions. By presenting theatrical objects not necessarily remaining from a precise 'live' event, such exhibition practices experiment with an alternative relation between display and performance. In the exhibition catalogue for *The World as a Stage*, Wood defines performance as a 'liminal space in which we expect something to happen.'[93] Situating theatre as a threshold of expectancy, Wood's definition locates performance as a boundary zone, transitional between two states or situations. Though constructed substantially from aesthetic objects and images, *The World as a Stage* and *Renoir at the Theatre* extend notions of the ways in which performance might be seen to occupy institutional gallery spaces by engaging with and attending to unspecific referents of performance.

Staging again intersections between theatre and gallery, these exhibitions situate the atemporal object in direct relation to the shifting, temporal terms of performance, and it is in this that their reference to established paradigms of the displayed and the performed becomes expanded. The object no longer appears within these frames as the record of a time-bound event but reveals instead an alternative relation premised on the symbiosis of performance and display. Arresting motions of movement and stasis, exchange and solidity in order to progress revised rules for the display of performance, *The World as a Stage* and *Renoir at the Theatre* enable the proposition of a model which, borrowing once again from Bergson's theory 'escapes us as soon as we try to fix it at either of the two extremities, it consists in the double current which goes from the one to the other'.[94] These events and the artworks they contain are not definable within the remit of the autonomous art object out of time in the gallery or within the domain of performance conceived as something transitory and disappearing; rather these exhibitions experiment with a new temporality for performance and transcend distinct theatrical and art historical models precisely in the duality of their operations, their functionality as both displayed *and* performed.

Notes

1. Peggy Phelan, *Unmarked: The Politics of Performance* (London and New York: Routledge, 1993), 165 and 146–47.
2. Ibid., 165.
3. Vicente Todoli, 'Foreword' to *The World as a Stage* [Exhibition Catalogue], ed. Jessica Morgan and Catherine Wood (London: Tate Publishing, 2007), 5.

4. Tate, *The World as a Stage* [Exhibition Leaflet]. Produced on the occasion of *The World as a Stage* exhibition, Tate Modern, London, 24 October 2007–1 January 2008.

5. Catherine Wood, 'Art Meets Theatre: The Middle Zone,' in *The World as a Stage* [Exhibition Catalogue], ed. Jessica Morgan and Catherine Wood, 19.

6. Ibid., 18.

7. Ibid., 22.

8. Hal Foster, *The Return of the Real: The Avant-Garde at the End of the Century* (Cambridge, Mass.: MIT Press, 1996), xi.

9. '*Renoir at the Theatre: Looking at La Loge*,' Courtauld Gallery, accessed 20 August 2015, http://courtauld.ac.uk/gallery/what-on/exhibitions-displays/archive/renoir-at-the-theatre-looking-at-la-loge.

10. '*The World as a Stage*,' Tate, accessed 20 August 2015, http://www.tate.org.uk/node/237078/default.shtm.

11. Wood, 'Art Meets Theatre: The Middle Zone,' 19.

12. Ibid., 25.

13. Aileen Ribeiro, 'The Art of Dress: Fashion in Renoir's *La Loge*,' in *Renoir at the Theatre: Looking at La Loge* [Exhibition Catalogue], ed. Ernst Vegelin van Claerbergen and Barnaby Wright (London: The Courtauld Gallery and Paul Holberton Publishing, 2008), 61.

14. Sarah Hibberd and Richard Wrigley, eds. 'Introduction' to *Art, Theatre, and Opera in Paris, 1750–1850: Exchanges and Tensions* (London: Ashgate, 2014), 9.

15. Marcel Proust, *In Search of Lost Time Volume III: The Guermantes Way*, trans. C. K. Scott Moncrieff and Terence Kilmartin (London: Vintage, 2000), 38 and 42.

16. Ibid., 36.

17. '*Renoir at the Theatre: Looking at La Loge*,' Courtauld Gallery, accessed 20 August 2015, http://courtauld.ac.uk/gallery/what-on/exhibitions-displays/archive/renoir-at-the-theatre-looking-at-la-loge.

18. Proust, *In Search of Lost Time Volume III: The Guermantes Way*, 36–37.

19. Ribeiro, 'The Art of Dress: Fashion in Renoir's *La Loge*,' 50.

20. Proust, *In Search of Lost Time Volume III: The Guermantes Way*, 36.

21. Jessica Morgan, 'The World as a Stage' in *The World as a Stage* [Exhibition Catalogue], ed. Jessica Morgan and Catherine Wood, 8.

22. Wood, 'Art Meets Theatre: The Middle Zone,' 21.

23. Pip Laurenson and Vivian van Saaze, 'Collecting Performance-based Art: New Challenges and Shifting Perspectives,' in *Performativity in the Gallery: Staging Interactive Encounters*, ed. Outi Remes, Laura MacCulloch, and Marika Leino (Bern: Peter Lang, 2014), 35–36.

24. Ibid., 36.

25. Catherine Wood, 'People and Things in the Museum,' in *Choreographing Exhibitions*, ed. Mathieu Copeland (Dijon: les presses du réel, 2014), 121 and 115.

26. Ibid., 115.

27. Nicholas Ridout, 'You look charming. You look enchanting. You look dazzling. You look breathtaking. You look unique. But you don't make an evening. You are not a brilliant idea. You are tiresome. You are not a rewarding subject. You are a theatrical blunder. You are not true to life,' *Tate Etc.* 11 (2007), 107.

28. Henry M. Sayre, *The Object of Performance: The American Avant-Garde Since 1970* (Chicago and London: University of Chicago Press, 1989), 12.

29. Wood, 'Art Meets Theatre: The Middle Zone,' 21.

30. The place of performance documentation is a contested one, particularly in relation to the gallery wherein it might be seen to offer a return to the sort of commodity status live art has often sought to evade. Amongst a range of key texts engaging with documentation in the performance field and its relation to questions of ontology, one version of this conversation might follow Peggy Phelan's *Unmarked: The Politics of Performance* (London and New York: Routledge, 1993), via Amelia Jones's '"Presence" in Absentia: Experiencing Performance as Documentation,' *Art Journal* Vol. 56, No. 4 (1997): 11–18, to Diana Taylor's *The Archive and the Repertoire: Performing Cultural Memory in the Americas* (Durham: Duke University Press, 2003), to Philip Auslander's 'The Performativity of Performance Art Documentation,' *Performing Arts Journal*, 84 (2006): 1–10, and Rebecca Schneider's *Performing Remains: Art and War in Times of Theatrical Reenactment* (London and New York: Routledge, 2011).

31. Tate, *The World as a Stage* [Exhibition Leaflet]. Produced on the occasion of *The World as a Stage* exhibition, Tate Modern, London, 24 October 2007–1 January 2008.

32. Rebecca Schneider, *Performing Remains: Art and War in Times of Theatrical Reenactment* (London and New York: Routledge, 2011), 144.

33. Sayre, *The Object of Performance: The American Avant-Garde Since 1970*, 1.

34. Nicolas Bourriaud, *Relational Aesthetics*, trans. Simon Pleasance, Fronza Woods, and Mathieu Copeland (Dijon: les presses du réel, 2002), 29. Original emphasis.

35. Schneider, *Performing Remains: Art and War in Times of Theatrical Reenactment*, 29 and 140–41. Original emphasis.

36. Philip Auslander, 'The Performativity of Performance Art Documentation,' *Performing Arts Journal*, 84 (2006), 2. Original emphasis.

37. Morgan, 'The World as a Stage,' 7.

38. Matthew Reason, 'Archive or Memory?: The Detritus of Live Performance,' *New Theatre Quarterly*, 19:1 (2003), 82.

39. Joe Kelleher, *The Illuminated Theatre: Studies on the Suffering of Images* (London and New York: Routledge, 2015), 27. Original emphasis.

40. Morgan, 'The World as a Stage,' 11.

41. Boris Groys, 'Art in the Age of Biopolitics: From Artwork to Art Documentation,' in *Art Power* (Cambridge, Mass., and London: MIT Press, 2008), 53.

42. Ibid., 53.

43. Ibid., 54.

44. Schneider, *Performing Remains: Art and War in Times of Theatrical Reenactment*, 154.

45. Auslander, 'The Performativity of Performance Art Documentation,' 1.

46. Groys, 'Art in the Age of Biopolitics: From Artwork to Art Documentation,' 64.

47. Schneider, *Performing Remains: Art and War in Times of Theatrical Reenactment*, 28.

48. Morgan, 'The World as a Stage,' 10.

49. Wood, 'Art Meets Theatre: The Middle Zone,' 19.

50. Ibid., 22.

51. Morgan, 'The World as a Stage,' 10.

52. Wood, 'Art Meets Theatre: The Middle Zone,' 23.

53. Ibid., 23. It is significant to note here a long history of relations between artists and performance makers, particularly in the domain of dance, including

designs by Robert Rauschenberg, Claes Oldenburg, and others for the Merce Cunningham Dance Company, as well as more recent designs by Sarah Lucas and Cerith Wyn Evans for the Michael Clark Company.

54. Nancy Ireson, 'The Lure of the *Loge*,' in *Renoir at the Theatre: Looking at La Loge* [Exhibition Catalogue], ed. Ernst Vegelin van Claerbergen and Barnaby Wright, 14–15.
55. Ernst Vegelin van Claerbergen, 'Catalogue,' in *Renoir at the Theatre: Looking at La Loge* [Exhibition Catalogue], ed. Ernst Vegelin van Claerbergen and Barnaby Wright, 86.
56. Barnaby Wright, 'Catalogue,' in *Renoir at the Theatre: Looking at La Loge* [Exhibition Catalogue], ed. Ernst Vegelin van Claerbergen and Barnaby Wright, 68.
57. Ibid.
58. Proust, *In Search of Lost Time Volume III: The Guermantes Way*, 37 and 54.
59. Schneider, *Performing Remains: Art and War in Times of Theatrical Reenactment*, 145.
60. Sarah Hibberd and Richard Wrigley, eds. 'Introduction,' 10.
61. Charles Baudelaire, 'The Painter of Modern Life' [1863], in *Baudelaire: Selected Writings on Art and Artists*, trans P. E. Charvet (Cambridge: Cambridge University Press, 1972), 435.
62. Patrick Ffrench, 'Spasms: Moving Bodies from Baudelaire to Beckett,' Inaugural Lecture, King's College London, 25 October 2010.
63. Wood, 'Art Meets Theatre: The Middle Zone,' 21.
64. Patrick Ffrench 'Spasms: Moving Bodies from Baudelaire to Beckett.'
65. Laura Mulvey, *Death 24x a Second: Stillness and the Moving Image* (London: Reaktion Books, 2006), 21.
66. Wood, 'Art Meets Theatre: The Middle Zone,' 21.
67. Schneider, *Performing Remains: Art and War in Times of Theatrical Reenactment*, 140.
68. Ulla von Brandenburg quoted in Jessica Morgan and Catherine Wood, 'It's All True,' *Tate Etc.* 11 (2007), 75.
69. Schneider, *Performing Remains: Art and War in Times of Theatrical Reenactment*, 142.
70. G. K. Chesterton quoted in Walter Benjamin, *The Arcades Project*, trans. Howard Eiland and Kevin McLaughlin (Cambridge, Mass., and London: Belknap Press, 1999), 438.
71. Patrick Ffrench 'Spasms: Moving Bodies from Baudelaire to Beckett.'
72. Henri Bergson, *Matter and Memory*, trans. Nancy M. Paul and W. Scott Palmer (London: George Allen & Unwin Ltd., 1950 [1911]), 270, 19 and 267. Original emphasis.
73. P. A. Skantze, *Stillness in Motion in the Seventeenth-Century Theatre* (London and New York: Routledge, 2003), 28. Original emphasis.
74. Markus Schinwald quoted in Jessica Morgan and Catherine Wood, 'It's All True,' 72.
75. Rita McBride, quoted in 'Rita McBride Interview by Discoteca Flaming Star,' in *UBS Openings: Saturday Live - Arena* [Event Leaflet], Saturday 27 October 2007, Tate Modern, London.
76. Rosalind Krauss, *Passages in Modern Sculpture* (Cambridge, Mass., and London: MIT Press, 1981 [1977]), 217–21.
77. Alan Read, *Theatre, Intimacy and Engagement: The Last Human Venue* (Houndmills: Palgrave Macmillan, 2009), 223.

78. Krauss, *Passages in Modern Sculpture*, 229.
79. Wood, 'Art Meets Theatre: The Middle Zone,' 20.
80. Jessica Morgan and Catherine Wood, eds. *The World as a Stage* [Exhibition Catalogue], back page summary.
81. Wood, 'Art Meets Theatre: The Middle Zone,' 25.
82. John House, 'Modernity in Microcosm: Renoir's *Loges* in Context,' in *Renoir at the Theatre: Looking at La Loge* [Exhibition Catalogue], ed. Ernst Vegelin van Claerbergen and Barnaby Wright, 30.
83. Michael Baxandall, 'Exhibiting Intention: Some Preconditions for the Visual Display of Culturally Purposeful Objects,' in *Exhibiting Cultures: The Poetics and Politics of Museum Display*, ed. Ivan Karp and Steven D. Lavine (Washington, DC, and London: Smithsonian Institution Press, 1991), 37.
84. David Wiles, *A Short History of Western Performance Space* (Cambridge: Cambridge University Press, 2003), 259.
85. Krauss, *Passages in Modern Sculpture*, 221.
86. Bergson, *Matter and Memory*, 74.
87. Wood, 'Art Meets Theatre: The Middle Zone,' 20.
88. Ibid.
89. Baudelaire, 'The Painter of Modern Life,' 403.
90. Tino Sehgal quoted in Jessica Morgan and Catherine Wood, 'It's All True,' 74.
91. Ibid.
92. Bergson, *Matter and Memory*, 324.
93. Wood, 'Art Meets Theatre: The Middle Zone,' 19.
94. Bergson, *Matter and Memory*, 211.

3 Visitor & Performer
The Return of the Relational

I want to begin this third chapter with a phrase, 'not yet unstill titled.' These words, strung together, seemingly refer to two instances of arts practice. First, they appear to me to address, invert, and realign a work made in 1992 at the 303 Gallery in New York by Rirkrit Tiravanija, called *Untitled (Still)*, in which the artist transferred objects and articles habitually housed in the offices and storage areas of the gallery into rooms for exhibition wherein they received a different kind and mode of attention. Making visible the backstage operations of a contemporary arts venue, *Untitled (Still)* overturned expected designations of accessible and inaccessible institutional structures, upsetting assigned locations for preparation and administration, and staging and display. In a move regularly cited as paradigmatic of the sorts of aesthetic with which this chapter is concerned, Tiravanija also installed a temporary kitchen within the gallery and prepared food for exhibition visitors, while, according to the analysis of installation and participatory art critic Claire Bishop, 'the detritus, utensils and food packets became the art exhibit whenever the artist wasn't there'.[1] Although British artist Liam Gillick has contested this interpretation in his searing reproach of Bishop's position, asserting that the 'whole situation was the work, not one element of it', I reference this reading here because it speaks to an exchange between the display of objects and practices of performance explored throughout this book and signals something of the challenging terrain surrounding relational aesthetics with which this chapter is engaged.[2]

The second work recalled by this text, 'not yet unstill titled', was produced by Gillick and displayed from 24 October 2008 to 7 January 2009 as part of the *theanyspacewhatever*, an exhibition curated by Artistic Director and Chief Curator Nancy Spector at the Solomon R. Guggenheim Museum in New York. Appearing in black unspaced letters and a reflected font, and suspended from the ceiling of the gallery, this phrase forms part of *theanyspacewhatever Signage System* (2008). Moving upwards through the Guggenheim's signature rotunda, it is possible to read these words only after visitors have passed them by, looking back down the slope up which we have just traversed. Legible only in this direction, from behind, everything about these words, which literally hang in the air, looks backwards. The museum's description of Gillick's piece as referential of the work of other artists participating in the show prompts me to interpret these words as pointing towards Tiravanija's landmark project as something which, up until now, remains untitled in stillness, something 'not yet unstill titled', an unmoving trace which might be reanimated and recalled. This hanging object looks back to Tiravanija's previous installation-performance, just as it looks backwards through the exhibition it occupies within the Guggenheim Museum, an exhibition which itself looks again to the work of an oft associated cohort of artists. Engaging with a contested field of practice, *theanyspacewhatever* reconnects ten figures, including Tiravanija and Gillick, brought together by French curator and art critic Nicolas Bourriaud within his designation of 'relational aesthetics,' constructed during the 1990s. Engaged in practices of reversal, transferral, and revisiting, Gillick's words, *theanyspacewhatever*, and the exhibition I will examine alongside this, titled *Double Agent* and co-curated by Bishop and former Director of Exhibitions Mark Sladen, at the Institute of Contemporary Arts (ICA) in London from 14 February to 6 April 2008, still and untitled or unstill and named, all engage with and enact, what I am terming here, a 'return to the relational'.

Back to Bourriaud

Operating through events constitutive of a revisiting of relational theories and practices, this third chapter engages with a set of relatively new yet increasingly hegemonic vocabularies within the field of performance studies. Revolving around the relational and the spectatorial, such expressions are relevant to ideas of *Theatre, Exhibition, and Curation* in terms of questions of field and, while not the original conception of this book, form a significant sidebar on which the project sheds light. Examining two exhibitions demonstrative of what I am identifying as a 'return to the relational,' *theanyspacewhatever* and *Double Agent*, this chapter engages directly with notions of activated spectatorship in order to progress a more enhanced understanding of the relationship between gallery visitor and performer. Throughout this project, I have chosen to use the term 'visitor' to signal a distinctive relation to contexts of exhibition which differs both to the consideration given by the spectator to a single artwork on display within the gallery and to the contributions of the participant within an interactive project, performance, or curated event by signifying an embodied act of attending which does not necessarily involve taking part.

Approaching these contexts of exhibition making from the perspective of performance studies, it is important to acknowledge, with theatre scholar Nicholas Ridout, that, founded in communication, referentiality, and the giving and receiving of attention, 'theatre is always already relational, long before Nicolas Bourriaud proclaimed the arrival of relational aesthetics.'[3] In the essays collected together under his title for this aesthetic movement, Bourriaud admits too that 'art has always been relational in varying degrees'.[4] From the perspectives both of theatre practice and of art history, ideas of relationality have, then, always been integral to conceptions of creative practice and to its reception. Evident in the exchanges between performers onstage and theatre-goers in the audience, between art objects on display and visitors within a gallery, it may be because of this ubiquity that critics, curators, and scholars, including Bourriaud, as well as Claire Bishop, Anthony Downey, Jen Harvie, Shannon Jackson, and Jessica Morgan, to name but a few, continue to construct discourses around works which claim overtly to address this notion of what has variously been called social engagement, participation, collaboration, and relation.

Such claims to the prevalence and pervasiveness of what has been termed in the US context 'social practice,' invite me to qualify my use of ideas of 'return' with regard to addressing projects and artists collected together under the auspices of the relational. The 'return' evident in the title of this chapter signals a moment of heightened interest in participatory practice. In introduction to *Fair Play: Art, Performance and Neoliberalism* (2013), theatre and performance scholar Jen Harvie positions her book as a 'response to the recent proliferation of performance and art practices that engage audiences socially – by inviting those audiences to participate, act, work and create together; observe one another; or simply be together. This trend has been growing exponentially since the 1990s in, for example, much public art, immersive theatre, one-to-one theatre, and relational and delegated art.'[5] Whereas Harvie narrates this contemporary tendency towards socially engaged or engaging practice as a 'growth', I am interested in characterising the specific exhibitions addressed in this chapter as involved in a form of return because these particular examples seem to me to be symptomatic of a resurgence of artistic and academic commentary on relational aesthetics more so than a progressive expansion of social practice which participation, rather than relation, might designate. Indeed, in her *Artificial Hells: Participatory Art and the Politics of Spectatorship* (2012), Claire Bishop updates her 2006 designation of a 'social turn' in contemporary art to refigure this 'more accurately as a *return* to the social,' in acknowledgement of the historical legacy of artworks concerned with investigating participation, collaboration, and collective making and encounter.[6]

Each of the critics referenced so far in this chapter favours a different terminology and emphasises particular qualities and iterations of work, as well as a specific range of practitioners, within the broader field of socially engaged art.[7] Indeed, following her polemical readings of 'relational aesthetics', Bishop distances her current work from this designation, suggesting that the projects to which her most recent writing is addressed 'emerged in the wake of *Relational Aesthetics* and the debates that it occasioned' whereas the artists with whom Bourriaud works as a curator are 'less interested in intersubjective relations and social context than in spectatorship as more generally embedded within systems of display, temporality, fiction, design and the "scenario".'[8] Bearing in mind Bishop's position, the fact that she curates one of the exhibitions to which this chapter is addressed, and a broader distaste for this terminology, I have chosen here to engage specifically with the language of the relational because it seems to me to offer a number of affordances for thinking about *theanyspacewhatever* and *Double Agent*, not least, as Bishop states, through its connection to ideas of display and temporality. In Bourriaud's definition, given for ease of reference as a glossary entry at the end of his collected essays, the premodifier 'relational' designates an 'aesthetic theory consisting in judging artworks on the basis of the inter-human relations which they represent, produce or prompt' (112). Relational aesthetics, in these terms, proposes a revaluation of artworks founded in their connection to, and creation and manifestation of, human interactions in a given social context. In this rendering, art is recognised as 'a state of encounter' wherein an 'exhibition will give rise to a particular "arena of exchange"' (17–18). In what follows I want to extend these ideas of 'encounter' and 'exchange' to posit the terms of this 'state' or 'arena' as between display and performance.

Stressing, quite judiciously, the necessity of critiquing artistic practice according to criteria appropriate to the moment of its construction, Bourriaud reminds his readers of a traditional conception of the artwork as 'situated in a transcendent world' (27). From this initial investment in perpetuity, Bourriaud suggests, art 'gradually abandoned this goal, and explored the relations between Man and the world' (27). Attaining their 'formal and theoretical marks' in the kinds of minimalist arts practices with which Chapter 1 of this book is engaged, under the designation of relational aesthetics 'all manner of encounter and relational invention thus represent, today, aesthetic objects likely to be looked at as such' (46 and 28). In keeping with the other case studies examined in *Theatre, Exhibition, and Curation: Displayed & Performed*, Bourriaud's discourse extends the definition of the traditionally static and transcendent art object to incorporate live and experiential actions of meeting and performance. It is this investment in a 'theory of form' (19), in the customary or alternative modes through which art objects might be expressed or manifested, that Bourriaud's designation of relational aesthetics becomes relevant to the current project. Of course, commentators including Bishop and Downey have identified performance art as an historical precursor to the sorts of practice Bourriaud collects under the remit of the relational but I want to think the correlation somewhat differently. Described as a 'social *interstice*' (16, original emphasis), a relational artwork is an intervening space between two component parts. Focusing in on this image of the interstitial, relational art appears as a form which might be reimagined as occupying the intersection between the displayed and the performed.

Back to Bishop

With Bourriaud and Ridout, artist historian, critic, and curator of *Double Agent* Claire Bishop agrees that there exists a 'long tradition of viewer participation and activated spectatorship in works of art across many media'. In contrast to Bourriaud's writing and its focus on what she calls 'the "togetherness" of relational aesthetics', however, Bishop has promoted in her contentious studies a mode of 'relational antagonism,' that is to say a 'tougher, more disruptive approach to "relations"' that might more thoroughly enable democratic debate.[9] Indeed, in referencing surrealist André Breton's assertion of the potential of social disturbance, the title of her most recent monograph, *Artificial Hells* (2012), also 'appeals for more bold, affective and troubling forms of participatory art and criticism.'[10] Bishop's concern with regards to Bourriaud's theory has been, following her 2004 essay, that within the 'hybrid installation/performance of relational aesthetics, which rely so heavily on context and the viewer's literal engagement,' the quality of those produced and endorsed relations are not thoroughly interrogated; it is, she writes, 'no longer enough to say that activating the viewer *tout court* is a democratic act'.[11] Without analysing the means by which an artwork solicits the participation of the visitor and the value of the relations it thereby produces, Bourriaud's discourse, according to Bishop's reading, 'redirects the argument back to artistic intentionality rather than issues of reception'; it may be that an artist *intends* to produce work which triggers social engagement, however the terms and worth of this association too often remain unscrutinised. If, as Bishop summarises, Bourriaud wants to 'equate aesthetic judgment with an ethicopolitical judgment,' the next logical step is to consider how we might measure and compare the corresponding qualities and gains of the relationships generated.[12]

Beyond this focusing of attention away from visitor reaction and back towards intentionality, Bishop also takes issues with Bourriaud's theorisation of relational aesthetics precisely in terms of his formalism, something of particular value to the concerns I want to explore further in this chapter. Moving away from Tiravanija and Gillick, whom she positions as exemplary of Bourriaud's argument, in 'Antagonism and Relational Aesthetics' Bishop comes to focus instead on the work of Thomas Hirschhorn and Santiago Sierra because these artists, she suggests, 'set up "relationships" that emphasize the role of dialogue and negotiation in their art, but do so without collapsing these relationships into the work's content.' Bourriaud's conflation of structure and subject matter is problematic for Bishop because the 'erratic relationship' between these two components makes the former difficult to isolate. Inconsistent and changeable, the structural formations of a relational work are complex to identify, Bishop proposes, precisely because of the claims, made by Bourriaud, towards the attainment of a certain open-endedness in the manifestation of art objects awarded this designation. Relational art is, in its format, associable with installation art, not least in the sense, as Bishop reminds us, that its 'use of diverse media divorces it from a medium-specific tradition'.[13] This dissociation of installation and, by extension, relational art from the confines of a particular physical mode correlates with the definition of performance as an 'art form that lacks a distinctive medium' cited from performance scholar Barbara Kirshenblatt-Gimblett in the introduction to this book.[14] Connecting these descriptions, it seems appropriate to suggest that it is in terms of the approaches and paradigms usually associated with performance practice that it might be most useful to evaluate, critique, and re-position the contemporary return of relational aesthetics.

Indeed a related connection is also made by Bishop in *Artificial Hells* wherein she defines participation, her preferred term for socially engaged practice, as a mode in which 'people constitute the central artistic medium and material, in the manner of theatre and performance.' Participatory engagement, Bishop writes, 'tends to be expressed most forcibly in the live encounter between embodied actors in particular contexts' and it is, therefore, useful to employ the 'lens of theatre' in order to address contemporary forms of participation.[15] Revealingly, Bishop openly acknowledges the need to import terminology and theoretical positions from theatre history and performance studies in order to more thoroughly analyse participatory art and the associated politics and potentialities of being a spectator. 'The worlds of music, film, literature, fashion and theatre have a rich vocabulary to describe co-existing authorial positions,' she writes, whereas, the 'lack of an equivalent terminology in contemporary visual art has led to a reductive critical framework'. According to Bishop it is 'impossible to adequately address a socially oriented art *without* turning to these disciplines,' precisely because such 'interdisciplinarity parallels (and stems from) the ambitions and content of the art itself.'[16] Despite her critique of the collapse of structure and subject in Bourriaud's thesis, Bishop locates the interdisciplinary nature of participatory art not only in its form but also in its content. The focus of this work is interdisciplinarity itself, much as the thematic of the exhibitions addressed in the previous chapter of this book is theatre. By way of introduction, Bishop emphasises that 'participatory art is not only a social activity but also a symbolic one'.[17] Its terms are both actional and representational: participatory art exists at the juncture of display and performance.

In this more recent work, Bishop concedes that one of the successes of Bourriaud's theory was to 'render discursive and dialogic projects more amenable to museums and galleries' and to prompt a range of critical and creative projects demonstrating a more developed and questioning analytic engagement with and around participatory art.[18] Developing Bishop's earlier critique of the formalism of Bourriaud's argument, scholar of contemporary art Anthony Downey identifies that it is 'precisely this emphasis on formal, functional and relational concerns that signifies what is both promising and yet problematic in his thesis.' Although Bourriaud's theory maintains a quantity of 'critical abbreviations', such as those already mentioned to do with the modes, qualities, and politics of socialisation, as well possible precursors to relational forms, Downey recognises that it is important in its ambition to 'reconsider the schema of contemporary art criticism and, perhaps more momentously, to define a "movement" of sorts that has come to delineate a prominent body of work and artists working in the 1990s.' In terms of these aspirations, *Relational Aesthetics* still merits critical attention and it might be, Downey suggests, in the 'conceptual cul-de-sacs which Bourriaud's thesis leads us down that we find most purchase'.[19] Certainly these prove useful for addressing the exhibitions in this chapter.

One such impasse, of particular significance to the current book project, concerns Bourriaud's role as a curator of works he associates with relational aesthetics. This professional investment leads Downey to question whether this form in fact originates in 'actual artistic activity or the increasingly ascendant patterns of contemporary curatorial practices'.[20] Inseparable from issues of institutional preference, *theanyspacewhatever* and *Double Agent* play out Downey's inkling that relational aesthetics appear via curatorial ambition. Both of these exhibitions are premised on the associations and proclivities of particular prominent curators and critics. The artists included by Nancy Spector in *theanyspacewhatever* are all named by Bourriaud in his designation of *Relational Aesthetics* and 'perennial favourites of a few curators who have become known for promoting their preferred selection of artists'.[21] Despite her critique of such curatorial influence, *Double Agent* is co-constructed by relational aesthetics commentator and participatory art critic Claire Bishop even as she admits that dominant narratives around the latter have 'frequently come to lie in the hands of those curators responsible for each project'.[22] With that framing in mind, it is suggestive that Bishop does not include any commentary on *Double Agent* within her recent *Artificial Hells*. Indeed, she mentions the exhibition only in passing in a couple of notes to the chapters and most often to quote from the accompanying catalogue, co-edited with Silvia Tramontana. I will offer here a more sustained reading of the project, since *Double Agent*, and its US counterpart *theanyspacewhatever*, act as curated stagings of the conceptual concerns of this chapter and constitute the basis of its formation and analysis.

Returning to the Relational

In her writing on what she calls 'aesthetically turned' socially turned art and performance, Jen Harvie suggests that the 'enormity and spread of this trend raises questions about why these practices are proliferating, what they say about contemporary culture, what they can actually do for audiences, and what they can offer contemporary social relations.'[23] To this list of concerns I would add another; that is, how might they expand current understandings and conceptions of performance? In recent years, a number of major institutions on the international art scene have engaged in what I am terming a 'return to the relational' by means of temporary exhibitions founded on concepts of relationality and drawing together artists who have been commonly associated with this theory since the 1990s. Curated by Claire Bishop, *Double Agent* involves the Institute of Contemporary Art (ICA), mentioned briefly in the introduction to this book, more deeply within the remit of a project concerned with contemporary intersections between the displayed and the performed. The ICA represents another high-profile London-based institution, in addition to Tate Modern, The Courtauld Gallery and the Old Vic Theatre already discussed, working at this interface, and one that, in the same year as presenting this exhibition, announced the closure of its Live & Media Arts department. *theanyspacewhatever*, on the other hand, is important in providing a non-UK-based example of this sort of curatorial, exhibition-based practice, particularly since the Guggenheim Museum in New York, also referenced in the introduction, has become increasingly associated with an international context of live re-performance, having housed, for example, performance artist Marina Abramović's much commented on *Seven Easy Pieces* in 2005.

Keeping in mind these instances of live museological encounter and re-enactment, with which the field of performance research has recently been so preoccupied, it is useful here to involve the Guggenheim Museum in an analysis of exhibitions operating in dialogue with practices of performance through operations and objects functioning for the most part outside of the ephemeral 'live'. Invested in a variety of creative media and artistic theories, including those promoted as relational, both *theanyspacewhatever* and *Double Agent* claim, in their publicity materials, to engage with a view of exhibition practice that is expansive, dynamic, and performative. In the context of the former, the recognisable structural design of the Guggenheim's central white-painted rotunda not only directs the pathways of visitors within the museum but also, according to Thomas Krens, director of the Guggenheim Foundation from 1988 to 2008, challenges artists to respond with 'expanded manifestations of their work.' This spiral passage forms the location for *theanyspacewhatever* and it is with this situation that the contributing artists are first invited to contend so as to use the 'museum as a springboard for work that reaches beyond the visual arts'.[24] Previously incorporating architectural, design, and theatrical elements into their practice, all of the artists involved in *theanyspacewhatever* have produced installations and objects considered by Bourriaud as typical of the form he describes.

For curator Nancy Spector, the work made by these artists during the 1990s was 'elusive and allusive, quietly offering its own veiled commentary on how art can exist in the world today.' Curious and suggestive, referential and 'yet to be effectively categorized', Spector finds in this art, in terms resonant with those of Bourriaud's theory, a 'still open-ended story.'[25] The practices, to which *theanyspacewhatever* returns, like many explored in this book, are presented as uneasy to categorise, as still and enduringly indefinite. *Double Agent*, too, featured works described in the marketing materials for the exhibition as 'often slippery in meaning or disquieting in effect.'[26] Presenting art objects and installations made by a number of international artists working in a variety of media, *Double Agent*, according to the Teachers' Pack produced for the ICA by researcher and artist Emily Candela, forms an exhibition context in which 'performance art, socially-engaged artwork and political action come together.'[27] Linking participatory art and performance, both *Double Agent* and *theanyspacewhatever* promote exhibition-based practices that look beyond traditional forms of visual arts display precisely by investing in social engagement and drawing on adjoining disciplinary tropes and paradigms.

Appropriating *theanyspacewhatever*

Double Agent and *theanyspacewhatever* ostensibly seek to alter the experience of the exhibition environment for gallery visitors and engage with questions of participation. These events share with *Marina Abramović Presents...* (Chapter 1) and *The World as a Stage* (Chapter 2) a claim to the apparent disruption of visitors' expectations but such disturbance is, in each case, carefully designed and regulated. In the setting of the Guggenheim Museum and in relation to a show in which artists act as co-curators, the actual potential for alternative perspectives, associations, and relations must be tempered against the reality of institutional and creative controls. Despite such constraints, the premise of *theanyspacewhatever* follows a mode of construction resonant with the terms of Bourriaud's *Relational Aesthetics* by presenting an 'ensemble of units to be re-activated by the beholder-manipulator' (20). The title of the exhibition emphasises this possibility of renewal and reanimation. A cinematic term appropriated from philosopher Gilles Deleuze, the any-space-whatever designates a setting wherein the linkages between component parts can be drawn in any 'infinite number of ways.' Enabling multiple connections and conceived as '*deconnected or emptied spaces*,' the language of the any-space-whatever facilitates an extended application of the possibilities inherent in the empty space for performance, a motif recurring throughout this book and examined in its introduction with reference to the *Empty Stages* project of Tim Etchells and Hugo Glendinning; both the empty space for performance and Deleuze's any-space-whatever exhibit a sense of 'pure potential'.[28]

In Deleuze's rendering, the any-space-whatever is a disassociated place of possibility, a framework in which constituent fractions have the potential to be connected and re-connected in any number of ways which look towards revised and re-imagined formulations. How much of this conceptual agency is transferred to gallery visitors is a paramount concern in relation to *theanyspacewhatever* and the relational theories it appears to propagate; and it is this possibility of constructing an idiosyncratic and original trajectory through a curated space of exhibition, as well as points of intersection with filmic and other modes of screen-based presentation, which initiates the investigations forming the spine of the following fourth chapter. Despite claiming to create a space of interpenetration between different artists and modes of operation, an exhibition involving, what the Guggenheim's webpages call, a 'series of individual projects that intersect and overlap', within the space of the spiralling rotunda the exhibits feel for the most part disconnected and lacking in any shared communicative or affective thrust beyond this banner of the unspoken yet omnipresent 'relational.'[29] In her review for art-world magazine *Artforum*, curator and art historian Linda Norden dwells on the fact that the 'much-maligned, rarely elaborated concept of "relational aesthetics," is never mentioned by name' within the confines of the museum venue.[30] This underlying model remains unspecified, notably untitled, still, within the exhibition space.

In the catalogue accompanying *theanyspacewhatever*, Spector acknowledges that the term 'relational,' 'like any overarching assessment of an aesthetic trend or shared sensibility, can delimit as much as it can define.' Rather than be constrained by the, perhaps unavoidable, paradigms and expectations associated with this designation, Spector is eager to reinforce the connections among the contributing artists as more theoretical than compositional such that the practitioners are 'unanchored from any specific stylistic or technical premise'. In contrast to established critiques of aesthetic factions and unlike movements, such as minimalism, which are identified through shared material and visual conventions, Spector celebrates, at least on paper, the ways in which the artists represented within *theanyspacewhatever* all employ 'markedly different aesthetic strategies.'[31] Repeatedly employing the term 'polymorphous' to describe the multiform nature of the work produced by this loose collective of artists, it may be precisely because of this collision between that which is conceptually shared and that which is physically and visibly disparate that Spector takes up the title suggested by artist Liam Gillick, that is *theanyspacewhatever*. Their collaborations are, in Spector's terms, 'ephemeral, contingent, and ever elusive' and it is for this reason, perhaps, that she attempts to make an any-space-whatever, incorporating the individual within the relational and resurrecting practices definitive of a past creative moment so as to register its significance and safeguard its perpetuation.[32]

Opening *theanyspacewhatever*

Seeking to save, extend, or perhaps re-imagine the contingent relations between practitioners brought together by Bourriaud's curatorial practice and theoretical texts, Spector and her co-curating artists are most likely drawn to Deleuze's any-space-whatever because of its potential for the construction of new narrative and spatio-temporal arrangements. In keeping with ideas of a relational return, French Artist Pierre Huyghe's contribution to the *anyspacewhatever* engages in a structural re-imagining of sorts which, despite referencing the inauguration of the event, in fact works, as in the artist's earlier practice, to elongate and disperse the opening night across the temporal duration of the exhibition. Bourriaud noted the 'growing importance of the opening as part of the exhibition programme' (30) particularly with regards to the work of Huyghe, as well as artists Rirkrit Tiravanija and Philippe Parreno, in *Relational Aesthetics* wherein he suggested this emphasis as presenting, in each case, a 'model of an ideal public circulation' (37). Titled OPENING, Huyghe's event, staged three times over the course of *theanyspacewhatever*, invites visitors to explore the exhibition in the dark, using headlamps to illuminate our trajectories and the exhibits we encounter. Involving the immersion of gallery visitors in a state of near darkness, this experiential framework and the torches it employs, makes visible visitors' interactions within the context of exhibition, illuminating our attentions and revealing how, and at what, we choose to look.

Norden's description of the movement of focused lights throughout the gallery as something 'wonderfully fluid, leaving barely perceptible trails, like slow-motion traffic in time-lapse film' anticipates the methodology for tracing visitors routes within exhibitions environments presented in the following chapter, as well as the filmic and digital works which accompany its analysis. Introducing images of motion almost imperceptibly slowed and ideas of intervals in action, Norden's evocation of OPENING speaks to the forms of objects at the boundary of stillness and mobility encountered so far in this book. Making visitors' movements perceptible as remnants of fading light, streaks across the space which speak to the possibility of a slower encounter, OPENING offers visitors the opportunity to experience the museum outside of usual opening hours and as what Norden calls a 'spectral mine' – an ethereal cavity wherein we might engage with the works and fabric of the gallery space by means other than 'tracing the spiral optically'.[33] Inviting a more slow-moving and deliberate form of engagement, OPENING appeals to the potential of *theanyspacewhatever* as an exhibition in which unexpected and unprecedented explorations and interpretations might be discovered, by initiating the event multiple times from a blacked out rotunda associable with theatre's commencement in the dark.

Although lights and electronic displays were turned off and windows covered to make essential the illumination from the spotlights, in OPENING the prospect of transforming the museum into a black box is limited, in a sense acknowledged and anticipated by Huyghe, because of the 'impossibility—for security reasons—of making the museum truly pitch-black.'[34] Institutional restraints related to regulations for visitors' health and safety moderate the possibility of creating an empty space for performance or a dark crater for display within the confines of the Guggenheim. Despite this compromise, OPENING represents one of a minority of works produced for *theanyspacewhatever*, and indeed *Double Agent*, which take the form, at least in one iteration, of a 'live' event. Another, Dominique Gonzalez-Foerster and Ari Benjamin Meyers's orchestral performance NY.2022 (2008), shown on Tuesdays and Fridays in the Peter B. Lewis Theatre Mezzanine between 10 a.m. and 2 p.m., and thereby occupying a time-frame more in keeping with a theatre venue than a museum, was not playing during my visit to the Guggenheim. For the most part, these exhibitions are composed not of installed performers or performances which seek to initiate public participation but rather through what I am calling 'referents of the relational' and, in this way, they speak to the case studies addressed in the previous chapters of this book which operate comparably through referents of performance.

Eschewing Art Objects

While Bishop recapitulates that the 'hallmark of an artistic orientation towards the social in the 1990s has been a shared set of desires to overturn the traditional relationship between the art object, the artist and the audience' such that the artist is imagined not so much as a maker of material artefacts but more as a 'collaborator and producer of *situations*;' she also affirms that 'these shifts are often more powerful as ideals than as actualised realities'.[35] Rather than entering a situation which might promote an experience of interrelation with other visitors, within *theanyspacewhatever* we encounter, rather, for the most part referents of this sort of practice. The relationship between the contributing artists, for example, is staged in a number of material forms which speak to a mode of self-preservation. Examining a prominent instance of this sort of allusion, Rirkrit Tiravanija's documentary film *CHEW THE FAT* (2008) displays interviews with each artist on individual monitors housed within a single gallery space off the main rotunda, as well as in the museum's theatres in an abridged form. Shifting relational aesthetics' emphasis on sociability onto the interconnections between the cohort of artists, willingly or otherwise, collected under this term, Tiravanija's project reminds us that Bourriaud's definition affirms the evaluation of artworks on the basis of the interrelations they both produce *and represent* (112). In other words, relational aesthetics is concerned with interactions both performed and displayed.

Bourriaud's theory does not separate 'live' forms of encounter irreconcilably from the domain of the object but rather puts forward two modes through which relational artworks might come into being: 'a/ moments of sociability' and 'b/ objects producing sociability' (33). In Bourriaud's rendering, relational artworks operate through the ephemeral moment and the productive object. It is with these two formal propositions that the next sections of this chapter are concerned. Despite Bourriaud's claims for a relational aesthetic manifest, in addition to immediate experience, in physical things, in 'experiences publicised by surface-objects' (32), curator of *theanyspacewhatever*, Nancy Spector, narrates the practice of the 1990s to which this exhibition refers as a mode that 'eschewed the discrete aesthetic object'.[36] Framed by an historical narrative involving the rejection of the static artwork and an investment in dynamism and transformation, visitors to the Guggenheim Museum might expect Spector's exhibition to continue this 'shift from a focus on the individual aesthetic object to more ephemeral, situation-based work'.[37] Though presented as privileging experiential and performance-based exhibits over more object-centric museum display, *theanyspacewhatever*, and indeed *Double Agent*, in fact operate predominantly through tangible objects which may or may not prompt relations.

One such exhibit, produced by Berlin-based artist Angela Bulloch in collaboration with the musician David Grubbs, and titled *Hybrid Song Box.4* (2008), appears as four solid cubes stacked on the gallery floor, each patterned with circular holes through which the upper two of these boxes are lit. The most recent in a series of 'Pixel Boxes' instigated by Bulloch during the late 1990s, these cubic installations combine a minimalist appearance with technological illumination. A succession of coloured lights and musical sounds, introduced through digital programming, instigates changeability within these aesthetic objects which thereby exceed the stability suggested by their wooden frame. Changeable and transient, *Hybrid Song Box.4* performs in a manner true to the fusion made pre-eminent in its title, instilling action within an object and affecting visitors through an encounter that is momentary and composed of variable and fluctuating compositional elements. Like the spasmodic motion of *Bob,* found within *The World as a Stage* and discussed in Chapter 2, this animation creates an object which functions beyond the stillness associated with the museum vitrine and the ephemeral terms of performance by incorporating shifting and alternating displays of visual and musical scores. In choosing to install these wooden boxes, Bulloch does not merely 'privilege experiential, situation-based work over discrete aesthetic objects' as the documents produced to accompany *theanyspacewhatever* suggest.[38] Rather, as Bourriaud observes of relational artworks more broadly, Bulloch animates these substantial objects by incorporating '*immediacy* in their visual writing' (43, original emphasis). Intervening in their traditional aesthetic of stasis by means of light and music, in *Hybrid Song Box.4* Bulloch positions the 'transitivity of the cultural object as a fait accompli' (Bourriaud, 25), constructing an art object that, while sturdy and rigid, is also time-specific and transitional.

Relational Objects of Performance

Looking once again in their plywood construction to the influence of minimalist practices discussed in Chapter 1 of this book, Bulloch's Pixel Boxes incorporate motion and dramatic dynamism and thereby indicate, what art historian Branden W. Joseph calls, a deconstruction of any dichotomy between kinetic and minimal art via their 'ambivalent form of *objecthood*.'[39] Bulloch's objects are concerned with ideas of transformation and exhibit a certain animation that functions equivocally between two modalities. Like the kinetic sculptures described by Rosalind Krauss, *Hybrid Song Box.4* was 'intended to theatricalize the space in which it was exhibited'.[40] Affecting a space for performance, Bulloch's Pixel Boxes return to an earlier and less thematic kind of theatricality than those addressed so far in this book. These wooden cubes, not white but timber, are characterised by transition, passing through different stages and forms, and enacting

Bourriaud's representation of transitivity as a 'tangible property of the artwork' (26). In relational terms, the aesthetic object is defined by occupying an intermediate position which, in my reading, shifts between designations of the object on display and the ephemeral performance.

Constructing 'relations between individuals and groups, between the artist and the world, and, by way of transitivity, between the beholder and the world', it is in terms of performative interpretation and transitional qualities that any 'artwork might thus be defined as a relational object' (Bourriaud, 26). Acknowledging the economic value of encounter, Bourriaud laments, with regard to contemporary communal relations, what he calls a 'general reification', suggesting that the 'social bond has turned into a standardised artefact' (9). While remaining cautious of the objectification of present-day public encounters, Bourriaud, at the same time, seems to promote this union of object and social exchange within the framework of aestheticism. In his terms, 'form only assumes its texture (and only acquires a real existence) when it introduces human interactions' (22). Founded precisely in acts of contact, and in relations specific to the art community, *you'll never work in this town again* (2004-ongoing) displays, within the framework of the *Double Agent* exhibition, referents of the relational, objects apparently constructed through physical interface and forms of sociability, specifically altercation. Seeming to exhibit the sort of 'tougher, more disruptive approach to "relations"' sought by curator Claire Bishop, the five images from *you'll never work in this town again* on display within the ICA form a series of portraits of figures from the art world community.[41] Including critics, collectors, and notably the two curators of *Double Agent*, Bishop and Sladen, these images are taken, we are told by the gallery guide, immediately after Glasgow-based artist Phil Collins had slapped each person in the face and therefore depict and perpetuate an appearance of, what Shannon Jackson calls, the 'kind of subjection any curator now expects to endure when a "relational" artist comes to town.'[42]

Curated within an exhibition which openly seeks to disrupt visitors' engagements, this narrative must be approached with caution. Being careful not to presume too easily the veracity of this action, these images at least bring to the fore the role of the curator. Positioning contributors usually implicit within the project of exhibition as visible performers and possible collaborators in a creative deception, Collins' portraits make apparent the ways in which artists and curators determine in association what is on display in gallery institutions. Within these photographs this essential relationship between artist and curator becomes, at least conceptually, the determining situation for artistic creation. In *Artificial Hells* Bishop asserts that 'photo-documents of participatory projects have their own experiential regime' such that we should not approach these photographs as 'objects of a new formalism,' but rather assess the ways in which they 'reinforce the social and artistic experience being generated.'[43] Like the *Empty Stages* photographs produced by Etchells and Glendinning and examined in introduction to this book, *you'll never work in this town again* draws out performances through processes of documentation and narrative construction. Invested in the performance and communication of particular encounters, these images, following Rebecca Schneider, raise the question of when and 'where, then, does the event (or the scene) take place' and beyond this if, indeed, it did.[44] Like the artists discussed in *Relational Aesthetics*, Collins does not demonstrate a preference for performance, rather *you'll never work in this town again* displays performed 'relations between people and the world, by way of aesthetic objects' (42). Disturbing the relationships between artists and curators, and questioning what Bourriaud calls the 'arbitrary division between the gesture and the forms it produces' (47), Collins' stricken photographs operate through and in relation to performance.

Exhibition as Mode of Practice

While Collins associates performance with objects framed by guiding museological documents, the artists represented within *theanyspacewhatever* create an environment wherein, according to the publicity for the project, 'an exhibition can be a film, a novel, a shared meal, a social space, a performance, or a journey.'[45] Directly aligning exhibition and performance, the architecture and fabric of the gallery emerge throughout *theanyspacewhatever* as materials with which to work. Considering the installations on display within the Guggenheim in their curation together, I will give examples briefly of a number of exhibits which appropriate and alter the museum structure through the following paragraphs so as to think further about the ways in which certain artists have 'claimed the exhibition itself as a medium.'[46] For a second and more prominent contribution, titled *Firmamental Night Sky: Oculus.12* (2008), Angela Bulloch installs a dark and twinkling skyscape within the zenith of the Guggenheim's rotunda, creating an illusory night. By means of this installation, Bulloch conceals the daylight, which even between October and January, usually accompanies at least some part of the Guggenheim's daily opening times, and situates *theanyspacewhatever* beneath a perpetual and starry darkness, or at least one maintained throughout the exhibition's opening hours. Visible immediately on entering the gallery, *Firmamental Night Sky* resituates museum visits in relation to concepts of time and illumination, inviting museum-goers to reflect on the context in which their engagement and attentions occur.

Further up the rotunda, other exhibits alter the spatial situation of gallery visitation. Covered with inkblot-shaped cut-outs and lit from within, Los Angeles–based artist Jorge Pardo's *Sculpture Ink* (2008) works to extend the usual reach of the gallery walls so that these encroach into the museum's spiral path. Constructed from sixteen beautiful cardboard-like screens which resemble jigsaw pieces, *Sculpture Ink* situates these temporary partitions on alternating sides of the Guggenheim's rotunda such that the panels interrupt the flow of visitors' movements and alter the speed at which it is possible to progress through the gallery. On these screens are exhibited prints made by Pardo in collaboration with the other contributors to *theanyspacewhatever*, including Paris-based artist Dominique Gonzalez-Foerster, a practitioner also keen to alter the fabric of the gallery. For *Promenade* (2007) Gonzalez-Foerster installs a white scrim to construct a screen which envelops the third ramp of the Guggenheim's rotunda. Moving through this enclosed section, the visitor is enfolded in sounds of birds and flowing water audible through speakers on the left side of the gallery ceiling. Despite its title suggesting a place in which to walk and be seen, within this *Promenade* vision is limited. It is not possible to see what is around the next bend. Visitors cannot tell how far through the exhibit we have progressed and, on emerging, are greeted by a sign which reads 'halfwayhalfway'. Suspended from the ceiling and composed in black letters, these words form part of Liam Gillick's *theanyspacewhatever Signage System*, the installation with which I began my analysis in this chapter.

Impinging on the operational machinery of the museum environment, some of these texts act as labels demarcating the location of public amenities or identifying the rotunda's 'ramps one to six', while others suggest that visitors 'stay here sometimes' or 'disintermediate now'. Parodying and intervening within the confines of curatorial and institutional directives and written instructions, Gillick's signs draw attention to and highlight the constructed nature of the gallery experience. In this way, his *Signage System* articulates gallery systems as a space in which to make art and highlights the situation of the visitor within these operations. In Gillick's practice, the 'unveiling of the institutional apparatus seemed to require varied forms of stage management' such that, as Jackson notes, 'each institutionally critical gesture re-engaged one or more registers of theatricality.'[47] Often referential of the museum context, Gillick's marking of 'halfwayhalfway' alludes to a midpoint in the progress of the Guggenheim's spiral incline, inviting visitors to travel 'that way that way' or to 'start from the top down'. Whether imperative or suggestive, Gillick's interventions reveal the ways in which visitors' experiences within exhibition contexts are inflected by the designed character of the gallery and its texts and it is, as explicated further in my introduction to this book, for this reason that such written framings are substantially referenced throughout my project. Borrowing the Guggenheim's language, in deference to this sort of institutional qualification, *theanyspacewhatever Signage System* has the potential, to 'subtly reorient visitors' experiences of the exhibition itself' by intercepting and thereby revealing directives which might otherwise fade into the background and offering alternative engagements within the framework of the gallery and its institutional protocols.[48]

Arresting and Reorienting

Many of the exhibits on display within *theanyspacewhatever* speak to the possibility of physical reorientation and reveal the ways in which thinking about performance in the art museum, following Jackson's terms, necessitates an 'encounter with some very difficult problems that are both formal and institutional.'[49] Irresolute between display and performance, Stockholm-based artist Carsten Höller's *Revolving Hotel Room* (2008) is constructed on three transparent, rotating disks which continually shift the familiar trappings of temporary accommodation positioned on one sphere in relation to those objects of white furniture located on the others, as well as to the gallery framework. Although Höller's orbs promise to involve, or revolve, the actions of gallery visitors, the installation is not open for public occupation. To enter the room, an exclusive reservation must be made in advance with New York's luxury Waldorf-Astoria Hotel. Giving visitors who can afford this privileged engagement, and are aware of the booking system, the opportunity to spend a night in the gallery, Höller's installation offers only those able to take up this elite invitation an alternative experience of this context and thus draws attention to issues of institutional accessibility, exclusivity, and parity of experience within the museum.

In addition to *Revolving Hotel Room*, Höller contributes another work to *theanyspacewhatever* which is also founded in rotary motion. *Krutikow's Flying City Revolving* (2008) is presented within the exhibition in the form of a live transmission from a rotating video camera which tracks the motion of transparent towers installed, and also spinning, on the roof of a city-based building. These spherical forms are, according to information provided by the museum, based on Russian architect Georgii Krutikow's 1928 imagining of an airborne community and appear on three screens within the gallery, providing different and changing perspectives across the city conveyed through unsteady projection. Both of Höller's installations generate what the Guggenheim describes as 'unstable situations that challenge the assumptions of the viewer and explore the influence of unanticipated movement on human perception.'[50] Exploring the effects of delicate motions on gallery visits, of turning and shifting positions, Höller's objects, and the representations he constructs of these, offer to visitors the possibility of being moved. Those guests who do inhabit the bed, desk, or dressing area of *Revolving Hotel Room* might leave this accommodation in a different orientation within the gallery to that from which they boarded the turning disks. During gallery opening hours, though, Höller's flying city and rotating bedroom wait empty for future occupants, and it is telling in this regard that the curatorial texts narrate the force of these projects in terms of viewing and perception.

Unable to access the mobile spaces of Höller's installations, the majority of visitors encounter these works from the position of spectator rather than participant. Most museum-goers arrive at these systems without being granted the agency to enter and act within their frameworks. Here, a complication of ideas of display and performance means that, though some visitors do experience *Revolving Hotel Room* through an embodied occupation, most of us must be content to view the work as an inaccessible exhibit. In *Fair Play: Art, Performance and Neoliberalism*, Jen Harvie suggests that socially turned art practices, rather than divesting agency to visitors, sometimes offer instead a 'spectacle of communication and social engagement' and, by creating opportunities for involvement that are temporary and limited, raise questions of 'who can participate and on what terms?'[51] Höller's projects reveal a certain amount of control over who can occupy and take up particular positions within exhibition environments. Leaving spaces vacant, or enterable only according to specific regulation and agreement, *Revolving Hotel Room* draws attention to the hierarchies of engagement operating within contemporary arts institutions and the discrepancy that some visitors will encounter this work as an object producing sociability while for others it will remain as an artwork to be looked at in distanced contemplation. Observing this room unoccupied, as I did on my visit to *theanyspacewhatever*, for the most part visitors experience this space as a venue that remains in the domain of display and excludes capacity for performance.

Artistic Occupancy

Within *Double Agent*, we find galleries of the ICA also allocated for specific purposes and employments which exceed the usual format of gallery display and require particular kinds of occupation. Bishop is keen to stress that this exhibition is not related to her previous writings on participation but rather concerned with a 'mechanism of delegation, of outsourcing performance to other people' and related to participatory concerns only through a retained interest in work that is 'ethically uncomfortable'.[52] Alert to the possibility that the exhibits on display might be challenging in some way, on the first floor of the ICA visitors discover a gallery turned into a studio. In this context, we are told by the exhibition leaflet, US-based artist and critic Joe Scanlan 'presents the up-and-coming artist Donelle Woolford'.[53] According to this introduction, Scanlan's installation initially appears to operate in symmetry with Marina Abramović's presentation of live artists reviewed in Chapter 1. Assimilating studio and gallery, this work raises questions about the relative worth of processes of making aesthetic objects as compared with constructing relations and participations within and beyond contexts of display. Presented within the gallery on selected Saturday and Sunday afternoons throughout the course of *Double Agent*, visitors, during these particular moments, find Woolford employed across three benches, surrounded by cut pieces of wood of different sizes, tools, protective eye glasses, filing cabinets, shelves, a radio, chairs, plants, cupboards, and other paraphernalia that implies the artist at work.

Apparently crafting, what the exhibition information describes as, 'wooden assemblages that reference Cubism and which are designed to coincide with (and challenge) the 100th anniversary of that movement', two such compositions, constructed from fragments of wood, hang on the wall of the gallery.[54] Cubism plays a significant role in Bourriaud's narrative of the development of, what he terms, a 'new, relational, dialectical order' since it is owing to the challenges brought about by this movement that the relational framework was 'applied to more and more limited objects' (27–28). Bourriaud writes that artists working within the cubist discipline 'attempted to analyse our visual links with the world by way of the most nondescript everyday objects and features (the corner of a table, pipes and guitars), based on a mental realism that reinstated the moving mechanisms of our acquaintance with the object' (28). Examining human relations with the physical world through a more restricted range of commonplace objects, what is especially interesting about Bourriaud's designation of the formations and methodologies of cubist art, in relation to a book project concerned with complicating associations between the static eternal art object and the ephemerality of performance, is the return to motional systems for understanding and explaining objects which this analysis encodes.

Instilling a sense of mobility into our perceptual and experiential processes, Bourriaud's description of the effects of the cubist movement resonate with Höller's *Revolving Hotel Room* and the rotation this work infuses within visitors' observations in the Guggenheim. By installing accommodation more integral to creative acts of making than to tourism and visitation within the ICA, Scanlan's work involves not only references to cubist concepts but also to past instances of artistic studio-based occupation within gallery environments. Bourriaud recalls, for example, artists Philippe Parreno, Pierre Joseph, and Philippe Perrin's occupation of the Air de Paris Gallery in 1990 and their transformation of this institution into a 'production workshop' (38). In keeping with Bourriaud's assertion of the ways in which relational aesthetics does not re-make or re-enact past artistic traditions, however, Scanlan's studio installation does not merely re-perform previous relational acts of this kind, but rather appropriates this action to the ideological and aesthetic agendas of the contemporary moment through the addition of an act of surrogacy. During an interview staged at the ICA by curators Bishop and Sladen, Woolford reveals an alternative identity. Onstage and outside her studio-gallery Woolford admits: 'by the way, my name is Abigail Ramsay and I'm an actor hired by Joe Scanlan to play the role of Donelle Woolford, just as other actors have been hired to play her in different locations.'[55] Multiply represented, displayed, and performed, Woolford is a construct imagined and presented by an artist and embodied by a performer. Taking on this role, in a performance with regards to which Scanlan is credited as creator, Ramsay is remunerated for her creative labour, involved in an exchange financial, aesthetic, and misleading. Ramsay is not, in fact, engaged in the production of cubist art objects, or at least this is not the main emphasis of her situation within the gallery.

Acting the Artist

Undertaken within this context of display, Woolford's work is necessarily performative, at least a representation of her daily experience as artist, and, in fact, more illusive, more performed even than that. Assuming the character of a sculptor for the duration of *Double Agent*, Abigail Ramsay acts the artist at work and thereby participates in what Nicholas Ridout calls in his essay for the exhibition catalogue, following Antonio Negri, Maurizio Lazzarato, and Paolo Virno, '"immaterial labor": work that does not produce goods, but instead produces social relations, communication, the movement of information. This is the labour of the service and the knowledge economies' and the purpose of her presentation is performance.[56] Interestingly, Bishop's writing on 'delegated' performance within *Artificial Hells* centres on practitioners employing and instructing 'non-professionals or specialists in other fields to undertake the job of being present and performing at a particular time and a particular place on behalf of the artist'.[57] Focusing on practices which involve the outsourcing of 'presence' to participants asked to represent certain social factions, rather than to professional performers such as Ramsay, in this related discussion Bishop suggests that delegation 'maintains a comfortable relationship to the gallery,' noting that it has 'accelerated with the institutionalisation of performance art and facilitates its collectability.'[58] Alongside their relationship to performance, delegated modes have a particular connection to ideas of display and collection that I want to tease out further.

During an event publicised as a 'Discussion with Donelle Woolford at the ICA,' Sladen cites correspondence from Scanlan with regards to his installation which situates the performer therein as a 'fully-fledged artist in her own right: she has a body and opinions and a developing oeuvre. Her only drawback is that by conventional measures she is not real.' Exploring what might be acceptable, or at least accepted, as a 'real' artist, Scanlan asserts that his invention of Woolford is akin to 'any other author who invents a character whom they hope will enter the public imagination' and that her character is still expanding and developing 'even as she moves through the stage of the art world, with all its characters and props.'[59] In his presentation of Woolford, Scanlan figures not only the gallery but also the 'art world' as a place for performance filled with portable objects and dramatis personae, but not all visitors to the ICA are aware of this play. During the same conversation, Bishop recounts how many gallery attendees were 'completely convinced that this was an artist who had set up a studio in the space. So there's an element of deception there that's more or less convincing and more or less troubling.' The curators are keen to reveal Woolford's duplicity through the event of live discussion because, in Sladen's terms, if the work appears as a 'flawless façade then I don't think it operates.'[60] Visitors who encounter the artist unaware that she is, in fact, an actor, do not experience the full capacity of the exhibit; the installation miscarries if the performance therein is not recognised as such.

Following Ridout's writing on the ways in which 'various forms of theatrical failure or undoing bring about moments of affective discomfort,' it is through specific and intentional 'undoings' that Scanlan's presentation of Woolford might be identified as performance and the 'deception' or 'discomfort' of that action realised and acknowledged.[61] The display of Woolford must fail in order for the performance to appear. In addition to the revelation made during the moment of live discussion, textual clues insinuating the ruse of Scanlan's project permeate the *Double Agent* literature. The theatricality of Scanlan's presentation is, Bishop and Sladen propose, 'hinted at through the tone of our language in the gallery guide', for example in the use of the phrase "up and coming" to describe Woolford's aesthetic prominence which, apparently, the curators would 'never use in relation to the other artists' and also in the promotion of the interview with Woolford as addressed to the subject of her "double life in London."[62] Although flagged by the curators, such indications of the equivocal nature of the installation are, I would suggest, quite specific and require a somewhat specialist and privileged knowledge regarding the rhetoric operative in arts institutions in order to be discerned. Perhaps more accessible indications of Woolford's status as performed are evident in Ramsay's live enactment of this part and the documentation by which it is framed.

Visual Discrepancies

It is through the textual and visual discourses surrounding his installation for *Double Agent* that Scanlan does successfully 'seed discrepancies into the project'.[63] Instating not just a working artist's studio into a gallery context, but also a performer within a situation of display, Scanlan's presentation reveals the ways in which, borrowing from Ramsay, these 'two don't exist in the same world.'[64] It is through a divergence of display and performance that Woolford's performative status might be understood. Taking directives from a practitioner trained and used to practicing within a visual arts context, rather than a theatre-maker, or at least a stereotypical imagining of a director working within a script-based tradition, differs in terms of methodology, priority, and stimulus. Bishop notes, for example, that this distinction is evident in the emphasis on the '*visuality* of Donelle: what she's wearing is important, how she looks in the space and what the space looks like that she's operating in. There's much less emphasis on motivation for the character.'[65] Being careful not to exclude the significance of visuality from the remit of the theatre, it is suggestive that, at least in Bishop's analysis, the character of Woolford is conceived in terms of visible display rather than convincing or compelling psychological performance.

Played previously by other actors and represented by different performers in the later iterations of *Double Agent* at the Mead Gallery, Warwick and the BALTIC Centre for Contemporary Art in Gateshead, Woolford's appearance is always of paramount concern such that we might imagine the construction of this artistic persona more in terms of the formation of an aesthetic object than a developed theatrical character. It is in terms of visual cohesion that Scanlan inserts inconsistencies into Woolford's representation and on the basis of this aspect of the work that gallery visitors might first identify the performers appearing as the artist as such. Referring to a picture of another actor's performance of Woolford reproduced within the framework of the *Double Agent* literature, Ramsay laughs 'everyone has that guide and clearly that woman is not me!'[66] Engaged in a performed exercise of spot-the-difference, it is, then, as curator and critic Polly Staple also observes, in the discussion following Woolford's interview, the 'moment when the visuality starts to creep in ... that's really powerful.'[67] It is in relation to the images picturing Woolford that Scanlan's presentation of that character is destabilised and his reference to performance within a context of display becomes apparent.

Employing these sorts of delegatory and performative strategies can work to undermine any clear sense of what the exhibition leaflet for *Double Agent* terms 'the authentic or authoritative artist,' a figure who is substituted instead by a number of actors and proxies who may themselves prove to be 'partial or unreliable.' Scanlan's alignment of the figure of the artist with a shifting cast of performers recalls the case studies of Chapter 1 and particularly Elmgreen & Dragset's play *Drama Queens* wherein canonical art objects were substituted with props. Developing the concerns of the exhibitions explored so far in this book, within *Double Agent* each 'artist uses other people as a medium' and such acts of surrogation, borrowing again from the gallery literature 'raise questions of performance'.[68] Explicitly addressing the relation between customs of performing and visual arts practice, the title of the exhibition signals the intricacy of the positions of artist, curator, collaborator, and visitor and the relative agency available to these individuals within exhibition environments. This heading suggests immediately that the performers operating within this context are multiple.

People as a Medium

A related kind of doubling characterises the work of Amsterdam-based artist Barbara Visser and her contribution to *Double Agent,* a video installation involving footage from a series of lectures in which she cast actors to appear as herself. Once again exploring the relation between artist and performer, Visser hired actors to present her work in lectures not identified to the audience as staged. In a first iteration, performed in 1997 and titled *Lecture with an Actress*, Visser fed a presentation and responses related to a question and answer session to a performer through an earpiece. For a second, meta-performance titled *Lecture on Lecture with an Actress* (2004), Visser employed yet another actor to interpret a film of the previous address. In 2007, Visser herself appeared for the first time within this frame, not as a 'live' presence, but rather as a shadow cast onto a screen showing footage from the event in 2004 and as a voice, dubbing the words of the second actor. Involved in notions or replay and return, this final performance forms the basis for the video, titled *Last Lecture* (2007), screened in the ICA for *Double Agent*. Manifesting through a layering of lectures, as with Scanlan's installation of Woolford, clues concerning the performed nature of these public events are manifest within the strata of the constructed film and accompanying commentary. Enacting intentional inconsistencies embedded by Visser within the composition of this cumulative lecture series, at the end of her performance, the first actress visibly removes the earpiece through which her words have been fed, while the second performer, who comments on this filmed action, bears little physical resemblance to her predecessor. The first actress is blonde, the second, brunette and, even from a viewing position in which we are alerted to the deceptive planes of the project, visitors to *Double Agent* never learn which appearance is closer to Visser herself, who materialises only as a silhouetted character.

Contradictions occur also in relation to the film's subtitles. Presumably a remnant from the project's second iteration, these do not cohere with the speech later dubbed by Visser, into which she incorporates further playful discrepancies. As *Last Lecture* begins, Visser's shadow enters while the second actress also arrives onscreen to introduce the film of the first lecture. The dark-haired actress, or rather Visser's dubbing of her presentation, explains, 'I've just started a performance where I prompt an actress playing me.'[69] In this layering of voices and instructions, Visser introduces an early incongruity into the working of the film by drawing attention to the placement of an earpiece through which the first script is relayed; her speech tells of a 'small device in her left ear', the subtitles of a 'small device in her right ear.' Mirroring and reformulating the levels of construction, these contradictions between spoken and written narration continue to appear. The voice tells viewers, that it is 'hard to find any resemblance' between the performers, whereas the subtitles interpret the similarity as 'striking'.[70] Early in the film we are informed that Visser is concerned specifically with the question: 'what can I do to wake up the audience'? The employment of different, and noticeably unalike, performers, and the intended inaccuracy of the subtitling, require visitors to be more discerning and, following Bourriaud's description of relational aesthetics, demand a more activated form of spectatorship.

Insisting within the film's commentary that 'what we see depends on what we are looking for', Visser's work articulates a position in which a play 'is not a play when the audience doesn't know what they're looking at.' Being cautious of accepting too easily the fidelity of any element of this multifaceted installation, the words onscreen suggest that, for visitors to an earlier iteration of this duplicitous project, their encounter 'counts as a real experience' because, without any awareness of the presentation as performance, this appears as relatively 'honest' and 'genuine'.[71] Assuming each actor to be Visser herself, the understanding of those spectators unaware of the lectures as performed is partial. Their insight is limited in symmetry with that of those visitors naive to the fictional status of Woolford in Scanlan's work. Within *Double Agent* and the confines of the ICA galleries, we encounter *Last Lecture* with some awareness of its deceptive layers and our attentions attuned to the presence of performers. Visitors here are informed that the lectures are designed and invaded by theatricality. Not only involved with an association between artist and actor, *Last Lecture* brings attention to the situation in which the work positions layers of audience, viewer, and visitor. It is indicative of the exhibitions addressed in this chapter that, rather than creating a further performance in this series, Visser's contribution takes the form of an, albeit doctored, mode of documentation. On Visser's website her practice is described as concerned with 'the uncertain relationship between registration and dramatization'.[72] Examining the relationship between recording or cataloguing and theatrical presentation, *Last Lecture* draws attention to the experience of gallery visitors through the mode of an object referent of two previous performances concerned with the position of the spectator.

An Exhibition of the Audience

The contemporary focus on the situation of the gallery-goer, and our relation to the work of art, the artist, the institution, as well as other visitors within the museum, develops in certain arenas, following Bourriaud's theory, not merely as an aspect but 'the quintessence of artistic practice' (22) such that 'human relations have now become fully-fledged artistic "forms"' (28). In this rendering, the mode of expression exists not in relation to but rather becomes embodied interrelation and within *Double Agent* we see an iteration of this form which returns us to the object. Whereas, in the case studies that formed the substance of the first chapter of this book an interchange between actor and art object was evident, developing the remit of Chapter 2, here this exchange comes to involve visitors rather than professional performers. Not just taking up the exhibition itself as a medium, within the events explored in this chapter visitors are confronted with, what contributing artist to *theanyspacewhatever* Pierre Huyghe calls in the Guggenheim's literature, 'an exhibition of the audience.'[73] By displaying those who move and interpret, and therefore perform, within the confines of a gallery environment, the concerns of these exhibitions look to the following chapter on digital practices, sharing an investment in the performative and productive nature of visitors' engagements. Contributing to exhibitions which intersect between practices of the displayed and the performed, visitors are acknowledged here as agents at work within gallery spaces, constructing and decoding, while at the same time subject to regulation and direction, by artists, curators, and other spatial and institutional instructions.

Within *Double Agent*, many of the installations require visitors to interact physically with the projects on display. In order to engage with the artworks, gallery-goers must perform under their direction. Filmmaker, actor, and theatre director Christoph Schlingensief's *The African Twin Towers— Stairlift to Heaven* (2007), for example, incorporates an 80-minute film made in Namibia, with a cast including Irm Herman and Patti Smith, as well as non-professional performers, designated by the first part of the work's title. At the same time, this piece also draws exhibition visitors into the space of the installation so as to witness a shorter film displayed in a small box fixed high up within the projection of the first. This smaller-scale film, in the words of the exhibition leaflet, 'requires viewers to literally incorporate themselves into the work, as it is visible at the top of a stairlift that cuts across the main projection.'[74] Seated within this hoist, I travel across the varying shape of the larger projection such that my silhouette casts a shadow on the illuminated screen. Reaching a modest white box, I lift the black curtain which covers an opening into that cube and look inside. Through this slit, a black-and-white film is visible which shows two figures sucking each others' fingers and touching faces. The visitor who journeys to this hidden display before me refuses to disclose what he has seen: 'I can't tell you what's behind the screen.' 'Why', asks his companion? 'It's a secret.' In order to share in this secret, visitors must occupy the stairlift and, thereby, position themselves on display within Schlingensief's installation, looking out to other gallery-goers watching the larger projection.

As visitors take turns to make this journey, within Schlingensief's installation, as Alan Read adopts from Walter Benjamin, a 'profoundly theatrical project is underway in which *truth* is no longer a matter of exposure which destroys the secret, so much as a *revelation* which does justice to it.'[75] The process of moving through the projection and up in the ascending chair is the means that constructs the secret, or at least the illusion of it. This mechanism of viewing makes the visitor curious to see what is hidden, only to be met with something perhaps not as titillating as the work's title and approach might suggest. In this way, Schlingensief's artwork captures the interest of gallery visitors and requires this curiosity to be enacted physically through a bodily investment in the piece. Of course, in this example, visitors may choose not to mount the lift and scale the screen and rather to watch *The African Twin Towers* at a distance. Elsewhere within the exhibition, however, such incorporation is not so easily avoided. In *Instant Narrative (IN)* (2006–8), the project on display in the next room of the gallery, participation is not, by contrast, optional and the volition which visitors may exert with regards to our engagements with this work is therefore significantly altered. This installation, conceived by Barcelona-based artist Dora García, is narrated on the ICA's website as bringing a 'live component into the exhibition'[76] and does so not, or at least not primarily, in the guise of professional, hired performers, as was the case in Scanlan's studio, but rather by drawing on non-elective visitor-performers.

Staring at an Empty Room

Operating at the intersection of the displayed and the performed, García's gallery-based performance works have, like Visser's, investigated the relation between artist, audience, and performer through acts of delegation involving hired actors. For *Double Agent*, rather than employing professional performers, García stationed what the ICA's exhibition leaflet calls 'observers' within the gallery who construct a narrative based on the actions of visitors which is then projected onto its white walls. Technologically mediated and transferred, according to the ICA's framing of this performance-installation, the 'authorship of this narrative is a function of continual displacement—from the artist to the writer to the visitor' and, in its investment in surveillance, observation, and the relation between predetermined and improvised behaviours, *Instant Narrative* looks to the following digitally committed chapter of this book.[77] Recording something of visitors' movements through this part of the exhibition, this act of narration shares with those projects reviewed in Chapter 4 an idea of visitor as performer; both speak in terms of 'trajectory,' tracking gallery-goers as they 'trace the usual routes' or the 'radical routes' and asking visitors to imagine, how 'would it be if you had a thread tied to the back of your trousers? Which trace would you have left in here?'[78] Drawing visitors' attention to our occupation of the galleries, *Instant Narrative* records, re-imagines, and affects these possible positions and stances.

Figure 3.1 Dora García, *Instant Narrative*, 2006. Performance, computer software, video projection. Photo: ICA, London, 'Double Agent,' 2008. Photo Lyndon Douglas. Courtesy of the artist and Michel Rein, Paris/Brussels.

Constructed within a gallery environment, the emerging text of *Instant Narrative*, from which I will draw extensively in these paragraphs so as to demonstrate something of the effect of this installation in my writing, necessarily incorporates references to this context as well as to modernist ideals associated with institutional architecture. Transliterating not only surrounding exhibits, the authors of this narrative return frequently to unfolding scenarios founded in the legacy of the white cube for display and the coeval empty space for performance. Their words speak of 'staring at an empty room. Writing about an empty room' and there is a sense that, even when visitor-performers do occupy the gallery space, soon 'the room will be empty again.' Enacting a task delegated by an artist, the writers also consider their own relation to this emptiness, as well as the potential for production inherent within this setting. 'Without him recording the nothing,' one proposes, 'there will be nothing', and so, he continues, 'it falls to words', to the combination of 'imagination and monotony in astonishing smudges' and, if the words fail to come 'he. disappears.' Poised by its authors and its protagonists, and their inevitable exit from the gallery, towards disappearance, *Instant Narrative* draws not only on museological terminology but also on tropes of theatricality within its discourse. Visitors are presented as 'standing alone like being on stage' and critiqued for positioning themselves out of the writer's view 'in the dead area when there's a chance for making theatre from life.'[79] Despite foregrounding disappearance in its writing, García's project, by operating across domains of the displayed and performed, exceeds the ephemeral. The work exists during gallery opening hours in a performed iteration but continues in text-based form via the words collected and transcribed.

In symmetry with the performances enacted through the photographs of Collins' *you'll never work in this town again* and the digital objects produced in Chapter 4, it is through the construction of *Instant Narrative*, in part a textual object projected onto the walls of the exhibition space, that the performances inherent in each visitor's movement through the gallery, as well as those of writer-observer, are made visible. Extended and, perhaps also, inhibited through this articulation, the action of the gallery-goers, and García's delegated attention on our movements, becomes involved in an interplay of creation and display, performance and object. Perplexing these relations, visitors who seem aware, in their physical behaviour and attitude, of their role as performer, or who seem to take pleasure in playing this part, are publicly ridiculed in terms of the aesthetic object, for pretending to be 'from a painting, he is a muse, a model, a pre-Raphaelite?'[80] Each of the writers read imaginary stories and interactions onto visitors' behaviours, much as gallery-goers might construct a tale based on the subject of a painting or the shape of an art object. Within the framework of *Instant Narrative*, the relations between gallery visitors are imagined as much as they are enacted. Extended into a fictional realm, the actions and gestures of visitor-performers become the subject of the work by being translated into a form which intermingles observable mannerisms with creative and performative interpretations.

Flickering Attentions

Challenging once again any clear distinction between performance and object, the accounts projected by *Instant Narrative* as almost instantaneous text document motions made moments before while also working to intervene within these behaviours, prompting changed directions and altered attentions. On visiting García's project, I became aware of my involvement in an invented and extended narrative via a question legible on the gallery wall and apparently interpretive of my entrance to the installation: 'should I trust the writer and head for the dark room or run now?' The writer's words raise questions about the confidence I, as visitor-performer, might have in the expressions of this delegated writer and the kinds of expectations and confidences at work between us within the gallery. Looking for a page on which to make a note of my thoughts, the author interprets this activity into a fiction wherein I begin to 'scribble an escape plan' in my notebook, while rummaging to find the floorplan of the ICA. The writer imagines my actions into a narrative about invention and, significantly in relation to my coming fourth chapter, about way finding in galleries. In fact, anticipating that this exhibition might be critical to the current book project, I was not, as the observer pretends, contriving a getaway, but rather jotting down the text which the writer constructs responsively in relation to my actions. The narrator's words are prompted by my impulse to keep a record of the exhibit, and these expressions, in turn, instigate the continuation of my own annotations. In my experience of *Instant Narrative*, the integral action of note making becomes reciprocal and propagating.

Within this installation, which works to make self-reflexive the act of exhibition attendance, visitors who attempt to conceal themselves from the writer's view almost certainly receive the attention they are trying to avoid. Here each 'performer is without choice' and, since visitors who retreat from this domain also find their withdrawal translated into text, the mechanisms of the installation ensure 'the performers always participate'.[81] In this way, García's work points to the debt Bourriaud's defence of relational aesthetics owes to the theory of philosopher Louis Althusser and perhaps particularly to his assertion that 'ideology has always-already interpellated individuals as subjects'.[82] Applying this notion of pre-existing subjects to visitors attending an exhibition, within *Instant Narrative* each gallery-goer is always-already operating as a performer through our proximity to this context. It is the situation of display that compels the visitor to perform. Recognising ourselves within the framework of *Instant Narrative*, visitors are coerced by the installation to acknowledge and respond to this representation and to negotiate our behaviour with this in mind. In this way, García's exhibit operates through, what Schneider calls, 'the circulatory aspects of the hail'.[83] Instigating a reciprocal performance between visitor and writer, in which both are affected by the other's actions, *Instant Narrative* arrests the attentions of each visitor through acts of relational interpellation.

Exceeding both the normative rules of the fixed, unchanging text or art object and of performance as non-object-centric, *Instant Narrative* highlights and extends the inherent summoning of the anticipated visitor by museological and curatorial structures. Both performing and displayed, visitors to this installation must always be 'in both worlds at the same time'. 'Connecting otherwise disconnected details something else can take place' within García's construct precisely because 'the laws in here work differently. Performance occurs in the act of doing it. Rules are established in their making.' It is not true, in this hybrid space, as one writer projects, that 'time doesn't matter for this is a white box with no apparent connection to the outside (although this has not yet been finally proven.)' Rather, *Instant Narrative* makes reference to temporalities different from traditional figurings of the gallery which entail endurance and perpetuity. This installation invokes not only the traditional ephemerality of performance, but also the duration of film, the 'endless loop of images projected onto the shadow-enveloped wall.'[84] Engaging with the works that surround it, *Instant Narrative*, unlike other displays completed in advance of the exhibition, responds to its situation within a curatorial arrangement and performs in relation to the projects alongside which it is presented. Like the works of Visser and Schlingensief, García's installation invests in a screen-based mode of presentation, taken up in detail in Chapter 4 of this book. The flickering images characteristic of filmic representation are read by the observer onto the acts of viewing those works compel. Here, 'attention flickers between both films' which operate across this flutter and the loop on which they are played, thereby resonating with a project central to *theanyspacewhatever*.[85]

A Lull in the Action

Halfway up the rotunda of the Guggenheim Museum visitors encounter *Cinema Liberté/Bar Lounge*, a makeshift movie theatre and coffee shop which returns to and reenacts a project of the same title presented in different contexts by Douglas Gordon and Rirkrit Tiravanija. For the first iteration of *Cinema Liberté/Bar Lounge* at the FRAC Languedoc-Roussillon in Montpellier in 1996, the two aspects of the setup were located on different floors of the venue but connected by a video link which streamed the action from the cinema to the bar, including not only the films but also those watching. Focusing on visitors' attentions, the project combines an interest in relational aesthetics with, what Director of MoMA PS1 and Chief Curator at Large at the Museum of Modern Art in New York, Klaus Biesenbach calls, an exploration of 'performance through new media' wherein viewers 'act out their movie watching behavior in a more conscious and public fashion.'[86] In this version, as in the recapitulation presented in the Guggenheim, the cinema screens a selection of films banned at the time of their first release while offering to museum visitors refreshment and time for recuperation. During my visit, the film on display was *The Salt of the Earth* (1954), made by blacklisted Hollywood director Herbert Biberman and including in its cast participants from mining communities in New Mexico. Narrated by Mexican-born actor Rosaura Revueltas, arrested during filming, the first line of the movie asks, 'How shall I begin my story that has no beginning?' Functioning without a clearly defined starting point, the narrative, like the filmic loop on which it is played within the gallery, and the political hail, the call for a politicised response with which it was associated, is circulatory.

Invested in realities of socio-political labour and salaried performance, the films shown within the repertoire of *Cinema Liberté* were chosen because, a guide within the Guggenheim Museum tells me, they are 'still shocking' today and, in this persisting capacity to provoke, might initiate conversation. Arresting the attention of gallery visitors, these films might prompt visitors to take a seat on one of the bean bags scattered around the cinema, inter-pellated by the summons of these movies which 'still', enduringly, might, at least according to Gordon and Tiravanija, as well as the Guggenheim staff who support their project, astound and incite reaction. Hanging near to *Cinema Liberté*, one of Gillick's signs reads 'running backwards'. Looking again to a former presentation, this cinema moves in reverse, contradicting the oft-pretended endurance of the museum, as well as the ephemerality of performed modes. Relocated to the middle of an exhibition which sits at an interchange between concepts of the displayed and the performed, *Cinema Liberté/Bar Lounge* integrates spaces for projection and social relaxation. The walls are tagged with four statements which point to a certain com-plexity of experience and understanding: 'You never knew'; 'I always knew'; 'they never knew; 'you always knew'. Operating between the constant, per-manent, forever of the 'always' and the inaccessibility of 'never', this café offers a brief period of intermission or quiescence within the exhibition.

Collecting my complimentary coffee, a barista in the Bar Lounge informs me that here 'we're at a lull in the action'. This place of respite and filmic distraction forms, within *theanyspacewhatever*, a space in which to pause and be still, to reflect on and respond to the exhibition and gallery sur-roundings. Offering rest, an interlude within the persistent flow of the exhibition, this café and cinema reveal how, through what Bourriaud calls 'little services rendered, the artists fill in the cracks in the social bond' (36). Fusing breaks within the culture of gallery visitation, *Cinema Liberté/Bar Lounge* works to 'patiently re-stitch the relational fabric' (36). With regard to small actions of service, Bourriaud uses terminology associated with mending and re-making the failures of the relational project so that the lull provided by the cinema and café, in fact, becomes the most active gesture towards social interaction. This moment of care, this intermission in which visitors receive attention and remain still, have a break, stretching and relaxing for an instant, is the dynamic moment within the exhibition. According to Spector, the *anyspacewhatever* invites visitors to 'encounter a cluster of seeming opposites – collectivity and individuality; the past and the present; active engagement and quiet contemplation – in a fluid, transitional space.'[87] Intermediate between contemplation and relation, it is the interval within the exhibition which becomes its most critical and communicative point. *Cinema Liberté/Bar Lounge* represents a striking conjunction of provocation and motionlessness.

Unconscious Optics

One of a number of film-based installations on display within the Guggenheim, *Cinema Liberté/Bar Lounge*, like an associated collaboration with Anna Sanders Films, resists, what the exhibition website calls, 'any distinction between the art film and the art of film.'[88] Displaying popular movies within a museum context, Anna Sanders Films, a production company founded in 1997 by Pierre Huyghe, Philippe Parreno, Dominique Gonzalez-Foerster, Charles de Meaux, and the Association for Diffusion of Contemporary Art, is significant to the current project for the ways in which it operates at a point of intersection. Opposed to interpretations wherein cinema has 'long been separate from the visual arts', this film production company seeks to instigate, what the Guggenheim's webpages narrate as 'a third term, in which art and film intertwine and commingle.'[89] This is comparable to the ways in which this book is concerned with the interface between the displayed and the performed. Complimentary to my interests here, the films on display within *theanyspacewhatever*, selected by film director and artist de Meaux, share an interest in relations between different modes of operation and the use of one approach to extend and further develop another. One of the films presented by Anna Sanders, *El sueño de una cosa* (*The Dream of a Thing*, 2001) by Parreno, comprised a minute-long film, and the panels, reproductions of Robert Rauschenberg's 1951 *White Painting*, on which it is projected, as well as a silence of four minutes and thirty-three seconds in a gesture towards that seminal work by composer John Cage.

In an essay co-written for the exhibition catalogue, art curators and critics Hans Ulrich Obrist and Daniel Birnbaum propose *El sueño de una cosa* as a film 'undeniably and overwhelmingly present', occupying a 'territory of expectation' and instilled with its own 'peculiar chronology.'[90] While Parreno's cinematography is aligned with performance in terms of its presence and immediacy, its temporality does not belong to the ephemeral. For Obrist and Birnbaum, established forms of sequentiality are inadequate in describing this piece which prioritises a temporality open to multiple reconstruction. Throughout *theanyspacewhatever* film is emphasised as a 'quintessentially time-based medium.'[91] This temporal quality, associated with the playing and re-playing of film, is exploited by Douglas Gordon in another cinematic work which he contributes to the exhibition. Titled *24 hour psycho back and forth and to and fro* (2008), this video installation forms a new iteration of *24 Hour Psycho* (1993) for which Gordon stretched Alfred Hitchcock's thriller *Psycho* (1960) to a twenty-four hour duration. Altering the momentum and speed at which the film is usually presented and experienced, *24 hour psycho back and forth and to and fro* is formative of another lull, another form of delay and interruption, within *theanyspacewhatever* and bestows on moving images something alike to the established stillness of a museum object. American writer Don DeLillo begins his short novel *Point Omega* (2010) through an encounter with an earlier iteration of this film project, a 'more or less moving picture' which might enable perceptive spectators 'finally to look and to know you're looking, to feel time passing, to be alive to what is happening in the smallest registers of motion' and attuned to the subtleties of such gradual transitions.[92]

Exceeding object status in its protracted, yet still present, movement, Gordon's film is shown in its entirety three times during the course of the *theanyspacewhatever*. Played across two screens, which show, simultaneously, the decelerated film running forwards and backwards, this form of presentation allows for, what the exhibition literature calls, 'startling moments of concordance.'[93] Arresting when two of the film's images coincide, Gordon's work reminds us that film acting, unlike that of the stage, is not sequential but rather, in the terms of Walter Benjamin, a 'frightened reaction can be shot now and be cut into the screen version.' In this way film production, Benjamin notes in his influential essay 'The Work of Art in the Age of Mechanical Reproduction' (1936), affords 'a spectacle unimaginable anywhere at any time before this.' Generating a display previously inconceivable, *24 hour psycho back and forth and to and fro* makes visible the mechanics of filmmaking, 'its interruptions and isolations, its extensions and accelerations, its enlargements and reductions', its capacity to be stilled. Revealing what Benjamin calls 'unconscious optics', images of the world not visible to the human eye, Gordon's installation presents a time which viewers of Hitchcock's original were not intended to see.[94] Slowing down a filmed performance and enlivening this in two different directions within one installation space, Gordon's filmic work expands our conceptions of time and of motion. In DeLillo's rendering too, the 'depths of things so easy to miss in the shallow habit of seeing' which this project reveals are mesmerising.[95] Responding to a cultural moment in which it was possible to 'see things on TV and then never see them again', Gordon sees *24 hour psycho back and forth and to and fro* as a way of placing 'something monumental and perpetual into the world.'[96] Seeking security in monumentality and perpetuity, Gordon's filmic installation looks to the terminology and refuge of the museum in response to the threat of missing and being missed.

Eternal and Ephemeral

24 hour psycho back and forth and to and fro speaks to the relationship between concepts of display and performance. This work appears, borrowing Spector's reference to Manuel Castells' conception of time in a networked society, both seemingly '"eternal" in its endless and instantaneous accessibility and "ephemeral" in its ultimately contingent status'; since the exhibit was not showing on the day I visited *theanyspacewhatever* I could not watch it. In reaction to what Spector calls, an 'unprecedented *immediacy* of current events and cultural expressions', made possible by digital television and the ubiquity of the internet, the artists, including Gordon, who contribute to this exhibition employ a concept of time beyond that of the stable object or the disappearing performance by making time a 'malleable material, a medium unto itself.'[97] In symmetry with other case studies examined in this book, this exhibition materialises through tangible objects which, like Gordon's film and Bulloch's *Hybrid Song Box.4*, exceed the traditional stasis of the museological exhibit by incorporating durational and experiential actions. Operating between the temporalities traditionally associated with paradigms of display and those of performance, the artists working within the Guggenheim explore ways in which, following Spector, a 'kind of vibrating temporality could produce new narratives'. Constructing a sporadic momentum through which to instigate alternative modes, *theanyspacewhatever*, in Spector's interpretation too, reveals that the 'exhibition format has provided a particularly rich model to explore ways in which time can expand, loop, and fold around new scenarios that extend well beyond the conventional paradigm of object-orientated, chronologically limited events.'[98]

While exhibits such as Pardo's *Sculpture Ink,* Gonzalez-Foerster's *Promenade*, and Gillick's *theanyspacewhatever Signage System* appropriate and disrupt the fabric and functional systems of the museum environment, Bulloch's *Firmamental Night Sky* and the subtle motions and intermittent rhythms of Höller's revolving installations speak to the possibility of reorienting visitors' perceptions of, if not our engagements with, the exhibition environment in relation to concepts of time. Inviting alternative positions, formed from existing modes of display and encounter, the exhibitions examined in this chapter interrupt any linear and progressive narrative of art history by recollecting a past form of production and interrupting the possible disappearance of this way of working. Though defined by Bourriaud as 'not the revival of any movement,' the relational aesthetic forms, to which *theanyspacewhatever* in particular returns, share with Bourriaud's designation a 'thinking about the fate of artistic activity' (44). Comparably invested in defining, and questioning, conventional paradigmatic tropes and looking to future modes of practice which might rethink and exceed them, these exhibitions, which operate between the relational practices associated with the 1990s, contemporary responses to such forms of social engagement, and current artistic and curatorial concerns, follow a strategy of return. *theanyspacewhatever* and *Double Agent* work to construct a kind of caesura in the genealogy of art history by returning to the relational and resisting the confines of traditional models both of display and of performance.

Making complex the exchanges between document and performance, recorded event and theatrical act in *you'll never work in this town again*, and between artist performer and aesthetic object in Scanlan's presentation of Donelle Woolford and Visser's *Last Lecture*, within *theanyspacewhatever* and *Double Agent* 'the work of art represents a social *interstice*' (16). Returning to this definition of relational art, cited from Bourriaud earlier in this chapter, we find here a conception of the art object as something intermediate and transitional, an intervening space between two actions, which might be thought broadly in terms of display and performance. With neither mode emerging as straightforwardly medium-specific, it is useful to reconsider relational aesthetics in connection to approaches and paradigms usually associated with performance and in this regard the interval, the lull evident in Gordon and Tiravanija's *Cinema Liberté/Bar Lounge*, becomes a space of production and interrelation, making viable new rhythms and ways of being working within gallery environments. In closing this chapter, it seems only appropriate to return finally to Huyghe's *OPENING* of *theanyspacewhatever* and to visitors' torch-lit heads and the corresponding flashes of light in the dark museum which mark an alternative pace for its occupation. Like many of the works on display within this exhibition, including Gordon's *24 hour psycho back and forth and to and fro,* for which the museum remained open throughout the film's duration, this *OPENING* event stretched the usual temporal frames of museum operations.

Figure 3.2 Pierre Huyghe, *Transfer Book*, 2008. Stapled booklet. 21.8 × 27.9 cm / 8.5 × 11 in. Courtesy of the artist and Marian Goodman Gallery.

Interrupting any sequential progression of beginning, middle, and end, on entering the Guggenheim museum, visitors encounter first Italian artist Maurizio Cattelan's *Daddy Daddy* (2008), a work in which a statue of a recognisable character, Pinocchio, appears face down in the gallery's fountain. Acting as what critic and writer John Kelsey calls, a 'false ending that greets you upon entering the show', visitors are hailed into the gallery initially to the call of a fictitious finale.[99] Correspondingly, the final image of the exhibition makes reference to Huyghe's *OPENING*. Near to the top of the Guggenheim's rotunda, travelling upwards, visitors discover a large greyed image, an imprint of performance referential of the second iteration of Huyghe's project, *theanyspacewhatever Transfer Book* (2008), a collection of iron-on transfers depicting the architecture of the museum within which the exhibition is displayed. 'Passing from the positive (of the journey) to the negative (of its transcription)', Huyghe's work pictures the opening event and thereby, like the return to the relational addressed in this chapter more broadly, 'translates forms from one state to another' in a transformational action particularly resonant for the current project.[100] Contemporary intersections between display and performance rely on intermittent acts of transfer and transition, each manifesting, like relational aesthetics, via display practices which employ, what Bourriaud calls, a 'transitive ethic' (24). Invested in an ethics of the fleeting and the transitional, the transitive, in grammatical terms, speaks of an action transferred to an object.

Capable of passing between forms and conditions, the return to relational aesthetics enacted by *Double Agent* and *theanyspacewhatever* speaks audibly at the interface of the displayed and the performed, particularly with regard to the kinds of interpellation inherent in the impetus on visitors to recognise and respond to our position as agents operating within the museological project. Within *Double Agent*, exhibits including Visser's *Last Lecture* and Schlingensief's *Stairlift* bring awareness to the situation of the gallery visitor, with the latter requiring attention manifested in the body. Engaging with actions of visitation through a screen-based mode of presentation, García's *Instant Narrative* makes visible the performances inherent in each visitor's movements, extending and inhibiting these participations through written articulation. Within *theanyspacewhatever*, Huyghe's *Transfer Book* is similarly representative of the ways in which an event, in this case of people moving within an exhibition, might materialise once again in the act of reception. Not, in Norden's terms, so 'elegantly theatrical as his transfer-book image', Huyghe's *OPENING* gains performative status in terms of the object.[101] Positioning visitors' behaviours as both displayed and performed, these relational returns, for me, look to the next chapter, producing alternative and 'relational space-time elements' (Bourriaud, 44) through which acts of museum visitation and performance might be reformulated, extended, and re-imagined. Telling here is a creative, curatorial, and discursive interruption of the disappearance of forms.

Notes

1. Claire Bishop, 'Antagonism and Relational Aesthetics,' *October* 110 (2004), 56.
2. Liam Gillick, 'Contingent Factors: A Response to Claire Bishop's "Antagonism and Relational Aesthetics",' *October* 115 (2006), 102.
3. Nicholas Ridout, 'You look charming. You look enchanting. You look dazzling. You look breathtaking. You look unique. But you don't make an evening. You are not a brilliant idea. You are tiresome. You are not a rewarding subject. You are a theatrical blunder. You are not true to life,' *Tate Etc.* 11 (2007), 106.
4. Nicolas Bourriaud, *Relational Aesthetics*, trans. Simon Pleasance, Fronza Woods, and Mathieu Copeland (Dijon: les presses du réel, 2002), 15. Since this

chapter engages in detail with Bourriaud's theory, further citations to this work are given in the text.

5. Jen Harvie, *Fair Play: Art, Performance and Neoliberalism* (Houndmills: Palgrave Macmillan, 2013), 1.

6. Claire Bishop, *Artificial Hells: Participatory Art and the Politics of Spectatorship* (London and New York: Verso, 2012), 3. Original emphasis.

7. For a detailed tracing of the terminology of 'social practice' see Shannon Jackson's *Social Works: Performing Art, Supporting Publics* (New York and London: Routledge, 2011).

8. Bishop, *Artificial Hells*, 2 and note 2 to the Introduction (page 287).

9. Bishop, 'Antagonism and Relational Aesthetics,' 77–79.

10. Bishop, *Artificial Hells*, 6–7.

11. Bishop, 'Antagonism and Relational Aesthetics,' 64 and 78.

12. Ibid., 62 and 65.

13. Ibid., 70 and 64.

14. Barabara Kirshenblatt-Gimblett quoted in Richard Schechner, *Performance Studies: An Introduction* (London and New York: Routledge, 2002), 3.

15. Bishop, *Artificial Hells*, 2–3.

16. Ibid., 9 and 7.

17. Ibid., 7.

18. Ibid., 2.

19. Anthony Downey, 'Towards a Politics of (Relational) Aesthetics,' *Third Text* 21:3 (2007), 268 and 275.

20. Ibid., 271.

21. Bishop, 'Antagonism and Relational Aesthetics,' 79.

22. Bishop, *Artificial Hells*, 6.

23. Harvie, *Fair Play*, 1.

24. Thomas Krens, 'Preface' to *theanyspacewhatever* [Exhibition Catalogue], ed. Nancy Spector (New York: Solomon R. Guggenheim Museum, 2008), 6.

25. Nancy Spector, '*theanyspacewhatever*: An Exhibition in Ten Parts,' in *theanyspacewhatever* [Exhibition Catalogue], ed. Nancy Spector, 13–14.

26. 'Double Agent,' ICA, accessed 4 August 2015, https://www.ica.org.uk/whats-on/double-agent.

27. Emily Candela, '*Double Agent* Teachers' Pack,' accessed 4 August 2015, https://www.ica.org.uk/sites/default/files/downloads/ICA%20Educator's%20Resource%20Pack%20Double%20Agent.pdf, 10.

28. Gilles Deleuze, *Cinema 1: The Movement-Image*, trans. Barbara Habberjam and Hugh Tomlinson (London: Continuum, 1986), 109 and 120. Original emphasis.

29. '*theanyspacewhatever*,' Solomon R. Guggenheim Museum, accessed 4 August 2015, http://www.guggenheim.org/new-york/exhibitions/past/exhibit/1896.

30. Linda Norden, 'Night at the Museum,' *Artforum* (2008), accessed 4 August 2015, http://artforum.com/diary/id=21388.

31. Spector, '*theanyspacewhatever*: An Exhibition in Ten Parts,' 16.

32. Ibid., 24.

33. Norden, 'Night at the Museum.'

34. Ibid.

35. Bishop, *Artificial Hells*, 2.

36. '*theanyspacewhatever*,' Solomon R. Guggenheim Museum.

37. Spector, '*theanyspacewhatever*: An Exhibition in Ten Parts,' 15.

38. '*theanyspacewhatever* Online Exhibition,' Solomon R. Guggenheim Museum, accessed 4 August 2015, http://web.guggenheim.org/exhibitions/anyspace/exhibition.html.

39. Branden W. Joseph, 'Ambivalent Objects,' in *theanyspacewhatever* [Exhibition Catalogue], ed. Nancy Spector, 35–36. Original emphasis.

40. Rosalind Krauss, *Passages in Modern Sculpture* (Cambridge, Mass., and London: MIT Press, 1981), 204.

41. Bishop, 'Antagonism and Relational Aesthetics,' 77.

42. Shannon Jackson, *Social Works: Performing Art, Supporting Publics* (New York and London: Routledge, 2011), 98.

43. Bishop, *Artificial Hells*, 8.

44. Rebecca Schneider, *Performing Remains: Art and War in Times of Theatrical Reenactment* (London and New York: Routledge, 2011), 140.

45. '*theanyspacewhatever*,' Solomon R. Guggenheim Museum.

46. Ibid.

47. Jackson, *Social Works*, 107.

48. '*theanyspacewhatever* Online Exhibition.'

49. Jackson, *Social Works*, 41.

50. '*theanyspacewhatever*,' Solomon R. Guggenheim Museum.

51. Harvie, *Fair Play*, 3.

52. Claire Bishop and Mark Sladen, 'Discussion with Donelle Woolford at the ICA,' in *Double Agent* [Exhibition Catalogue], ed. Claire Bishop and Silvia Tramontana, 86.

53. '*Double Agent*' [Gallery Guide], produced on the occasion of the *Double Agent* exhibition, Institute of Contemporary Arts (ICA), London, 14 February–6 April 2008.

54. Ibid.

55. Bishop and Sladen, 'Discussion with Donelle Woolford at the ICA,' 84.

56. Nicholas Ridout, 'Performance in the Service Economy: Outsourcing and Delegation,' in *Double Agent* [Exhibition Catalogue], ed. Claire Bishop and Silvia Tramontana, 129.

57. Bishop, *Artificial Hells*, 219.

58. Ibid. and note 2 to Chapter 8 'Delegated Performance: Outsourcing Authenticity' (page 349).

59. Joe Scanlan quoted in Bishop and Sladen, 'Discussion with Donelle Woolford at the ICA,' 87.

60. Bishop and Sladen, 'Discussion with Donelle Woolford at the ICA,' 87–88.

61. Ridout, 'Performance in the Service Economy,' 127.

62. Bishop and Sladen, 'Discussion with Donelle Woolford at the ICA,' 89.

63. Ibid.

64. Abigail Ramsay quoted in Bishop and Sladen, 'Discussion with Donelle Woolford at the ICA,' 85.

65. Bishop and Sladen, 'Discussion with Donelle Woolford at the ICA,' 86.

66. Ibid., 85.

67. Polly Staple quoted in Claire Bishop and Mark Sladen, 'Discussion with Donelle Woolford at the ICA,' 90.

68. '*Double Agent*' [Gallery Guide].

69. In an attempt to maintain something of the complexity of this piece and my experience of it, the references to *Last Lecture* (2007) in this and the following

paragraphs relate to my own recollections and notes made during my encounter with this work as it appeared within *Double Agent* at the ICA in London in 2008. A transcript – which seems, according to my notes, to record the subtitles for the work – is also available in the Exhibition Catalogue: Barbara Visser, 'Transcript of *Last Lecture*, 2007,' in *Double Agent* [Exhibition Catalogue], ed. Claire Bishop and Silvia Tramontana, 66–73.

70. Ibid., 69.
71. Ibid., 71–2.
72. 'About,' Barbara Visser, accessed 4 August 2015, http://www.barbaravisser.net/about/.
73. '*theanyspacewhatever* Online Exhibition.'
74. '*Double Agent*' [Gallery Guide].
75. Alan Read, *Theatre in the Expanded Field: Seven Approaches to Performance* (London: Bloomsbury, 2013), 61–62. Original emphasis.
76. 'Double Agent,' ICA, accessed 4 August 2015, https://www.ica.org.uk/whats-on/double-agent.
77. '*Double Agent*' [Gallery Guide], produced on the occasion of the *Double Agent* exhibition, Institute of Contemporary Arts (ICA), London, 14 February–6 April 2008.
78. Roy Brendan et al., 'Transcript of *Instant Narrative (IN)*, 2006–08,' in *Double Agent* [Exhibition Catalogue], ed. Claire Bishop and Silvia Tramontana, 43 and 47. The quotations referring directly to my personal encounter with this work as it appeared at the ICA in London in 2008 are taken from my own notes made during that event since this particular section of the text is not transcribed within the excerpt contained in the Exhibition Catalogue.
79. Ibid., 41, 43, and 46–47.
80. Ibid., 41.
81. Ibid., 47.
82. Louis Althusser, 'Ideology and Ideological State Apparatuses (Notes towards an Investigation),' in *Lenin and Philosophy and Other Essays*, trans. Ben Brewster (New York: Monthly Review Press, 1971), 175.
83. Schneider, *Performing Remains*, 140.
84. Brendan et al., 'Transcript of *Instant Narrative (IN)*, 2006–08,' 42–43 and 46.
85. Ibid., 46.
86. Klaus Biesenbach 'Sympathy for the Devil,' in *Douglas Gordon: Timeline*, ed. Douglas Gordon and Klaus Biesenbach (New York: The Museum of Modern Art, 2006), 25.
87. Spector, '*theanyspacewhatever*: An Exhibition in Ten Parts,' 9.
88. '*theanyspacewhatever*,' Solomon R. Guggenheim Museum.
89. Ibid.
90. Hans Ulrich Obrist and Daniel Birnbaum, 'Philippe Parreno: Dust,' in *theanyspacewhatever* [Exhibition Catalogue], ed. Nancy Spector, 100.
91. '*theanyspacewhatever*,' Solomon R. Guggenheim Museum.
92. Don DeLillo, *Point Omega* (London: Pan Macmillan, 2010), 11 and 6.
93. '*theanyspacewhatever*,' Solomon R. Guggenheim Museum.
94. Walter Benjamin, 'The Work of Art in the Age of Mechanical Reproduction' [1936], in *Illuminations*, ed. Hannah Arendt, trans. Harry Zohn (London: Jonathan Cape Ltd, 1970), 232, 234, and 239.
95. DeLillo, *Point Omega*, 13.

96. Douglas Gordon quoted in Christy Lange, 'Douglas Gordon: Ten Years Ago Today,' in *theanyspacewhatever* [Exhibition Catalogue], ed. Nancy Spector, 70–71.

97. Spector, '*theanyspacewhatever*: An Exhibition in Ten Parts,' 22. My emphasis.

98. Ibid.

99. John Kelsey, 'theanyspacewhatever,' *Artforum* (2009), accessed 4 August 2015, http://artforum.com/inprint/id=22123.

100. Nicolas Bourriaud, 'The Reversibility of the Real: Nicolas Bourriaud on Pierre Huyghe,' *Tate Etc.,* Vol. 7 (2006), accessed 4 August 2015, http://www.tate.org.uk/context-comment/articles/reversibility-real.

101. Norden, 'Night at the Museum.'

4 Gesture & Object

Digital Display and Arrested Attention

On display within *Frank Auerbach: London Building Sites 1952–62*, an exhibition held in the Courtauld Gallery, London, from 16 October 2009 to 17 January 2010, was a black painting. The picture is titled *Shell Building Site: Workmen under Hungerford Bridge* and was produced by London-based artist Frank Auerbach between 1958 and 1961. The date for this work is given as a range because although Auerbach first composed, and then exhibited the painting in 1959, in earth tones, he later repainted the entire surface of the image in the black hues in which we encounter it today. Taking a perspective of the Hungerford Bridge on the river Thames which most likely positions the artist among the theatres and galleries of London's South Bank and behind the Royal Festival Hall, the work depicts the nineteenth-century railway arches, as well as the foundations for The Shell Building, a complex developed on the former site of the Festival of Britain (1951) and described by Courtauld curator Barnaby Wright as 'one of the largest and most dramatic areas of post-war rebuilding in central London'.[1] Depicting a space significant to the history of exhibition making, Auerbach's image is engaged with processes of demolition and reconstruction represented throughout the Courtauld's exhibition in terms of the theatrical.

For architect and writer Andrew Todd, 'theatres are by definition building sites,' both material spaces of possibility wherein cultural formations might be made, disassembled, and built again.[2] By swathing his *Shell Building Site: Workmen under Hungerford Bridge* in paint that renders the image almost entirely black, Auerbach makes it possible to read not only the depicted building site but also the image as something like a theatre. In its shape and shade the painting echoes the form of the ubiquitous black box studio, conflating planes and surfaces in a single colour and transposing the eponymous black walls of this particular type of theatre venue onto the white, or in this case grey, walls of the Courtauld Gallery. Associable both with processes of urban construction and practices of theatre making often minimalist or experimental, Auerbach's canvas is not blank in its blackness but rather textured and complex. It offers, what Wright calls, a 'sepulchral vision in which forms gradually emerge through the darkness as one's eyes become accustomed to Auerbach's light.'[3] Looking into the image one 'form' which emerges for me has to do with theatre. Excavational in its execution, this painting associates the monumental and the transitory in a way that makes it particularly relevant to performance and its documentation. It is not immediately perceptible. Rather our looking at it is perhaps more akin to our experience of watching a production in the theatre. We are at first in the dark, before figures and structures become illuminated and then dissolve before our eyes.

Figure 4.1 Frank Auerbach, *Shell Building Site: Workmen under Hungerford Bridge*, 1958–61.PrivateCollection.ImagecourtesyofTheCourtauldGallery,London.© Frank Auerbach, courtesy Marlborough Fine Art.

Screening Art and Performance

Thinking in more detail about acts of looking at visual artworks and events of performance, in this chapter I want to further my examination of the relationship between the displayed and the performed by engaging with digital technologies and their different functions in the gallery and in connection with theatrical acts. In what follows I will restage two digital methodologies for tracing perceptual engagements with *Shell Building Site: Workmen under Hungerford Bridge* and the Auerbach exhibition more broadly. The first involves an eye-tracking device that records viewing patterns in relation to a particular image. The second is an original digital methodology for tracing the movements and observations of visitors as they progress through exhibitions. Interrogating the potential of digital tools for the documentation of artistic and event-based practices, these methodologies address specifically how performative engagements might be recognised as such by means of digital objects. Such frameworks speak to the broader concerns of this book through technological engagement with acts of performance, exhibition, and reception. Each methodology produces a representation to be viewed on a screen, that is to say, on a flat vertical surface set up for the display of images. Turning to one of these approaches now, the former of these digital undertakings means that the first time I see the paintings brought together for the *Frank Auerbach: London Building Sites 1952–62* exhibition is on computer monitor.

Pressing the space bar to begin, my experience starts in a theatrical digital darkness waiting for an image to appear. I am in the Interaction Centre at University College London (UCL) beginning an experiment using their Eye Tracking System. Constructed from fourteen photographs, digital representations of paintings produced by Auerbach, the experiment shows each image for fifty seconds, returning to a black screen before the revelation of every new picture.[4] Viewing these paintings on screen, the programme traces the passage of my gaze, recording where my eyes look using infrared technology. As in the digital performances explored later in this chapter, this system relies on two key pieces of apparatus: a camera and a source of light, in this case an infrared beam, beyond the visible spectrum, focused onto my eye. Tracking the light's reflection, the camera records where I look, for how long, and in what order, the data then exported and represented on the surface of the image which prompted that behaviour. Looking at *Shell Building Site: Workmen under Hungerford Bridge* my eyes concentrate first on a lighter region discernable through the arch to the top left of the image. This illuminated space absorbs a substantial part of my attention. Adjusting to the darkness, my gaze is consistently drawn beyond the frame of Auerbach's railway arches to exposed structural outlines in the distance of the image. Lured downwards by thick textures of paint, my observations trace the strokes of the artist's brush, following, extending, and mimicking their shapes and directions.

Documenting something not normally visible, the experiment makes clear two elements of the act of viewing particularly significant to this chapter. First, it becomes clear that looking at an image, on screen or in a gallery, implicates the work in an experience that is time-based. Thus we might conceive looking at an art object as a practice situated between modes of static display and moving performance, that is to say between the digital representation still on screen, or the equivalent painting in situ within the gallery, and the motion of eyes across its painted surfaces. Second, looking at these records of viewing patterns, it becomes apparent that, as in the theory of philosopher and historian of media Vilém Flusser, the 'significance of images is on the surface' and to be discovered through acts of 'scanning' wherein 'one's gaze follows a complex path formed, on the one hand, by the structure of the image and, on the other, by the observer's intentions.'[5] The reconstructions from the Eye Tracking System re-enact the work of my own visual engagements and the ways in which these are influenced by and diverge from the marks and rhythms of painterly representation. Having engaged with these renderings on personal computers, I want to associate them with two different screen-based performances that were on display simultaneously in and around Tate Modern during 2012. In relating my approaches to *Frank Auerbach: London Building Sites 1952–62* with two works presented in Tate Modern, Berlin-based artist Tacita Dean's concluding contribution to the Unilever Series, *FILM* (2011–12), curated by Curator of International Modern Art Nicholas Cullinan, assisted by Iria Candela, and the inauguration of Tate's Performance Room, a digitally disseminated domain for the presentation of live work, this chapter brings together two London-based venues also paired in Chapter 2 of this book in order to take a digitally inflected approach to their programmes.

There is a curious politics to the parallel commissioning by Tate Modern of a work by Tacita Dean, most often interpreted as a celebration of analogue technologies, alongside the introduction of a space for performance aimed entirely at an online audience and conveyed through digital modes of transmission. To date, it is the affordance of the digital that works produced and distributed through this mode are typically presented on two-dimensional screens. Within the gallery, Dean's work appeared on a related surface, a large white column which received the images from a film projector. A screen-based presentational mode, and a concern for architectural structure, inflects all of the case studies with which this chapter is concerned, both Performance Room and *FILM*, as well as the digital objects produced in relation to *Frank Auerbach: London Building Sites 1952–62*. A screen is, of course, also a display. This synonymy between a flat monitor unit and modes of exhibition makes the format of screen-based representation, or digital display, particularly pertinent to the concerns of this book. Having begun this project with Tim Etchells and Hugo Glendinning's *Empty Stages* photograph, this work, along with the painterly and filmic objects discussed since, necessarily marks out as a significant concern how performance might be displayed in the domain of the two-dimensional.

Within his seven coeval approaches to performance's relations with theatre, Alan Read reverses the common chronological ordering of the technological and the digital. While adhering to the logic that, 'once the two-dimensional readings of "media studies" had developed, the three dimensions of "live performance" would have been recognised,' Read imaginatively extends Philip Auslander's fundamental premise in his book *Liveness* (1999) to suggest that it was 'only at the inception of the first media-screen that performance could be separated out and examined for its difference.'[6] For Read, this primary screen is a distinctly permeable fourth millennium BCE glazed ceramic tile; here, on London's South Bank, it includes frameworks and installations for digital and analogue display, as well as far-reaching computer and internet-based technologies. Within and beyond the screen, the digital is a medium perhaps still looking for its form. With the advent of film, cinema, in the first instance, replicated or recorded the theatre before finding its own distinctive modes of operation. This course is mirrored in recent digital performance documentation and the familiar single-perspective videos produced of stage performances. In this chapter I want to make the most of the specific possibilities offered by digital technologies to expand my engagement with a certain exhibition of work and to consider the possibilities of screen-based renderings, both of the gallery space and of performance itself.

In *Theatre & the Digital* (2014), theatre historian and scholar in digital methodologies, Bill Blake argues that the scope of the questions being asked of theatre has expanded under the auspices of the digital, despite the latter being, in his terms, 'an ever multiplying and mostly impossible-to-pin-down referent'.[7] This chapter marks a move from the performative and relational referents of my previous examples, to a more overt association between performance and the digital premised on the multimodal and the evanescent. Like performance in the context of the gallery, ideas of 'the digital' have, in the contemporary moment, become somewhat generalised and ontological. Encapsulating this perspective, Blake suggests that the digital 'has become uniquely conducive to a discourse featuring sweeping definitions and escalating assumptions.'[8] Leaving open the possibility of multiple delineations of digital practice, my concern here is how performance might appear and in what forms via its digital referents. Co-founder of Blast Theory, Matt Adams writes in his foreword to *Theatre & the Digital* that the latter 'demands new forms of performance and new spaces to show it in', while at the same time projecting that currently '"the digital" is so embedded as to become invisible.' Setting the task for performance, Adams suggests that the 'four fundamental theatrical particles that Brook identifies – the performer, the audience member, at this particular place and in this particular time – are all challenged in a world that is networked.'[9] The ubiquity of digital encounter and production prompts a rethinking of, what Blake calls in that same text, 'core arts values,' including 'the very idea of theatre and the nature and status of the audience.' By bringing into question the quintessential ideals of performance, including those of liveness, ephemerality, and presence, the context of the digital might, as Blake suggests, 'reveal to us the limit case of the theatre' and make possible new ways of imagining its essential project and ontology.[10]

Digital networks, at the very least, provide another perspective on the alternate frames of reference through which performance might appear with which this book is concerned. Looking at points of interconnection between particular institutions and operations, in this case between the theatre and the gallery, might enable a further consideration of the ways in which performance is currently exceeding its conventional artistic limits through digital media and in exchange with exhibition contexts. Philosopher Samuel Weber foregrounds how 'complex and contradictory the relation between "theater" and "media" has become.'[11] Avant-garde practices across the visual and performing arts have historically and continually experimented with technological innovation and the contemporary penchant for performance in the gallery necessarily brings digital modalities to the fore. In her investigation of the interface between theatre and the digital arts, performance and new media scholar Gabriella Giannachi traces a theory of remediation through philosopher of communication Marshall McLuhan's belief that 'the "content" of any medium is always another medium'.[12] Earlier chapters of this book have explored exhibitions and artworks that take theatre as their subject. The cases explored here give that approach a digital inflection. If, as Giannachi suggests, 'all media remediate other media at the level of both content and form', my concern in this chapter is with digital projects which focus their attention on performance and its associated ephemeral modes and the ways in which something of the latter might be presented in another, this time digital, configuration.[13]

Building Site and Performance Room

In this book, I am concerned with sites wherein, borrowing Alan Read's terms, 'the stage is just one social platform among many'.[14] *Frank Auerbach: London Building Sites 1952–62* was presented in the same section of the Courtauld Gallery previously occupied by *Renoir at the Theatre: Looking at La Loge* (2008) wherein, in Chapter 2, we saw painters from the nineteenth century turning their attention away from stage productions and towards other situations of social and cultural expression. The later exhibition, with which this chapter is concerned, re-collected all of the paintings of post-war building sites produced by Frank Auerbach and presented these alongside sketches in pencil and oil made to assist in the impulsiveness of their rendering. Looking at these drafts together with the large-scale paintings whose production they assisted, it is clear that, in accordance with a description given by art historian William Feaver, these sketches 'maintain the pace, feeding spontaneity into the day-to-day business in the studio'.[15] Concerned with preserving an impression of urgency and vigour, Auerbach's paintings necessarily relate to performance in terms of its established definition as that which is temporal and dynamic. Engaged overtly in theatrical practices as sometime performer in his youth, Auerbach 'ventured in to acting and design' and, later, aside from turning to the post-war building sites as a subject for art making, tracked pictorially the transformation of the Camden Palace Theatre from theatre to cinema to studio, 'witness to the pageantry of the theatre's changes of use'.[16] In Feaver's terms, this repurposing and transformation of practice is itself theatrical and concerned with spectacle, tableaux, and remarkable public display.

Scenes of activity and invention, in Auerbach's work it is possible to connect the theatre and the building site as places of performative practice and production. According to Feaver, for Auerbach the conditions of post-war London, in its 'decrepitude and pioneering renewal, were abundantly theatrical'.[17] Perceiving the decay and regeneration inherent to these construction sites in terms of an excess of theatricality, these spaces in this rendering exist somewhere between the performed and the displayed. The Shell Building site was, in particular, Auerbach describes in interview with curator Barnaby Wright, 'so superb in itself that you could have taken it and put it in a museum'.[18] Something about the shape and resonance of these sites invites their museological appropriation and this determining quality exists in their unification of collapse and restitution, their simultaneous making and fading away, in short in their theatricality and dramatic constructedness. Sketched on location and then completed in the studio and displayed in the gallery, Auerbach's paintings, thinking in terms of Robert Smithson's established dialectic and extending its terms to particular spaces allocated for building and invested in the same vocabulary, shift between the sited 'earth or the ground that we are really not aware of when we are in an interior room or studio' and the non-sited artist's workroom or exhibition venue in a 'back and forth rhythm that goes between indoors and outdoors'.[19] Oscillating between site-specific engagements and contexts of exhibition and display, Auerbach's practice intersects everyday construction sites and the gallery, 'the non-site, which is an abstract container.'[20]

Looking beyond the confines of the art museum, a similar relation between the inside and outside of institutional contexts is evident in Tate's Performance Room. The inaugural strand of an annual programme focusing on performance and digital curation, *BMW Tate Live 2012: Performance Room* is a series of works 'commissioned and conceived exclusively for the online space.'[21] Despite this claim towards an entirely digital domain, the performances presented in this setting take place, at least in one sense, within a designated gallery at Tate Modern, even as they are streamed 'live' on Tate's website and YouTube Channel. The pieces are staged within a specified non-site or gallery location but are watchable, at least for most of us, only outside of this space, in the sites wherein we house our own screens and digital devices. The frame for this work becomes then the context of Tate's website or the familiar surround of YouTube and, beyond that, the screen and the monitor, what researcher and interdisciplinary artist Steve Dixon calls 'the computer's flickering QuickTime proscenium'.[22] Watching the performances online, viewers must construct our own conditions of experience, generating a different sort of theatre outside of the Performance Room, or at least a different iteration of the latter, which is physically inaccessible to us. Given this interrelation of the non-sited performance and the sited digital encounter, in this chapter I want to ask what it might mean to designate a place in a gallery for live performance and then conceive of access to that space as via, what Tate calls, an 'online-only live performance'.[23] Since 2012, Performance Room has been programmed annually by Tate's Senior Curator of International Art (Performance), Catherine Wood, and Assistant

Curator at the time Capucine Perrot, and in 2014 all of the commissions to date were shown on loop in a Screening Room at Tate Modern. Despite these later developments, I want to focus here on the first series of performances since these projects initiate this curatorial framework and are coeval with all of the case studies presented in the chapters of this book across a six-year period of practice.

In his description of Performance Room, former Director of Tate Modern Chris Dercon asserts that contemporary audiences want to 'participate' and 'establish direct contact', suggesting that a simultaneity of time if not space might be enough to enable some of the qualities associated with the experience of live performance to be more expansively broadcast.[24] Since 2012, Tate record that more than 140,000 people across 90 countries have viewed Performance Room.[25] To curate a digital exhibition which expands across time and space necessarily involves a different set of relations between the works associated therein to that performed by objects on display within the context of a located gallery space, or indeed during a festival of live work. In this context, those who watch the work are not visitors to an exhibition, nor do they occupy a position within the body of an audience; in relation to the work presented on screen they are independent spectators. Within this different kind of curatorial association, Jérôme Bel, Pablo Bronstein, Emily Roysdon, and Harrell Fletcher all responded to the specific demands of this commission during its first season. The framework of Performance Room provides artists with a particular set-up – a gallery space and a single camera – through which they must devise a performance to be communicated by the latter. The presence of the camera within this arrangement reminds us of Philip Auslander's conception of the 'live' as *"that which can be recorded"* such that the existence of this documenting technology becomes definitive of the being of the performances produced.[26]

Like many of the examples collected in this book, Performance Room begins through an allusion to the empty space for performance but with the addition of digital equipment with which to record what passes in that venue. Within the context of the screened recordings, we encounter a logo that accompanies, or rather initiates, frames, all of the performances, as well as the interviews from Tate staff which support the series. The logo takes the form of a white cube, unless appearing on white webpage, in which case it appears as a black box, labelled 'Performance Room' and giving the link to the relevant pages of Tate's website. Inside the cube in white (or black) letters is the title of the series, 'BMW TATE LIVE,' and the date of the given performance so that the architecture of the gallery is still presented, in this visual symbol at least, as the major framing device of the performance which takes place somewhere at a specific moment. Occurring at a particular time, both in the gallery and online, Performance Room, following Giannachi, 'consists of a performative component, which is unique in time, and a remediated component, which is more or less permanent' since each piece might be watched again online at a later date.[27] Combining both the enduring and the ephemeral, Performance Room enacts an ontology conceptualised throughout this book as both displayed and performed.

At the beginning of each live streaming, viewers are warned via black letters on a white screen that we are 'are about to watch an art performance live from Tate Modern.'[28] This is perhaps the most appropriate term for this work, something that combines the modalities of visual art and live performance. These 'art performances' are, according to Tate's publicity materials, part of a series 'commissioned and conceived using online space as its primary medium.'[29] In this description, the medium is not performance but rather a computer network. According to Matt Adams, 'every digital platform has its own affordances and time cycles' and when 'platforms such as these enter the dramaturgical space they bring their own forms of "now" with them.'[30] Introducing alternative potentials and immediacies into the history of performance making, digital networks expand the temporalities and venues for performed endeavours. Within Tate Modern, the platforms are multiple; there is a room, which we cannot enter, wherein a performance happens that we watch through digital technologies on screens outside the institution and, in another space within the gallery, an installed screen which stages and draws attention to a different medium or mode of production, this time analogue. This co-occupation of Tate by analogue and digital forms speaks against discourses that narrate too easily a displacement of the former by the latter. Rather, the relation here is one of cohabitation.

Reflections on Different Media

Just as Performance Room commissions artists to conceive a work of art for the online domain, so the Unilever Series (2002–12) invites artists to create an installation for Tate Modern's iconic Turbine Hall. Tacita Dean's contribution to the series, *FILM*, ran from 11 October 2011 to 11 March 2012 and responded not only to this specific architectural framework but also constructed, as its title suggests, a 'portrait of the analogue, photochemical, non-digital medium of film.'[31] Conflating both form and subject, Dean's work attempts to take a likeness of a medium, this time not performance, but film. In an interview available on Tate's website, the artist expresses how the project began with a 'formal idea' which was to make a portrait format film but one which excluded human figures, the conventional occupants of this orientation and layout. For Dean, 'film and digital are just different media, they're very intrinsically different, they're made differently, they're seen differently'.[32] Within the gallery, Dean's eleven-minute-long silent 35mm looped film is projected onto a long screen stretching upwards from the floor of the Turbine Hall in the proportion of an enlarged strip of film. In keeping with this self-referential construction, white sprocket holes frame each side of the screen so that the means of presentation mimics the form and focus of the work. In a lecture on *FILM* given at Tate Modern in 2012, art historian Rosalind Krauss describes this effect in terms of the theatrical trope of a play within a play, or, more broadly, a mise-en-abyme, that works to emphasise a sort of self-reflexivity which might update ideals of medium specificity challenged by post-modern and conceptual art.[33] All of the works in this chapter are concerned with the possibilities of a specific mode of production, either analogue or digital, and all, I suggest, enable further reflection on the potentialities and problematics of performance in relation to these domains of (digital) display.

Watching *FILM*, layers of vertical lines intersect those on screen with the industrial architecture of Tate Modern such that I initially assume there to be a translucency to the scrim which enables rectangular windows to coalesce with the projection. In fact, the building, as well as housing the installation, also forms part of its content. Interspersing the context of the Turbine Hall with natural topographies and phenomena, skyscapes and sea-scapes, as well as planes of vivid colour, *FILM* includes frames that morph and transform the fabric of the gallery. In one moment, a grey sphere seems to rest on a windowsill, constructing an impression of three-dimensionality. In another, the east wall of Tate Modern appears to fold downwards on screen from a creased corner. One layer of the space peels away to reveal the same scene behind. Another sphere bounces out and transports a cut-out of the windows down towards the floor, without causing any empty space or gap in the representation. Some of the images in *FILM* speak to previous projects by Dean, to classic science fiction films, surrealist artworks and René Daumal's unfinished novel about the invisible *Mount Analogue* (1952). Re-enacting earlier works, as well as the space of the Turbine Hall, *FILM* seems to me to be related in subtle ways to the re-performance of past live works in large-scale international galleries in the period covered by this book and the years preceding it. Like performance, time-based media, including film, also presents challenges to curators in terms of collection and curation. It too deteriorates and the technologies for its presentation disappear. Flanked with sprocket holes *FILM*, borrowing Krauss' terms, is 'fascinated by its capacity to re-enact itself.'[34] Re-enacting its own modali-ties, Dean's installation is inherently concerned with performing again the resolutions, textures, contrasts, and motions of film. Through this installa-tion, visitors find themselves in a literal sort of art house, standing in the dark for the performance of a new version of an old event of cinema.

Occupying a digital domain, the first work presented within Performance Room is also a re-enactment of sorts. On Thursday 22 March 2012, French choreographer and dancer Jérôme Bel presented a version of his 1997 performance *Shirtology* wherein the performer, in this instance Frédéric Seguette, peels off multiple T-shirts layered so as to invite viewers to make associations across their slogans and digits. In his digital and technological approach to performance, Alan Read reminds us of the digital's primary association with the hands, the fingers, the digits – its '*digital* resonance' – and the fact that, 'the "digital age", for all its contemporary sounding urgency, had in fact long ago been initiated by the invention of the alphabet (digital refers to information representing a set of fixed symbols such as letters or digits)'.[35] In its playful sequencing of ciphers, *Shirtology* is invested in certain forms of the digital even before its transfer to Performance Room. At the beginning of this piece, a white door opens and Seguette enters wearing jeans and a white long-sleeved T-shirt. Maintaining contact with the handle, his digits keeping a material connection to the gallery, he rotates to close the door behind him. During this action we glimpse that Seguette's shirt has a coloured pattern on the front. He moves to the centre of the screen and the camera zooms closer to his torso. His head is bowed. We can no longer see his legs and his hands hang by his sides just out of shot. We see now that his shirt shows a sailing boat moving away from his chest into white-crested waves. Letters on the shirt read 'FORCE 6'. His fingers enter the shot and he peels the shirt upwards, his arms crossing in the action. The white shirt comes away in front of Seguette's body and conceals for a second the white number '5' which appears, crumpled and compressed at first, on an orange-red vest worn underneath. The performer straightens the vest, stretching it downwards so that its text elongates and clarifies. The number, character we might say, or digit, is streaked in printed text. After fifteen seconds or so of heavy breathing, Seguette begins the process again, taking off the orange vest to reveal the printed area of a purple pullover beneath which is embossed in orange letters with the phrase 'FINAL 4', the letters inscribed vertically next to the enlarged letter. The pattern now becomes evident. The numbers are descending in a countdown, towards another phase of the performance perhaps, and the colour of the layer removed remains as an echo or remnant in the colour of the printed lettering on the garment it reveals.

Bel's practice has been eloquently articulated across the fields of visual art and performance by thinkers including Claire Bishop, Tim Etchells, Adrain Heathfield, Bojana Kunst, André Lepecki, and others. In a recent article on his work, theatre scholar and writer Una Bauer quotes Bel's assertion that our understanding of the body is 'based on codes and language.'[36] Invested in the politics of decoding, of deciphering systems of symbols for expressing and transmitting information, this emphasis necessarily designates an active role for the spectator who is required to read the performance in light of these stripped back texts. Reconfigured as a digital performance, *Shirtology* occupies a different relation to its audience through Performance Room as compared with previous iterations of the work in more traditional physical venues. In an interview with Roselee Goldberg, Bel insisted that his practice must be experienced in a theatre, expressing fervently that 'a museum is not my place.'[37] Occupying the online domain, Performance Room is singularly neither a gallery nor a theatre. For much of the performance, Seguette's concentration is downwards to his chest, his head directing each spectator's gaze so that all attention is on the objects exhibited on his body. In this gallery setting, the performers form is not made equivalent with the exhibited art object but rather correspondent with the display cases; Seguette becomes the mode of presenting the object, the museum vitrine performed. Given the online context of Performance Room, the shirts in turn come to act as makeshift screens for communication and display on which texts are produced and images are formed. In an echo of the peeling away of the gallery walls enacted in Dean's *FILM,* later in the performance Seguette strips to a white shirt, inscribed in multi-coloured letters. The digits are blurred by the pixels on my screen or too small to read on the view embedded in Tate's website. As if anticipating its illegibility, the performer begins to read the text, rotating his shirt to his face by stretching it around a palm which levers the fabric from his chest. The final words in this articulation – 'DANCE' and 'MUSIC' – take us to performance.

In what follows, the phrases on the shirts become directives for action, musical scores, and imperatives that Seguette performs. A white garment shows a figure outlined in green, arms raised, one leg bent and toes pointed. The camera pans out as the performer begins to replicate this pose. He is unstable, he wobbles and struggles in the shape before falling forwards and out of it. He returns to his spot centre stage and resumes. The camera zooms in. The next shirt is orange and shows two silhouetted figures dancing with yellow ribbons, the one on the right of the shirt stands on pointed toe with one leg outstretched and arms raised. The other is mid-leap. They look towards each other. I wonder at this point if the performer knows which shirt he will encounter next and whether his reactions to it are pre-scripted. I wonder if he is worried, as I am, that he might attempt to replicate these motions. He thinks better of it and takes off the shirt. A later garment reads 'DANCE OR DIE'. Seguette chooses the former, humming and swinging his hips from side to side. Between the decrees on his shirt is an image, half black and half white. Two square-headed figures beat a drum that occupies a zigzagged line between the two spaces of the illustration, a white figure occupying the black box and a black figure the white cube. Seguette's dance resides too in this crooked border. The influences of his choreographer chart a history of contemporary art and dance practice, with Bel proclaiming to draw many of his strategies from the visual arts.[38] Despite this formal influence, once again Bel's subject is performance itself. In an interview with Bel, Bauer asserts that his 'work seems to be very general, dealing with the basic principles (of dance, theatre, of human existence)'. Interested in 'mapping the territory of the performing arts' and its boundaries, Bel claims to use the 'frame of the theatre (architecturally, historically, culturally and socially speaking) to analyse dance,' as well as broader questions of audience engagement and theatrical representation.[39] In a modus operandi that recurs throughout this book, Bel is using one form to explore another, dance through theatre, performance through (digital) display, and audiences through online networks.

Mirroring Performance

Other works presented in Performance Room share this concern for investigating one form via the modes of production and paradigmatic expectations of another. For the second event in the series, live streamed on

26 April 2012, Argentinean-born artist Pablo Bronstein created a new work titled *Constantinople Kaleidoscope*. For this performance, a screen of mirrors is installed at the far end of the gallery and a number of reflective pillars occupy the space. A camera on a tripod, along with other record-ing equipment, seems to be in front of us but is, of course, behind us, or rather the camera we can see on screen is also the camera which records the perspective available to us online. What we are watching is a mirror image. There are a number of performers in the room; one sits on the floor, dressed in white, another stands, some are visible within the physical space of the gallery, others only as reflections. Near to the camera Bronstein is cos-tumed in an outfit described by the artist later, in an interview following the performance, as being sculptural and 'vaguely Ottomanish, Turkish fantasy dress.'[40] A final figure, listed in the credits as choreographer Matthias Sper-ling, seems to operate the camera and give directions to the performers. This character determines the rhythm of Bronstein's shifting postures throughout the performance and directs the movement of the dancers and their manipu-lation of the mirrored flats, using shorthand phrases to do with gatekeeping, fortresses, spiral staircases, and caravans.

At the start of the piece, we see the performers put on white gloves so as to handle the mirrored objects without leaving a trace. The two mobile pil-lars are then driven closer to the camera and the effect of these approaching surfaces is disorienting. Music starts to play and the columns are rotated to reveal the reflection of Bronstein who stands still behind the plane of the camera. At times we can see the performers moving the pillars, at others, when the mirrored surfaces consume the viewpoint of the camera, space shifts and we watch Sperling, and another seated figure, also watching the performance. The movement of the mirrored flats alters the available angles and perspectives, zooming and directing our focus, while the position of the camera remains still and unchanging. For the next held position, the perform-ers create a reflective cube from their individual plinths and rotate slowly. There is, throughout this work, a multiplication of white walls. Drawing on architectural approaches, Bronstein's work is, according to Tate's promo-tion of *Constantinople Kaleidoscope*, characterised by a preoccupation with structural form and, in this case, constructs 'a baroque trompe l'oeil stage set that exaggerates the perspective of the room'.[41] In this performance, the appearance of objects and actors in the gallery, and their relative position and apparent distance from the viewer, is amplified and distorted by a com-bination of digital and mirrored apparatus that bring into question their materiality through deceptive techniques and the creation of visual illusions.

Making any difference between three-dimensional performers and two-dimensional reflections indistinguishable, Bronstein's contribution to Performance Room draws on an historic architectural style dominant across fields of art and design during the seventeenth century. Incorporating a dynamic sense of motion and a commitment to the exuberant depiction of events, the baroque represents a compelling intersection of concerns as inspirant for performance. In his book *Digital Baroque: New Media Art and Cinematic Folds* (2008), Timothy Murray identifies the 'baroque' as a useful metaphor for describing digital practice, investigating the paradigmatic models which inform contemporary screen-based practices in relation to earlier conceptual forms. Following his theory, 'one of the enigmas posed by the baroque texture of the new media and its archival traces is the multidirectionality of temporal flow.' Contradicting any inherent linear trajectory for performance, the digital baroque rather moves forwards and backwards in time. 'Inscribed in the simultaneity of juxtaposition that is rendered so forcefully by the digital platform,' text, films, and computers become, in Murray's rendering, 'charged phantasmatic carries of cultural and historical interconnectivity.'[42] Spectral and amalgamating, Murray's digital forms speak to the terms of this project. It is noteworthy that most of the pieces presented within Performance Room share a preference for dance which betrays curator Catherine Wood's established interest in relations between visual art and choreography. Bronstein's attentiveness to dance is multi-modal and he states during a post-show discussion, wherein Wood and Kathy Noble pose questions submitted by the online audience, that he is 'interested in dance through painting' and particularly in 'images of dancers.'[43] Attracted to representations of performance produced in another form, Bronstein's inspirations resonate with and perpetuate the circulation of tropes moving between the performing and visual arts with which this book is concerned.

For Bronstein, something particularly insightful for his work is the studied ease and pertained effortlessness of sprezzatura styles of performance, which he claims to have learnt not from any formal dance training but rather from 'looking at the Sistine Chapel ceiling or the Mona Lisa.' Once again, the frame of reference is a mode of performance, and one contested by the rise of interest in theatrical labour in recent discourses in the performance field, that is learnt by means of visual and architectural compositions. In response to a question concerning the relationship between the architectural space of the gallery and the networked domain through which *Constantinople Kaleidoscope* is disseminated, Bronstein expresses the difficulty of creating impressive optical effects in live performance as compared with the relative ease of 'sticking a mirror up against a camera lens.'[44] In all of the contributions to Performance Room, there is a sense that it is the presence of the camera, perhaps more so than the possibilities of live streaming, that transforms the work. Bronstein is quick to remind us of the surrealist legacies inherent to his techniques, as well as the influence of artist, writer, and curator Dan Graham, who also used mirrors to confront the viewer's gaze and interrogate the relation between art and audience, as well as the effects of spatial structures and arrangements. Distanced by the recorded nature of the performance and watching it online, spectators of Bronstein's *Constantinople Kaleidoscope* cannot identify our own image reflected in its planes. Rather, we must find other ways of locating and reflecting on our spatial relations to the performance. This seems to be of significance to Bronstein who is interested in interactions in space and the construction of tracks, lines of movement and spectatorial perception, which connect and associate figures and objects.

Referring to the searchability of networked spaces, Bronstein shares his belief that 'whenever you look at something online, you basically look at what you want to find.'[45] Visitors to Tate's website might stumble on Performance Room but continue browsing if the work does not take our fancy. Within acts of curatorial selection and architectural directives, visitors also retain a certain amount of volition regarding how long we spend looking at works on display and the order in which we approach these objects. The relational practices examined in the last chapter of this book perhaps inevitably look towards performance in the sense of social interaction and participation. So as to further my thinking about screen-based engagements with visual art and performance and the ways in which the digital informs contemporary relations between the displayed and the performed, I want now to introduce, alongside the installations at Tate Modern discussed in this chapter, a second methodology for surveying the transitory and associative encounters evident in the visitation and interpretation of exhibitions. Exploring the capacity of digital techniques for mapping and communicating individual engagements with artworks in their curation together, this process affords to visitors a productive and dynamic position within the space of exhibition. By acknowledging the distinctive experience of each gallery-goer, it is possible to recognise the ways in which exhibitions are, at least to some degree, structured by the attentions of visitors and the connections, physical and speculative, we make between objects. Re-animating the relation between performance and audience or artwork and visitor, digital tools enable the development of a more active conception of these relations which might shed light on points of connection between practices of display and performance.

Registering and Recoding Performance

In her detailed study of *Theatre Audiences*, Susan Bennett articulates the need for more developed theories of reception, observing that empirical studies, at least up to the point of her writing in 1990, have been limited and restricted in focus, only really considering audience demographics rather than attempting to engage with behaviours of reception and the cultural implications of these actions. In addition to 'studies of individual audience in their social, material, and historical specificities', it is, Bennett suggests, through the discipline of performance studies and the employment of new technologies that questions of how we engage with performative events in the contemporary moment might be more specifically addressed.[46] Tellingly, Bennett maintains an emphasis on interdisciplinary approaches to encounter in her writing on *Theatre & Museums*. Here, her argument suggests that is precisely an increased emphasis on visitor experience that aligns contemporary curatorial and performance practices.[47] By constructing a digital process for tracing, mapping, and visualising the personalised routes taken by visitors around *Frank Auerbach: London Building Sites 1952–62*, the methodology under consideration here designates exhibition environments as areas of performative production, viewing gallery-goers as implicated and necessary players within these spaces.

Courtauld curator Barnaby Wright confides that the conception behind this exhibition centres on the 'parallels between the process of rebuilding London (earth dug up and transformed into buildings, as it were) and Auerbach's process of "building" paintings (paint turned into composed images).'[48] This is an exhibition concerned with reflecting on and documenting constructive processes, both in terms of post-war regeneration and of art making, and it is this conceptual resonance which drew me to the event as a context in which to develop a digital approach for investigating visitors' engagements with art. Auerbach too was interested in the relation between ephemerality and documentation, seeking, as he describes in interview with William Feaver, to 'record the life that seemed to me to be passionate and exciting and that was disappearing all the time.'[49] Exploring, in a similar way to the work with the Eye Tracking System, the forms visitors' experiences and attentions might take, the devised methodology enables an examination of how spatial layouts, in conjunction with specific curatorial actions, act as stimuli, limitations, or directives on the behaviour of each visitor. So as to avoid disturbing visits, methods involving tagging or the installation of digital hardware were avoided. Rather, this project used manual observation techniques in order to generate data relating how gallery visitors interact with a particular display context and the time spent interfacing with certain objects and locations.[50] Shifting intermittently between acts of display and performance, the process trialled within *Frank Auerbach: London Building Sites 1952–62* is cyclical, moving from images of construction on building sites, to the subsequent recording of visitors' interface with those evidential paintings, to the presentation of this new documentation as onscreen digital objects.[51]

Like others encountered in this book, the approach begins with a gesture towards an empty space. The digital methodology originates from a simplified rendition of the exhibition, drawing on gallery floor plans, architectural descriptions of an unoccupied representational space. Observing movements around the gallery and dragging a digital pen correspondingly across this map, displayed on the screen of a mobile computer, I trace individual routes, charting experiences in space and time. As the pen is drawn across the screen the system defaults to tracking motion, but it is also possible to note the painting to which a visitor's attention is drawn, as well as specific actions, such as sketching, talking with another gallery-goer, or taking a photograph. Revealing what visitors look at, in what order, and for how long, the digital objects constructed from the observed data make possible the representation not only of visitors' pathways and engagements with exhibits but also give details of duration and activity. The term 'digital object' has a quite precise and specialist meaning within the vocabularies of library and information science and it is, therefore, prudent to mention that I am using these words advisedly to speak to the object-related paradigms of performance examined throughout this project. These digital objects represent, borrowing from Patrick Ffrench's translation of philosopher Marie-José Mondzain's writing on the birth of the spectator, 'the sense of a gesture, not the meaning of an object.'[52] What is at stake here is not the effect of interpretation but its embodied enactment.

These objects cannot reveal the personal intentions and proclivities which prompt each visitor's pathway, but they do encode some of the ways in which a particular exhibition is approached and apprehended. In the gallery, we are attracted to some works more than others, looking at certain exhibits closely and at others in passing or at a glance. We might step back to view art objects from a different perspective or otherwise alter the distance between our bodies and the exhibits on display. Marking and synchronising as one act the physical lines of action and reaction, the digital objects generated from the observations within the exhibition visualise each route as a line which rises as the visitor progresses through the gallery and through time.[53] Here, in contrast to the 'inherent immobility of the still image', interrogated by Matthew Reason amongst others, and challenged throughout this book, these digital images display duration and motion within a static rendering.[54] Borrowing from American composer, music theorist, and writer John Cage, here the representation of 'duration is in space, read as corresponding to time' and, in this way, each visitor's observed actions are 'productive of an object in time'.[55] Looking at these images of people looking at images, I am struck by certain similarities with screen-based works being presented by Tate, or at least by the affordances my consideration of the former offers for thinking about the latter and vice versa. Both the visualisations and the works curated in Performance Room have to be watched on screens outside of the gallery so that the performances happening therein might be perceived and appreciated as such.

Like Auerbach's paintings of processes of construction usually unobserved, these digital objects reveal what Rebecca Schneider might call 'the reverberations of the overlooked, the missed, the repressed, the seemingly forgotten.'[56] To make these images is, then, to make visible acts of spectatorship and to picture something not usually watched within the gallery. Investigating in a literal way the forms participation might take, my reflections on this methodology concern, what Schneider calls, 'our performative relations to documents and .... the document as perfomative act, and as site of performance.'[57] Capable of displaying multiple pathways within the same digital object, the visualisations enable the comparison of gallery visits and convey patterns and deviations of participation. By looking at these traces together, it is possible to identify the idiosyncrasy of each visitor's movement between exhibits and the individual performances at work within exhibition environments. In this way, borrowing the terms of art historian and critic Hal Foster, a performative act of engagement is 'only registered through another that recodes it'. In processes of tracing and visualising, visitors' experiences and investments become apparent only through, what Foster calls, 'deferred action'.[58] Personal encounters within gallery environments appear only as performative in retrospection, through acts of digital display. Knowing what visitors look at, in what order, and for how long is to acknowledge creative agency and admit deviance as well as collusion with curatorial directives. Within the gallery, curatorial actions of selection, sequencing, and contextualization condition our participations. Within these digital objects, visitors' individual attentions and interests are made visible and these may not correspond to the modes of viewing anticipated by curators and other gallery staff.

Each visualisation provides information previously unavailable and offers alternative perspectives as to how visitors use gallery spaces, our attentions to more or less prominent works, and what we, the formerly overlooked, in turn disregard. With multiple pathways presented within the same digital object, this onscreen interconnectivity conflicts with the individuality of the behaviours documented, suggesting these as coincidental rather than independently recorded. At the moment of another's trace, each visitor is elsewhere, exploring another part of the exhibition programme, in the café or gift shop, or yet to arrive at the gallery. In this way, these digital objects, borrowing Alan Read's terms, invert 'the common velocity from individual to group, from self to collective, it is here the situation of "being in common" that gives rise to the experience of being-self.'[59] The visualisations materialise the individuality of visitors' engagements within this displayed event by their very situation within a shared frame on screen. In this way, the digital objects allow us to enact, or at least acknowledge, what Jen Harvie suggests as, a certain caution with regard to the ways in which contemporary social apparatuses, including large-scale art installations, 'compel us to assimilate in a group identity.'[60] These digital objects highlight and emphasise distinctive participants within a specific gallery context.

Different Tones of Performance

Returning briefly to Tate Modern for another event in Performance Room, American Artist Emily Roysdon's contribution, the third in the series, also explores the relation between individual and collective encounters in the gallery. For the piece, titled *I am a helicopter, camera, queen* and streamed live on 31 May 2012, Roysdon recruited over one hundred volunteer performers who identify as feminist or queer to enact choreographed movements. Communicating these actions via 'directions mapped onto the floor of the room', this performance, like the visualisations of visitors' participations produced within the Coutauld, explores, at least according to Tate's narration, 'how a particular space can be reconfigured through the group action of the people within it'.[61] The performance begins with the camera positioned in one corner of the gallery. The volunteers, dressed in black and white, look directly into the lens for a moment and then turn and walk to the opposite corner of the room. A couple of figures break out from the crowd into discrete actions. The first spirals to the camera holding a newspaper marked with the title of the piece, while another lies on the floor before rejoining the group who turn again and move to face one side of the gallery. It is these moments of individuation that stand out amongst the orchestrated motions. As the assembly rotates and travels to the opposite wall, my eyes are drawn to a figure on crutches and the faces of those performers who sneak a sideways glance at the camera or seem somehow more aware of its presence. It is the digital nature of the work which prompts Roysdon to recruit these volunteers to occupy the gallery. In the absence of a located audience within the physical space of the room, the artist was keen, she says, to include a number of people who might 'work on each other, work off of each other and not have a single spectacle for camera' and online audience.[62]

Acts of speech within the work articulate an awareness of this digital context. There are individual utterances concerning a 'camera,' a 'territory,' a 'resource cloud,' and a 'technological confession.' There are also shared choral exclamations of 'clock' or 'block' or 'lock' in amongst actions of turning and choreographed motions which work like a harmonic round to mobilise different factions of the pack in related waves of movement. These interjections associate time with choreographic blocking and ideas of overcrowding and obstruction. According to the ambitions of the artist, such elements of the performance have to do with occupying a space, which first needs to be constructed. 'I wanted to build a scene within the room,' says Roysdon during the post-show interview with Wood and Noble, stating that, having begun with the idea of filling the gallery, an initiatory gesture contrary to that of the empty space, or perhaps prompted by its promise, she wanted to 'create a stage' and fill it with choreography premised on the idea of something 'taking shape in the room'. For the artist, the collective movements are about 'building space,' so that here, as in Auerbach's paintings and the digital objects produced within the exhibition of that work, there exists an interest in the creation of space, as well as an association between construction and action. Quietly echoing the 2011 international Occupy Movements, Roysdon is not unaware of the political context her work invokes. For her, an institutional invitation to think about how to inhabit a space necessarily inspires ideas of 'occupation' and the realities of the contemporary political climate that terminology connotes.[63]

Amongst verbal and rotating actions, an awareness of the persistence of digital filming is maintained. In the latter half of the performance, the volunteers cut down strings suspended from the ceiling and move close to the camera to divide this thread into strips which they suspend across its lens whereon the lengths register as blurred lines. This action of veiling the camera draws the attention of the spectator to the veneer and physical barrier of its lens, now a curtained screen. Involving a cloaking of this optic, this component of the performance is described by Roysdon as a moment wherein the volunteers 'dressed up the camera,' giving it a different external appearance and perspective. To dress up is to disguise, to camouflage the equipment there to record the performance as something other than it is, to make it a character in the space so that the covering conceals or at least alters its primary function, shifting its potential as a tool for display into an object of performance. Describing her conception of the work, Roysdon highlights her mindfulness of the camera, stating that she thought about 'the flatness of the screen, and of the venue,' thereby conflating the architectural space and the computer monitor in terms of a planeness of representation. The framework of digital dissemination via a screen-based mode of display required the artist to think 'more conceptually, more formally,' so as to engage with questions of ontology and devise, what she calls, 'other ways of being live.'[64]

For *I am a helicopter, camera, queen,* the floor of Performance Room is marked up with circular patterns, orange and purple dots, scribbles and dashes, and a black sphere that looks like a camera shutter, a further analogue reminder of the digital presence which forms, or at least transmits, the performance. These colorations represent a score on which the performance is based, the image of the lens indicating the place the camera should take when it moves from the corner of the room to occupy a space more centrally on stage. The directions on the floor, a kind of pre-emptive mapping of the performance, are, Roysdon expresses, 'about pushing back at the walls, making different kinds of space.' At one point in the performance, the crowd enacts this resistance physically, squashing together at one limit of the room, swaying and tittering. Referencing this moment, Roysdon comments almost as an aside: 'They've done that before and never laughed, it's just – that's the liveness.'[65] Within the digital domain, it remains the unexpected moments and unscripted reactions that suggest something particular to performance. Roysdon's piece seems to be concerned to some degree with where the latter might be found within the gallery and in relation to an audience online. As with the unanticipated reactions of the performers, the shift in position of the camera also inflects what it is that is being presented. In Roysdon's terms, 'when the camera comes in the room it's a different tone of performance, it's a different kind of thing.'[66] In this interpretation, the position of the camera as peripheral to or immersed within the action, while in both positions formative in terms of the impetus and distribution of the work, makes for distinctive qualities and manners of making performance.

This is also the case when the performers venture outside of the Performance Room and beyond their allotted station within the gallery. Towards the end of the performance, one of the volunteers opens a door at the back of the room and the performers begin to leave the space. At first the situation of the camera remains unaltered, though shouts repeating the words we have already heard articulated within the chamber and read inscribed on its floor are audible from beyond the frame of what is represented on screen.

Inside Performance Room a single row of volunteers remain. They too cry out: 'Live. No. Now. Live. Time. Anyone. Our Lives.' A different performer voices each word as they fall to the ground. They reconfigure themselves in a line across the perpendicular axis of the room and repeat this action. The camera scans along the performers on the floor and exits. Outside the bodies continue, splayed out on the solid foundation of the gallery, legs wide, their frames interconnected, uttering. The effect is harrowing; the chains of forms and noise seem continuous. Though it is dark, we can see the shadow of the camera and its operator shaded on the bodies and the grey surface of the institution. This concrete flooring gives a clue as to where in Tate Modern Performance Room is located. The only light comes from the open door to that space. The camera looks back along the track of corpora to its entrance, the last shot revisiting the area designated for performance.

Speaking of her decision to take the performers out of the gallery, the artist cites the proximity of Tate Modern's iconic Turbine Hall as the stimulus behind this move. 'We're in this small gallery,' Roysdon states, and nearby is this 'famously enormous space.' There is an interest here in the appearance of bodies in galleries. 'It's nice to see what 105 people in this room looks like taking up space somewhere else,' says Roysdon.[67] There is a politics to this attentiveness to the 'taking up' of institutional spaces for performance. In the confinement of Performance Room, the volunteers are crowded but not amassed; their individualism is in this location paramount. Outside its protection, in the vacuous Turbine Hall they become bodies immobilised on the glossy surfaces of the institution. Within Performance Room, Roysdon explains, 'we have an intimacy and a proximity and that's one kind of vibe and then out there we take up a different amount of space and we have to take a different form.' The scale and renown of the Turbine Hall, the venue for the prestigious Unilever Series and a space, though witness to a number of performance events, not named specifically for enactment, requires an alternative mode of production to that possible within Performance Room. Roysdon was interested to 'really see what different form we have to take to be out there,' suggesting that performers and performance must take up transformed and revised structures of expression in order to move beyond particular positions designated in advance for performance by art institutional venues.

Forming Together in the Individual

All of the case studies explored in this chapter share an investment in the occupation of space and retain, in their respective forms of presentation, a commitment to particular sites of representation: Auerbach to the building sites of London; Tacita Dean and the artists within Tate Modern to the distinctive respective demands of the Turbine Hall and Performance Room; and the digital visualisations to the specific terrain of a certain exhibition within a particular public gallery. The plan etched on the floor of Performance Room for *I am a helicopter, camera, queen* acts as a reminder of, what performance scholar Heike Roms calls, the 'performative nature of the map' by giving close and specific 'attention to that which conventional cartography does not map, the experiential plenitude of our actual sensual and emotional encounter with a concrete environment'.[68] Composed of phrases of movement and language to be performed by the volunteers, this score appears on computer screens to spectators as a two-dimensional representation of a three-dimensional design. Here, as is also the case with the digital images constructed within *Frank Auerbach: London Building Sites 1952–62*, the challenge is to 'translate the three-dimensional, embodied and ephemeral performative map back into the flat, diagrammatic and a-temporal surface of the page.'[69] In both cases, the two-dimensionality of screen-based display inflects the presentation and viewing of a three-dimensional rendering.

On screen, each visualisation provides alternative perspectives which expand the means by which it is possible to conceptualise visitors' movements within exhibition environments. These digital objects raise questions about how technology mediates the transmission of experiences and the potential for producing documentation of human behaviours. Drawing on the capacities of digital tools, the methodology tested within the Courtauld Gallery supports the statement made by Michel de Certeau that it is 'false to believe henceforth that electronic and computerized objects will do away with the activity of users.'[70] Rather, in this case, it is through such 'computerized objects' that the activities of visitors might be observed and acknowledged. These digital practices thereby bring into play the performance of visitors; a form which cannot be dissociated from what de Certeau calls 'an art of using.'[71] They simultaneously recognise the ways in which contemporary perceptions are being challenged by the ability to observe and be observed by advanced technological means. Taking into account specific locations of display and performative engagements with art objects, such digital approaches address the limitations and opportunities inherent in particular cultural settings and the ways in which we as visitors inflect the exhibitions to which we attend through the choices we make about how we look, from where, for how long, and at what. Looking at these digital objects it is possible to observe that an exhibition is ultimately enacted by the visitors who attend to and within its construction.

This can be made more explicit by brief reference to the final piece in the 2012 season of Performance Room at Tate Modern. For his *Where I'm Calling From*, broadcast live on 28 June 2012, Harrell Fletcher installed London busker Stanley Prospere, who performs under the stage name Bill Jackson, within the gallery. Relocating Jackson's performance from the Tube stations of London to an institutionalised art venue, Fletcher's collaboration, like Auerbach's building site paintings, transposes work from the city spaces of London into an exhibition space. Fletcher's practice is often involved with the ideals of social engagement and with *Where I'm Calling From* there is an explicit interest, as narrated by Tate, in the politics of a 'shift from playing to a local London audience to performing on a global online stage.'[72] The recording of the performance begins with an emphasis on its title, which is typed in black lettering onto a page of white paper attached to the gallery wall. Before we see Jackson, we hear his playing as the camera pans to introduce the musician by means of the same form of makeshift signage and black-on-white lettering. We see the shadow of the guitarist on the white wall before the performer is visible. His black guitar case rests in the corner of the room. The set-up is much the same as in the Tube, with the scenery including just a small amp and a bottle of water, except that here, between each song, French ballads and country music, Fletcher asks Jackson questions from his position off screen, about his life and his practice; and then there is the camera.

Jackson looks in the direction of the artist speaker and not at the camera when responding to each question. His attention remains in the live space of Performance Room and not with those watching from beyond its physical confines. He talks about growing up in St. Lucia and his move to London, about how he came to go by a pseudonym and his musical influences, as well as the means by which he became a busker and his favourite London sites in which to perform. Each song is announced by means of a placard held in front of the camera which reads 'Will You Be my Valentine?' or 'Where Will the Children Play?' These signs and their interrogatives do not prompt attempts to answer from the audience who hear Jackson's beautiful singing online but rather remind us that his performance is perhaps most acutely digital in the sense posed by Alan Read and cited earlier in this chapter, by drawing attention to the human digits which hold each notice in turn, as well as those that pluck each string. As Jackson finishes his performance, he looks to Fletcher for direction, nods in understanding, and unplugs his guitar from the amp. The camera rotates to reveal Fletcher, Wood, and Noble seated at the other end of the gallery and we see further digits as this live audience clap their hands. During the discussion that follows, Fletcher is asked, in an echo of the outsourcing of practice explored in the previous chapter, to reflect on the process of delegating his performance to another player. Reviewing the ever-fragile nature of the ownership of work of this kind, Fletcher locates the performance as 'collaborative' and 'shared' so that it is simultaneously a piece he was commissioned to produce, while also being 'the Tate's project, and Stanley's project.' Despite these assertions of collective endeavour, Fletcher does take some credit for the virtuosity of Jackson's performance, saying that he is 'good at appreciating things' and drawing a parallel to some degree between his own practice and the work of the 'programmer/curator/facilitator' in deference to the discomfort with which his method of organising and installing other performers in a space is often met.[73]

'Sometimes people get really unnerved that I'm like an artist who gets to ask other people to do things', says Flecther, 'for some reason that seems you know like not an ok thing for an artist to do.'[74] In the context of Performance Room we might see Fletcher's work as the means by which Jackson's performance comes to be displayed. For the former, *Where I'm Calling From* is about expanding institutional access by using an opportunity or 'platform,' in this case digital, offered to him as a result of his status as an artist, to bring in other performers who are normally excluded from this sort of commission and high-profile dissemination. In this regard, Wood reveals that Fletcher had originally proposed to invite a number of different buskers to perform and asks him to say something about the 'kind of typologies of performance' he initially had in mind. This question about classifications and characteristics of performance is particularly pertinent to its place in the gallery. Responding to the curator's question, Fletcher narrates his interest in the means by which we encounter the music of buskers as we travel. As we walk through the subway, the artist describes, we might hear multiple performers playing music of different genres which come together in a 'kind of mash up or sequence' and thereby 'form together in the individual who is experiencing them.'[75] The accumulation of different performances or artworks experienced in association within the body of an individual visitor has been a preoccupation within my project. In the Tube, we hear a collocation of music incidentally as we travel and move around the city in everyday acts of performance. In the gallery, we are, as visitors, invited to read particular works in combination and to draw conclusions with regard to their cumulative effect on the basis of curatorial programming, conceptualisation, and narration.

Illuminating Revelations

As should be evident by now, there is a concern throughout this book with thinking of objects and performances, online or in the gallery, in terms of their curation together. *Frank Auerbach: London Building Sites 1952–62*, with its shared concerns for cacophonies of experience, offers an opportunity to think further about this relation through a focus on the visitor and an emphasis that is digital. Through the process of visualisation we might perceive, as Fletcher's interest in buskers in the Tube also reveals, the ways in which every exhibition is ultimately constructed, every display performed, by and within each visitor in turn. Picturing an event over time, this digital process makes visible the ways in which, borrowing from Henri Bergson, 'external images influence the image that I call my body: they transmit movement to it'.[76] In gallery contexts, the moving body of each visitor marks one way in which an exhibition, temporary or otherwise, might be experienced in time and the way in which attractions to paintings and sketches within a specific curatorial layout might be played out. Active between curatorial edicts which condition a conventional engagement and more spontaneous impulses, gallery-goers are 'beings in whom present impressions find their way to appropriate movements', to physical progressions towards works which capture imaginations.[77] Rather than looking at art objects collected under a particular thematic title and analysing these works through the optic of that context as I have throughout this book, and continue to so do with regard to the Performance Room series, in *Frank Auerbach: London Building Sites 1952–62* I want to think more about how the connections between works of art united by the frame of a particular exhibition are materialised in the attentions of gallery visitors and how these might be perceived on screen.

Functioning both as displayed and performed, the digital objects produced from the observations made within the gallery show how visitors move between, what literary critic Frank Kermode calls, the 'permanent value' of the art object and the 'perpetual modernity' of their attentions to it.[78] The status afforded to a work of art in a specific cultural moment, by a gallery institution and by visitors who encounter this exhibit therein, impacts on the ways in which this object is addressed. Following Kermode, such 'valuations affect our ways of attending', of being in a room with, and performing in relation to, the exhibition on display.[79] At times the critical and curatorial understanding of an object diverges from the ways in which visitors engage with that work in the gallery. Let us return now to the painting with which this chapter began in order to tease that out. Apparently delaying any swift comprehension of the scene depicted, the hues of *Workmen under Hungerford Bridge* suggest to art historian William Feaver that the represented sites of London will 'prove slow to reveal themselves'.[80] Looking at Auerbach's paintings, Feaver suggests, we should 'peer at them initially through half-closed eyes,' adopting a stance, like that required by Markus Schinwald's *Bob* exhibited within *The World as a Stage* and explored in Chapter 2 of this book, that is askance and strange so as to look further into his shades and dim scenes of construction. The intricate and complex surfaces of Auerbach's paintings seem to invite sustained inspection and deliberate analysis. In contrast to the slow processes of connection which Auerbach's work, and this painting in particular, might theoretically appear to demand, the amounts of time visitors spent looking at *Shell Building Site: Workmen under Hungerford Bridge* within the Courtauld Gallery are striking in their brevity.

According to the behaviours of the forty visitors observed, the average time spent still, looking into the black depths of this painting, was just twenty-four and a half seconds.[81] Rather than receiving sustained feats of meditation, the dark spaces of this image are explored, for the most part, only momentarily and in passing. Despite the extraordinary shortness of these engagements, eight of the documented traces track movements which revisit this work and these returns are, for the most part, prompted by a preparatory sketch, displayed in a nearby glass cabinet, or otherwise appear as another look during a brief recapitulation undertaken before leaving the gallery. Alternating between draft and painting, at least some of the visitors' perceptions re-enact something of the artist's process. Shifting between the substantial and the disappearing, the material and the illusory, Auerbach's paintings occupy a position shared by all of the case-study exhibits examined in this book, interchanging between tropes associated with the displayed and those of the performed. If we take the time to attend to *Shell Building Site: Workmen under Hungerford Bridge*, Feaver suggests that 'the features resolve. Solidified yet animated, sculpturally pictorial and pictorially subtle'. Auerbach's painting occupies a space between the concrete and the dynamic, decoded through our vision and on the brink of fitful disintegration. In the thickness of his colours, the addition and subtraction of painted strata, Auerbach 'operated within a flicker of collapse', working unsteadily between solid structures, cavernous abysses and paint on the verge of subsiding to create images which appear, drawing on Feaver's terms for their echoes of performance, as 'simultaneously concrete and elusive'.[82]

Flickers of Performance

Following this terminology of the flicker, I want to conclude this digital chapter now by turning to look in closer detail at an expressly analogue artwork. According to Tate's website, Tacita Dean's *FILM* was 'the first work in The Unilever Series to be devoted to the moving image.'[83] This phrasing reminds us that film is a form of image making which creates or gives the impression of movement and signals something of the position of Dean's work here, in a project concerned with performance's relation to modes of presentation, including digital forms, more often characterised as static. Watching *FILM*, it is clear that the medium of film is itself like an exhibition; it is a collection of still images in distinct frames mobilised together towards a specific subject or sensation. Throughout Dean's project, the familiar architecture of Tate's Turbine Hall remains visible but with notable additions: painted colours and segmentations, reflections in fine textures, large spheres at different heights. I remember a sunset, or a sunrise, on screen which conceals the top block of windows and dapples those below. 'I wanted to look at old film techniques that were used to create illusion,' says Dean, who drew on classic filmic methods including masking, double-exposure, and glass matte painting to produce her Unilever commission.[84] Answering critiques of nostalgia, Dean asserts that her investment in analogue modes of production is rather precisely 'of now' and works to articulate, in Krauss' phrasing, celluloid film as a 'living medium.'[85] Expressing her practice in terms of a contemporaneity and liveness, there are obvious parallels to be drawn between this figuration and the established terms of performance, not least in the context of the Turbine Hall which, according to Dean, 'does call for the spectacular, for the occasion, for the epic.'[86] Something about this gallery setting requires a medium-specific project that speaks to the particular properties of performance.

Invested in spectacle, in excessive display, as well as ideas of eventhood and self-reflection, film is, for Dean, her 'medium just like oil is the medium of painters' and she needs for her practice 'the time of film.'[87] Film, like performance, has a particular temporality associated with its mechanisms. In her lecture on *FILM*, Krauss stresses the ways in which Dean is concerned with the 'indexical nature' of analogue photography, clarifying the latter as a term used by philosopher Charles Sanders Peirce to signify a 'trace causally registered on the film the way finger or footprints are left at the scenes of crimes.'[88] As in the case of the digital objects produced in the Courtauld Gallery which track the course of visitors through an exhibition, Dean's practice is likewise concerned with 'traces,' with vestiges or marks which act as remainders from an action, condition, or event which might have taken place. Explicating the indexical basis of film, Krauss explains how, by means of the 'phi effect' the transition between frames becomes imperceptible because each produces a 'ghostly trace' in the viewer's eye that hovers over the next.[89] Working between filmic frames, as between art objects in the gallery, the perceptions of the spectator mobilise the cumulative effect of the display. An index is a sign, an indication of something, and a major concern in Dean's practice, according to Tate's précis, has to do with 'capturing fleeting natural light or subtle shifts in movement' through 'static camera positions and long takes [which] allow events to unfold unhurriedly.'[90] A slowness and stillness in Dean's film making reveals images and motions that are ephemeral and evanescent.

Figure 4.2 Tacita Dean, *FILM*, 2011. 35mm colour anamorphic film, mute. 11 mins. Courtesy the artist, Frith Street Gallery, London and Marian Goodman Gallery, New York, Paris, London. Photographs by Marcus Leith and Andrew Dunkly © Tate.

Borrowing from Tate's press release, Dean has also 'celebrated what is normally considered waste in filmmaking, such as the picture fading at the tail end of a roll, flash frames of over-exposure as the camera stops and starts, and the shimmering metamorphosis of a colour filter change.'[91] And it is these flashes of something elusive that make *FILM* particularly pertinent to performance. Watching Dean's work in the Turbine Hall, the representation of this space on screen is divided and coloured, at one moment orange, turquoise, red, green, purple in rectangular segments. Orange turns to reds and greens, turquoise to blue, turquoise to red, red to green, red to yellow, green to purple, with flashes in between of yellow, orange, turquoise. Narrating this technique, Dean describes how 'between when the colour filters change you get a coloured flash frame' and, in the end, she decided to use these effects 'because they were so spectacular.'[92] These coloured instances speak to display and performance. Early experimental cinema, Krauss reminds us, also 'made reference to the intermittent flashes of the separate frames unavoidable by the sequential registrations of the filmstrip' which resulted in a particular genre of making called, by Austrian filmmaker Peter Kubelka '"flicker films," projections of opaque frames of black leader alternating with transparency to produce intermittent white flashes.'[93] Alternating between black boxes and white cubes, Dean explicates the flickers of *FILM* through reference to another, this time 16mm, film project with shared concerns made in 2001 and titled, after French director and critic Éric Rohmer's 1986 movie, *The Green Ray*. Dean describes this phenomenon as the 'last ray of the dying sun to refract and bend beneath the horizon' and relates her effort to 'see, if not film, something that [she] could not imagine.'[94]

According to her narrative, another camera, this time digital, attempted to film this refraction on the same evening on which Dean made her analogue attempt. Watching back the respective recordings, the phenomenon was not visible on the digital documentation and was also defiant of 'solid representation on a single frame of celluloid, but existent in the fleeting movement of film frames, was the green ray, having proved itself too elusive for the pixilation of the digital world.'[95] In Dean's account, the green ray functions as a metaphor for that which the digital, with no need of the 'phi effect', might exclude or forget. In this book project, however, this evasive flash addresses performance and the modes in which this ontology might appear. Dean affirms that 'the point about my film of the green ray is that it did so nearly elude me too' and this evasiveness is so often, and therefore notably, also the point of performance.[96] In *The Green Ray*, the movement of the film reel is able to capture something lost both in the pixels of the digital image and the still celluloid frames. The momentary event signalled by the film's title exists rather somewhere between the static renderings of analogue photography, visible only in animation, when the singular images coalesce. While making her film, Dean was also unsure about whether or not she had seen the green ray with her naked eye. The flicker is not securely visible either live or as a still image. Rather it is in the intermingling between these two modes that the fading effect of this light becomes visible. In this locus between the display of a single frame and the motion of the rolling film, something evanescent appears and this model of exhibiting the elusive suggests to me that this juncture might also be a place of performance.

The "It" of Performance

Speaking about *FILM*, Rosalind Krauss dwells on what she calls 'the sort of truculence with which Tacita Dean is refusing to replace the medium.' For Krauss, there is here a powerful emphasis on the particularities of a certain mode of production and a simultaneous investigation of what the specificities of that form might be. Cinema, says Krauss in her lecture at Tate Modern, is a 'multi-faceted apparatus, making the "it" of itself hard to locate: is it the screen, or the beam of light that pierces the blackened void to highlight the image? Or is it the filmstrip, the camera, or the projector?'[97] The complexity of the mechanisms of cinema, its simultaneous location on screen, in the lens and on the film reel, makes its ontology difficult to extrapolate. Also concerned with projection and illumination from a darkened space, this problem of determining the "it" of medium-specificity is applicable also to the quintessence of the digital and, in keeping with the project of this book, of performance. In her analysis, Krauss suggests that different artists answer the question by accenting one distinctive quality; flicker films, she proposes, 'opted for the filmstrip, made present to vision by its very series of interruptions, as well as making the projection screen another "itself" when the blank frames make it interrupt into pure blooms of light.'[98] In this rendering it is an interruption, an intermittent flickering between screen and reel, that makes visible certain aspects of the substance of analogue film.

Keeping in mind this principle of fluctuation, it seems significant to recall in concluding this chapter that the analogue maintains in its terminology a sense of analogy, that is to say a particular connection to a modus operandi founded in relation, correlation, and equivalence. All elusive and difficult to pin down, there are certain suggestive parallels to be drawn between digital, analogue, and performed ontologies and comparisons to be made between these media which reveal something about the curation and exhibition of performance. Throughout this book the case studies have emerged as concurrently displayed and performed through just such analogy or correspondence and relation between these respective modes. In the body of digital examples presented in this chapter, the particular iterations of Performance Room and the original methodology for tracing and visualising visitors' attentions to the exhibition *Frank Auerbach: London Building Sites 1952–62*, digital platforms have become mediums for the creation and dissemination of performance. Flickering between a performance situated in a gallery and an online spectatorial domain, all of the commissions for *BMW Tate Live 2012: Performance Room* speak to and engage with alterative possible locations for performance. In Jérôme Bel's *Shirtology*, layers of costume become improvised screens for performance and display. Both Bel and Pablo Bronstein, in his *Constantinople Kaleidoscope*, employ the affordances of Performance Room to explore one form through the terms of another, while Emily Roysdon and Harrell Fletcher investigate strategies for extending and exceeding the positions delineated for performance in advance by curators and art institutional programming.

While investigating the characteristics of film, the substantial analogue case study informing this chapter, Tacita Dean's work for the Turbine Hall at Tate Modern, is also productive for probing further the particularities of performance as something emerging throughout this book via modes of production that are intermittent. Read in association with the other case studies examined in this chapter, *FILM* becomes insightful for the thinking about the positions which performance might take up within the gallery and the sorts of practices that might be housed therein. Despite Tate's developing appetite for live work, Performance Room represents a particular instance in which the viewing of performance takes us beyond the institutional confines of the exhibition space. The performances might, in certain iterations, take place within an allotted room within Tate Modern but the audience is not permitted to enter that space. Around the same time, a physical screen is installed in the gallery, begging the question as to why performance is identified as a form that it is possible to disseminate through another, this time digital, medium whereas analogue film is not. Presumably Dean's *FILM* could not be broadcast in this way to an online audience because of the specific, and increasingly abandoned, technologies required to project the 35mm format. Performance, on the other hand, communicated online, is implied as a mode which might operate through the capacities of another; there is something about its ontology that exists beyond a located live moment.

Despite the precise prerequisites for analogue projection, when *FILM* is installed within the Turbine Hall its particular ontology is perhaps even more difficult to locate. To the list of possible locales suggested by Krauss – screen, projector, filmstrip, camera – we might add being in a particular place at a particular time, a specific architecture, which frames certain available relationships to, and distances from the work. During the Q&A following her lecture, Krauss is asked about the importance of experiencing *FILM* in its gallery context in relation to the museological struggle to collect and preserve works across a range of technological forms. The question is posed by Pip Laurenson, Head of Collection Care Research at Tate and a conservator committed to developing strategies for collecting and conserving time and performance-based art, in relation to theatre and performance scholarship: 'I wondered if I could ask you, as an art historian and critic, how important it is for you to be able to continue to encounter those works as installed with those mediums or is it enough that is was done and that you can investigate that retrospectively almost like we might a performance?'[99] In her response, Krauss is compelled to admit that she wrote her lecture before visiting *FILM* as it is installed in Tate Modern, basing her paper on images of the work accessible in digital format online. Watching analogue film via a digital representation, one medium is encountered indirectly through the terms of another and this reflective, or this time pre-emptive, exploration speaks to the problematics of performance.

Notes

1. Barnaby Wright, *Frank Auerbach: London Building Sites 1952–1962* [Exhibition Catalogue] (London: The Courtauld Gallery and Paul Holberton Publishing, 2009), 74.
2. Andrew Todd, 'Environment, Image and Materiality in the Theatre Worlds of Peter Brook and Ariane Mnouchkine' (paper presented at the *Living Landscapes* conference organised by Mike Pearson and Heike Roms at the Department of Theatre, Film and Television Studies, Aberystwyth University, 18–22 June 2009).
3. Wright, *Frank Auerbach*, 77.
4. I am grateful to Maartje Ament and the UCL Interaction Centre for constructing and running this experiment so that I might observe the images for the first time through the Eye Tracking System and to Barnaby Wright, Daniel Katz Curator of 20th Century Art at the Courtauld Gallery, London, for supplying representations of Auerbach's paintings in digital form.
5. Vilém Flusser, *Towards a Philosophy of Photography*, trans. Anthony Mathews (London: Reaktion Books, 2000), 8.
6. Alan Read, *Theatre in the Expanded Field: Seven Approaches to Performance* (London: Bloomsbury, 2013), 22.
7. Bill Blake, *Theatre & the Digital* (Houndmills: Palgrave Macmillan, 2014), 11.
8. Ibid., 13.
9. Matt Adams, 'Foreword' to *Theatre & the Digital* by Bill Blake, viii–ix.
10. Blake, *Theatre & the Digital*, 24, 35, and 37.
11. Samuel Weber, *Theatricality as Medium* (Bronx: Fordham University Press, 2004), 99. For an extended discussion of the place and proliferation of theatricality in relation to modes of electronic media see in particular Chapter 3 of this text: 'Scene and Screen: Electronic Media and Theatricality.'
12. Gabriella Giannachi, *Virtual Theatres: An Introduction* (London and New York: Routledge, 2004), 4.
13. Ibid.
14. Read, *Theatre in the Expanded Field*, 94.
15. William Feaver, *Frank Auerbach* (New York: Rizzoli, 2009), 5.
16. Ibid., 8 and 17.
17. Ibid., 11.
18. Frank Auerbach quoted in Wright, *Frank Auerbach* [Exhibition Catalogue], 78.
19. Robert Smithson, 'Earth' (excerpts from a symposium at the Andrew Dickson White Museum of Art, Cornell University in 1969), in *Robert Smithson: The Collected Writings*, ed. Jack Flam (Berkeley: University of California Press, 1996), 178.
20. Ibid.
21. 'BMW Tate Live 2012: Performance Room,' Tate, accessed 15 July 2015, http://www.tate.org.uk/whats-on/tate-modern/eventseries/bmw-tate-live-2012-performance-room.

22. Steve Dixon, *Digital Performance: A History of New Media in Theater, Dance, Performance Art, and Installation* (Cambridge, Mass., and London: MIT Press, 2007), 141.

23. 'Curator, Catherine Wood on Performance Art,' Tate, last modified 20 March 2012, http://www.tate.org.uk/context-comment/video/curator-catherine-wood-on-performance-art.

24. 'BMW Tate Live 2012: Performance Room.'

25. 'BMW Tate Live: Screening of Performance Room series,' Tate, accessed 15 July 2015, http://www.tate.org.uk/whats-on/tate-modern/film/bmw-tate-live-screening-performance-room-series.

26. Philip Auslander, *Liveness: Performance in a Mediatized Culture* (London and New York: Routledge, 1999), 51. Original emphasis.

27. Giannachi, *Virtual Theatres*, 6.

28. 'BMW Tate Live: Performance Room Pablo Bronstein,' Tate, accessed 15 July 2015, http://www.tate.org.uk/whats-on/tate-modern/music-and-live-performance/bmw-tate-live-performance-room-pablo-bronstein.

29. 'BMW Tate Live 2015: Performance Room,' Tate, accessed 15 July 2015, http://www.tate.org.uk/whats-on/tate-modern/eventseries/bmw-tate-live-2015-performance-room.

30. Matt Adams, 'Foreword' to *Theatre & the Digital* by Bill Blake, x-ix.

31. 'The Unilever Series 2011: Tacita Dean,' Tate, last modified 10 October 2011, http://www.tate.org.uk/about/press-office/press-releases/unilever-series-2011-tacita-dean.

32. 'Tacita Dean on FILM: Interview,' Tate, accessed 15 July 2015, http://www.tate.org.uk/whats-on/tate-modern/exhibition/unilever-series-tacita-dean-film.

33. 'Rosalind Krauss on Tacita Dean's FILM,' Tate, last modified 8 March 2012, http://www.tate.org.uk/context-comment/video/rosalind-krauss-on-tacita-deans-film.

34. Ibid.

35. Read, *Theatre in the Expanded Field*, 82 and 102. Original emphasis.

36. Una Bauer, 'The Movement of Embodied Thought: The Representational Game of the Stage Zero of Signification in *Jérôme Bel*,' *Performance Research* 13:1 (2008): 38.

37. 'Why Dance in the Art World? Jérôme Bel and RoseLee Goldberg in Conversation,' last modified 13 September 2012, http://performa-arts.org/magazine/entry/why-dance-in-the-art-world-jerome-bel-and-roselee-goldberg-in-conversation.

38. Ibid.

39. Una Bauer, 'Jérôme Bel: An Interview', *Performance Research* 13:1 (2008): 45, 47, and 43.

40. 'BMW Tate Live: Performance Room Pablo Bronstein.'

41. Ibid.

42. Timothy Murray, *Digital Baroque: New Media Art and Cinematic Folds* (Minneapolis: University of Minnesota Press, 2008), 25, 9, and 20.

43. 'BMW Tate Live: Performance Room Pablo Bronstein.' All subsequent references to Bronstein and Wood's discussion of *Constantinople Kaleidoscope* (2012) in this and the following paragraphs are drawn from this source.

44. Ibid.

45. Ibid.

46. Susan Bennett, *Theatre Audiences: A Theory of Production and Reception* (London: Routledge, 1990), 86–87 and 210–11. Original emphasis.

47. Susan Bennett, *Theatre & Museums* (Houndmills: Palgrave Macmillan, 2012), 9.

48. Barnaby Wright, email message to author, 28 August 2009. I am extremely grateful to the Courtauld Gallery, London, and particularly Barnaby Wright, Kerstin Glasow, and Caroline Campbell, for their support in kind and for making space for this digital endeavour, as well as for discussing with me its practical and future implications.

49. Auerbach quoted in William Feaver, *Frank Auerbach*, 229.

50. That visitors' behaviours and attentions might be affected, influenced, and, in the extremity, limited by the application of this digital methodology is an ethical concern. My observations in the Courtauld Gallery were protected by ethical approval from the King's College London Social Sciences, Humanities and Law Research Ethics Subcommittee. In line with guidance from the Courtauld Gallery, Space Syntax, and the *Ethical Guidelines* of the Social Research Association (http://the-sra.org.uk/wp-content/uploads/ethics03.pdf, accessed 10 January 2012, 31), I received permission to obtain participants' consent post hoc (REC Protocol Number: SSHL/08/09–35). Within the Auerbach special exhibition (2009–10) I documented the pathways of forty visitors. All of the recordings were completely anonymous and the selection of which visitors to observe random and indiscriminate, based on the coincidence of one participant completing their viewing of the exhibition just before another enters.

51. A short article giving more practical details of the visualisation methodology on which this chapter reflects appears as 'Out of Sync: Curation, Participation and Reactional Pathways' in *Performance Research* 16:3 On Participation & Synchronisation (2011): 89–93 (http://www.tandfonline.com/). I am extremely grateful to Dr Stuart Dunn, Lecturer in the Centre for e-Research at King's College London, and Dr Nicholas Gold, Senior Lecturer in the Department of Computer Science at University College London, for their generous support of this digital project. The bespoke data capture software, which records the trajectory of each observed visitor in terms of an x,y placing reference and timestamp, was designed with Dr Nicolas Gold in 2009. The visualisation process was developed collaboratively with and supported by Dr Stuart Dunn and follows the principles of the space-time cube, developed elsewhere. The data collection within the exhibition was undertaken over three days per week for a period of two weeks, in addition to a pilot session in which to regulate the accuracy of the methodology. The latter is influenced by manual observation techniques and notations employed by Space Syntax Limited, and I would like to thank Maia Lemlij for meeting with me in 2009 to discuss observation methods and providing me with access to their *Observations Manual* (2008).

52. Marie-José Mondzain, 'Chapter 1 (Excerpt) The Images That Give Birth To Us,' trans. Patrick Ffrench for Mondzain's presentation at *Caves*, an event convened by Alan Read in the Anatomy Theatre and Museum, King's College London on 14 February 2011, 3. This section is published in French as 'Les images qui nous font naître,' in *Homo Spectator* (Paris: Bayard, 2007).

53. For examples of these visualised images, please see my publication describing this methodology: 'Out of Sync: Curation, Participation and Reactional Pathways,' *Performance Research* 16:3 On Participation & Synchronisation (2011): 89–93.

54. Matthew Reason, 'Still Moving: The Revelation or Representation of Dance in Still Photography,' *Dance Research Journal* 35–36 (2–1) (2003): 48.

55. John Cage, *Silence: Lectures and Writings* (Middletown, Conn.: Wesleyan University Press, 1973), 39.
56. Rebecca Schneider, 'Performance Remains.' *Performance Research* 6:2 On Maps & Mapping (2001), 104.
57. Ibid., 105.
58. Hal Foster, *The Return of the Real: The Avant-Garde at the End of the Century* (Cambridge, Mass.: MIT Press, 1996), 29.
59. Alan Read, *Theatre, Intimacy & Engagement: The Last Human Venue* (Houndmills: Palgrave Macmillan, 2008), 198.
60. Jen Harvie, 'Agency and Complicity in "A Special Civic Room": London's Tate Modern Turbine Hall' in *Performance and the City* ed. D.J. Hopkins, Shelley Orr and Kim Solga (Houndmills: Palgrave Macmillan, 2009), 216.
61. 'BMW Tate Live: Performance Room Emily Roysdon,' Tate, accessed 15 July 2015, http://www.tate.org.uk/whats-on/tate-modern/music-and-live-performance/bmw-tate-live-performance-room-emily-roysdon-i-am.
62. Ibid. All subsequent references to Roysdon, Wood, and Noble's discussion of *I am a helicopter, camera, queen* (2012) in this and the following paragraphs are drawn from this source.
63. Ibid.
64. Ibid.
65. Ibid.
66. Ibid.
67. Ibid.
68. Heike Roms, 'Eye and Ear, Foot and Mouth: Mapping Performance in Three Journeys and One Withdrawal,' in *A Cosmology of Performance: Testimony from the Future, Evidence of the Past*, ed. Judie Christie, Richard Gough, and Daniel Peter Watt (London: Routledge, 2006), 13.
69. Ibid., 11.
70. Michel de Certeau, *The Practice of Everyday Life, Volume 2: Living & Cooking*, trans. Timothy Tomasik (Minneapolis: University of Minnesota Press, 1998), 254.
71. Michel de Certeau, *The Practice of Everyday Life*, trans. Steven Rendell (Berkeley: University of California Press, 1984), xv.
72. 'BMW Tate Live: Performance Room Harrell Fletcher,' Tate, accessed 15 July 2015, http://www.tate.org.uk/whats-on/tate-modern/music-and-live-performance/bmw-tate-live-performance-room-harrell-fletcher.
73. Ibid. All subsequent references to Fletcher, Jackson, Wood, and Noble's discussion of *Where I'm Calling From* (2012) in this and the following paragraphs are drawn from this source.
74. Ibid.
75. Ibid.
76. Henri Bergson, *Matter and Memory*, trans. Nancy. M. Paul and W. Scott Palmer (London: George Allen & Unwin Ltd, 1950 [1911]), 4.
77. Ibid., 113.
78. Frank Kermode, *Forms of Attention: Botticelli and Hamlet* (Chicago: University of Chicago Press, 2011 [1985]), 62.
79. Ibid., xiii.
80. Feaver, *Frank Auerbach*, 14.

81. The shortest time spent by an observed visitor looking at *Shell Building Site: Workmen under Hungerford Bridge* (1958–61) by Frank Auerbach was just three seconds and this brief engagement was recorded during a weekday lunchtime. The longest time spent in a still examination of the painting was two minutes and nineteen seconds. This was recorded during the lunchtime of a weekend and the visitor was making a sketch of the painting. The longest observation of the work made without sketching was one minute and forty-four seconds. This act of looking also occurred during a weekend visit.
82. Feaver, *Frank Auerbach*, 14.
83. 'The Unilever Series 2011: Tacita Dean.'
84. 'Tacita Dean on FILM: Interview.'
85. Ibid. and 'Rosalind Krauss on Tacita Dean's FILM.'
86. 'Tacita Dean on FILM: Interview.'
87. Ibid.
88. 'Rosalind Krauss on Tacita Dean's FILM.'
89. Ibid.
90. 'The Unilever Series 2011: Tacita Dean.'
91. 'The Unilever Series 2011: Tacita Dean.'
92. 'Tacita Dean on FILM: Interview.'
93. 'Rosalind Krauss on Tacita Dean's FILM.'
94. 'Tacita Dean on FILM: Interview.'
95. Ibid.
96. Ibid.
97. 'Rosalind Krauss on Tacita Dean's FILM.'
98. Ibid.
99. A question posed by Pip Laurenson and recorded within 'Rosalind Krauss on Tacita Dean's FILM.'

Conclusion
Final Movement

Reflecting on the historical emergence of concepts and objects, philosopher and historian of science Ian Hacking suggests that, in order to discuss the categories and operations of things, it is 'convenient to group them together by talking about "what there is," or ontology.'[1] Performance occupies a complex relation to 'being there,' to exhibitable qualities and referents of presence. It is perhaps suggestive to note too that in these terms ontology associates things not 'here,' in a proximity and immediacy of attendance, but rather 'there,' and at a distance that is demonstrative and signifying. Like a traditional museological display, which communicates meaning via classifications presented as static and unshifting, ontology has been characterised as the analysis of general traits and kinds wherein, as Hacking reminds us, 'the emphasis has been on demarcation'.[2] Concerned with perceptions and theories according to which a field of knowledge and enquiry might be delineated, such definitions of historical ontology are easy to connect with the organisational, classificatory, and preservatory principles of the art museum and gallery. Hacking is interested in how our practices of naming interrelate with the things we designate, in the interactions between those things and our conceptions of them, and in this study my concern has been to take up these questions of being, naming, categorising, and conceptualising in relation to performance and through the optic of exhibition.[3] Bearing in mind established ontological distinctions in order to bring into focus objects and events through which these transform, it is useful to retain from Hacking's definition of ontology an emphasis on 'what there is,' on shared qualities and characteristics which might operate and move across paradigms.

The productive frictions evident in the sorts of recent exhibitions charted in this book suggest a model of performance which traverses between 'historical ontology', aligned with the traditionally static museum, and ontologies of performance, associated most often with movement and transience. In Hacking's terms, the historical ontologist is 'preoccupied by general and organizing concepts and the institutions and practices in which they are materialized.'[4] In the preceding chapters, I have worked through a range of case studies curated at high-profile theatre and exhibition venues over a period of six years. These events emerge in relation to an increasing curatorial commitment to live art and performance as a set of contingent fields and forces. Each brings into close association the displayed and the performed and reveals something about how arts institutions predominantly concerned with the visual are now emulating performance practices in material configurations through the form of exhibition. Concerned with historical, theoretical, and disciplinary intersections, these examples speak across terrains of display and performance, enabling connections to be made that are conceptual and associative and which allow for affiliation across paradigms and ontologies. The most striking of these cases offer models wherein, after Hacking, 'epistemological concepts are not constraints, free-standing ideas that are just there, timelessly' but rather coalesce and intermingle so that the ontologies attached to each mode of expression might be reviewed and expanded.[5]

Over the chapters of this book, I have employed gallery-based examples to talk about theatre. The project, therefore, expresses my conviction that it is important to acknowledge displayed and object-based practices in relation to conceptions of what might count as performance. P.A. Skantze has pursued in her work a 'way of writing about theatre, about audience, and about history that can move across the plane of analysis to display'.[6] In attempting to confront how complex interactions between traditions of display and performance might work to exhibit something of the latter in contemporary exhibition environments, this book aims to present something of theatre and performance by and through its analysis. Looking at a carefully selected range of artworks and events, my project has always been about testing these expressions as frameworks for thinking about and conceiving performance. Along with exploring specific instances of practice, what is at stake throughout is a concern for and commitment to, what Joe Kelleher calls, 'that dubiously abstract and universalizing entity *the theatre itself*,' and the ways in which it is evoked, challenged, and thought again in and as exhibition.[7] By way of conclusion, I would like to briefly illustrate how certain connections and conceits appear across all of the examples presented here by collecting particular insights and ideas around a final case in point.

Moving to Conclude

So as to draw together some of the threads emerging through this text and the case studies surveyed therein, I will turn my attention in these final pages to *Move: Choreographing You*, a temporary exhibition curated by Stephanie Rosenthal, then Chief Curator of the Hayward Gallery in London, from 13 October 2010 to 9 January 2011. Intersecting concepts of dance and visual art, the event, like this book, situates itself between two traditions and terminologies. Operating through a creative interface complementary to that which I have asserted throughout this project, *Move* exhibits a useful relation to the exhibitions discussed more substantially therein and proves helpful in collecting and consolidating emerging tropes, patterns, and theories, not least because the language through which it is articulated by curators and commentators speaks to, yet plays out differently, shared concerns. *Move* appears amongst a number of exhibitions staged by the Hayward in recent years, including *Light Show* (2014), which are conceived thematically and titled so as to signify their unifying subject. Marketed as exploring fifty years of practice occupying a liminal space between dance and visual art, *Move* is concerned with exhibiting an historical survey of the cooperation between two fields and consequently differs in focus to the models built up through this study. The event therefore offers an opportunity to situate the paradigms and reformations brought to light through the exhibitions addressed in the preceding chapters in relation to a longer history of practice without reiterating that well-attended to terrain.

Like the collection of events brought together and studied within the broader chapters of this book, *Move* exhibited both pre-existing and specially made artworks suggestive of an interface between display and performance. Including works by Boris Charmatz, William Forsythe, Robert Morris, Bruce Nauman, Yvonne Rainer, and Simone Forti, amongst others, *Move* draws together a spectrum of dance-related objects within a gallery context. The emphasis on motion involves the exhibition not only in the presentation of objects, but also with invitations, tasks, and instructions variously additional to or rooted within the materials on display. In his review of *Move*, performance scholar and media choreographer Johannes Birringer notes how 'Rosenthal's selection of works draws largely on sculpture and installation art, sets, and objects that can be played with or that "theatrically" emphasize their materiality in the manner that Michael Fried abhorred when writing on "art and objecthood" in 1967'.[8] It is this emphasis on sculptural works and material objecthood which makes the event particularly relevant to the terms of this book. Commenting on the staging of the exhibition, Birringer observes that the Hayward 'opted to present installations as a go-between – "propositions" in the sense in which Lygia Clark's *Elastic Net* (1973) functions as a curious "transitional object" for the spectators who get entangled in it, or Franz Erhard Walther's fabric elements (reproductions of *1. Werksatz*, 1967) allow two visitors to hold each other's balance as they lean backward'.[9] Sustaining two modes of production in elastic tension, in *Move*, as in the examples presented in this project, object-referents appear, following Birringer's phrasing, as mediators, assertions halfway between visual art and dance which advance each mode at fluctuating intervals.

Through an accumulation of aesthetic things, *Move* once again approaches the possibility of displaying performance within gallery settings and the ways in which concepts of performance might be seen to occupy these spaces via intermediate objects. Invested in the relation of previous and current iterations of the interface between dance practice and visual art, *Move* also incorporates within its frame an interactive digital archive, co-curated by Rosenthal and performance and dance scholar André Lepecki. Installed within the gallery on black flat-screen monitors stationed on white cube-shaped tables, and navigated via a concertina of selectable images, this contextual resource is introduced by Rosenthal and Lepecki as a 'dynamic vision of what choreographer Yvonne Rainer called the "concurrent" history of visual arts and dance since the 1960s.'[10] *Theatre, Exhibition, and Curation* has likewise proposed a mode of expression that is co-operative, conjoint, associating, and, like the digital format of the *Move* archive, object-based. In his scholarship, Lepecki is concerned with how visual arts practices have influenced, developed, and been incorporated into languages of dance and vice-versa, with the latter often involving the political potential of the body and strategies by which to 'resist, or bypass, politically compromised notions of the art object as commodity, fetish, or surplus-value.'[11] For Lepecki, dance scholar Erin Brannigan writes in her essay on 'Dance and the Gallery' (2015), the 'object is the link between dance and the visual arts'.[12] While Lepecki invests in ideas of choreographic objecthood and how objects might structure actions, this study addresses visual art objects which present something of, and thereby alter, performance's ontology.

Calling for a 'Concurrent Archive' Lepecki asks: 'What if we postulate that the history of dance and the visual arts in the past half-century is essentially a co-formative one?'[13] Lepecki's plea advocates a history that acknowledges and equally values reciprocal influence, exchange, and interaction. The models developed in this book take the 'co-formative' more literally, detecting exhibitions and objects that are twofold in their subject and expression, simultaneously displayed and performed and thus concurrently and co-determinately two forms. In order to put forward some final thoughts on this sort of co-animation, I want to draw on the shape of *Move's* archive and, occasionally, particular works presented within the physical exhibition at the Hayward. Browsable thematically, the *Move* archive is constructed across nine classifications which Rosenthal and Lepecki call 'resonating zones of compositional tactics,' suggesting that this archival arrangement 'scrambles linear historical narratives to produce unexpected constellations, revealing powerful connections between works – thematic, material, political and aesthetic.'[14] Like the non-sequential modes of production examined from Chapter 1 of this book, the structure of the *Move* archive encourages, at least conceptually, creative engagement with the limits of disciplinary paradigms. Over the next pages, I will draw on four of Rosenthal and Lepecki's archival categories so as to highlight certain tropes developing across the broader framework of this book and structure some final reflections, re-associations, and imaginings.

'Choreographing Things: People making things move and things making people move.'[15]

Concerned with recent choreographic practices, as well as work from the 1960s by Yvonne Rainer, Simone Forti, and others, which employ 'objects and things as the main activators and protagonists of dances,' Lepecki describes this zone of the *Move* archive as engaging with processes wherein 'things reveal their subjectivity, while humans reveal their thingness, to the point where it becomes hard to say who moves whom, who choreographs whom, and who is choreographed by whom.'[16] Working at the intersection of the human and the non-human, this subsection of the archive speaks to patterns emergent from the early stages of this book. Chapter 1 brought into association *Marina Abramović Presents...* (2009) and Elmgreen & Dragset's *Drama Queens* (2008), for which Tim Etchells provided a text, because of the direct reversal these events perform in their relative repositioning of 'things' of exhibition (sculptural objects) on stage and 'things' of performance (live artists) within the gallery. With the latter requiring the removal of the Whitworth Gallery's art collection, these events highlight the complexity of making space in which to navigate intersectional practices of display and performance, reverberating through gestures towards and associations of the idealism of the empty space for performance and the white cube for exhibition. Much of the legacy of the relation between dance and art, not least the *Anthropometries* of Yves Klein, also work through this analogy, inscribing what Lepecki calls 'an isomorphic correspondence between paper and stage'.[17] From their respective gallery and theatre venues, both *Drama Queens* and *Marina Abramović Presents...* challenge the physical conditions and perceptual arrangements of the spaces in which to view art.

In her essay on 'Choreographies in the Visual Arts,' Rosenthal teases out certain correspondences between dance and minimalism in the visual arts, remarking that, 'while some bade farewell to objecthood, turning the idea into the work, others emphasised it.' As sculpture was 'reconceived as a solicitation to action' so this focus on movement 'entirely dissolved the objecthood of art.'[18] Also playing with legacies of minimalist practice, *Drama Queens* and *Marina Abramović Presents...* make symbiotic pictorial and literal forms, complicating the relationship between theatre, objecthood, and performance. From this opening chapter, the book has engaged with a number of exhibitions which challenge traditional paradigms of the theatrical and exhibition event by showing material things choreographed to reveal something of the former; referents of performance which function within the more orthodox object-centric thinking of visual arts display. In *Move* too we find objects simultaneously displayed and performed: Lygia Clark's 'Sensorial' and 'Relational Objects,' for example, or William Forsythe's 'Choreographic Objects' which, as this book has sought models of performance operating in an alternative relation to the ephemeral, ask 'whether choreography can elaborate an expression of its principles that is independent of the body'.[19] Within the domain of dance, the objectness of sculpture offers new emphasis to stillness. Associating the sculptural and the performative, in *Renoir at the Theatre* (2008), examined in Chapter 2, and the paintings of Constantin Guys in particular, the theatrical experience is presented as statuesque. Within *The World as a Stage* (2007–8), installations such as Pawel Althamer's *Self-Portrait as a Businessman* (2002–4) and Geoffrey Farmer's *Hunchback*

Kit (2000) shift the place of the performance-document. By alluding to less specific theatrical acts, these object-referents reveal not disappearance but rather make visible some sense of performance more broadly. Whereas, notably in the formative actions of Marie Cool Fabio Balducci, Chapter 1 saw performance initiate not disappearance but display, in Chapter 2 display appears not as documentation but as performance.

Within *Move* too traditionally static object-based displays are instilled with motion and made performative. This is evident, for example, in Spanish choreographer and visual artist La Ribot's performance-installation *Walk the Chair* (2010). Composed of fifty folding wooden chairs which visitors may reposition throughout the gallery, each of these seats is marked with a quotation from an artist, choreographer, or philosopher offering some conception of movement. In order to read these inscriptions it is necessary to move from a seated position and alter our customary relation to the everyday object. Recalling the relational projects examined in Chapter 3, we find on these chairs the words of, amongst others, Nicolas Bourriaud: 'Artistic practice is always related to another person and at the same time it constitutes a relationship to the world.' Operating through events constitutive of, what I am calling, a 'return' to relational theories and practices, this third chapter engaged with a set of hegemonic vocabularies revolving around the relational and the spectatorial in order to assess what light these might shed on the interconnection of performance and display. *theanyspacewhatever* (2008–9) and *Double Agent* (2008) revisit a set of theoretical paradigms according to which the artwork is considered as a 'social *interstice*', an intervening space between two components which might be thought as display and performance.[20] In keeping with the other objects of study examined in this project, Bourriaud's theory expands the definition of the autonomous art object to incorporate actions of encounter and performance. Operating outside connotations of transcendence, Angela Bulloch's *Hybrid Song Box.4* (2008), for example, instills digitally arranged motions of light and sound within a seemingly stable object and thereby shifts between designations of the static artwork on display and ephemeral performance. In Bulloch's work, as has become clear more broadly through the case study exhibitions of this book, art objects appear through, what French philosopher Henri Lefebvre terms in his rhythmanalytical project, an 'apparent immobility that contains one thousand and one movements'.[21] Lefebvre's examination of rhythms will be useful to these concluding paragraphs for its focus on intermittence, something central to the terms of this project and to collecting together and theorising practices alternatingly displayed and performed.

'Tracing Movement: Tracking the body's imprint in space and time.'[22]

'Dance does not produce durable objects,' writes Lepecki, but 'belabours itself into visibility, sometimes leaving behind evidence of its fleeting acts.'

Investigating the means through which 'the visual arts and dance track the transient *par excellence* – movement,' this subsection of the *Move* archive revolves around an interest in the performer's body in space.[23] Through the progression of this book, a parallel concern for the gallery visitor's movement becomes increasingly apparent. Another of La Ribot's chairs suggests that when 'the roles of author, actor and spectator are not clear for any of the people playing those roles, then something interesting begins'. This book has presented a number of inversions in the respective situations of performer, object, visitor, and exhibit. Clear examples of such confusion of status are evident, for example, in *Double Agent*: in Joe Scanlan's presentation of Donelle Woolford (2008) and in Barbara Visser's staged lectures (2007) which not only involve an association of artist and actor but draw attention to visitors' positions in relation to the performer or object displayed. This contemporary focus on the situation of the gallery-goer signifies a situation wherein 'human relations have now become full-fledged artistic "forms".'[24] This is evident in Pierre Huyghe's *OPENING* of *theanyspacewhatever* and within *Double Agent* in Dora García's *Instant Narrative* (2006–8). By displaying those who move and interpret within the confines of gallery environments, these relationally conceived exhibitions anticipate the digital practices of Chapter 4, sharing an investment in the performative and productive nature of visitors' engagements. As has become clear throughout this book, one of the most frequently occurring intersections of the displayed and performed emerges through visitors' acts of attendance and attention.

In this book, we have seen works which interrupt visitors' movements, for example, within *theanyspacewhatever*, Jorge Pardo's *Sculpture Ink* (2008), Dominique Gonzalez-Foerster's *Promenade* (2007), and Liam Gillick's *Signage System* (2008). In keeping with such attempts to make the exhibition setting dynamic, *Move*'s investigation of dialogues between dance and sculpture also draws an association between gallery and stage. Pablo Bronstein, for example, whose *Constantinople Kaleidoscope* (2012) was examined in Chapter 4 as part of the first iteration of Tate's Performance Room, erects a *Magnificent Triumphal Arch in Pompeian Colours* (2010) within the Hayward Gallery. Bringing together dance and architecture, a performer's movement shifts from one form to another in the act of moving through this structure, from 'everyday' actions to heightened gestures of *sprezzatura*. Alternating from one mode of operation to another via architectural influence, Bronstein's transitional work speaks to models developed throughout this book. Within *Move*, choreographic practice often reveals the ways in which public and politicised spaces control the movements that are possible therein. Rosenthal reminds us that artworks 'invite visitors to an exhibition to perform certain movements, effectively creating a choreography for them.'[25] Simultaneously, another of La Ribot's chairs cites Adolfo Vásquez Rocca's belief that 'spectators become the organisers of their impulses and of their aesthetic experience.' Chapter 4 investigates this intersection and the potential for gallery visitors to develop their own trajectories within institutions preoccupied by external controls, including curatorial directives. Documenting acts not normally visible, this chapter invests in the digital to stimulate revised approaches to the displayed and performed.

Within a range of expanded formulations, choreography also refers to systems for notating movement. In a related way, Chapter 4 explores a range of objects and methodologies which reveal performance retrospectively. Displayed on screen, images of visitors' participations within the Courtauld Gallery's *Frank Auerbach: London Building Sites 1952–62* exhibition (2009–10) are reviewed alongside two projects curated at Tate Modern: Performance Room and Tacita Dean's *FILM* (2012). Whereas the history of dance and sculpture, as Lepecki recalls, has been founded on the moving body as that which might 'both supplement and shatter traditional surfaces of representation – paper, canvas, a beautiful serial sculpture' – here we see Tate reinstating the screen in relation to their (largely dance-based) performance programmes.[26] Performance Room raises questions about why performance is a form that might be displayed through digital media whereas analogue film, and Dean's project in particular, is not. Throughout this book there is a concern with encountering performance by alternative means. The digital images of gallery visitors correlate to the rest of this project by incorporating duration into apparently still object-based renderings, while *FILM* suggests something of performance through its attention to the green ray, a phenomenon that cannot be seen either live or within the stilled image of a single frame but rather appears in a flicker. Across the book an alternative temporality for performance emerges which is not a sequential transition from animate to inanimate, or visible to invisible, but moves from temporality to atemporality and back again.

'Transforming Time: Duration, repetition, accumulation, acceleration, and slowing down.'[27]

In the introduction to this section of the *Move* archive, Lepecki asks: 'How do visual arts and dance exchange between each other modes for extending, compressing and distorting temporality?'[28] The focus of my interest in this question differs to Lepecki's, whose response centres on a shared capacity for dance and the visual arts to transform our experience of time. The temporary events collected in this book represent a context wherein models of temporality associated with display and performance might be expanded and rethought. Focusing in on these performative exhibitions, the 'progress of attention results in creating anew not only the object perceived, but also the ever widening systems with which it may be bound up'.[29] The contemporary visual arts exhibitions investigated here take on the potentialities and problematics of performance and instil duration within apparently stable modes of display so that in order to assess these artworks, borrowing from Hal Foster, alternative 'models of causality, temporality, and narrativity are required'.[30] Within *Move*, American artist Bruce Nauman's contribution *Green Light Corridor* (1970) presents a final opportunity to recollect some associations between display and performance. Entering Nauman's work is sickly, disorienting, and cannot be achieved square-on but only sideways. In his theory of attention, French philosopher Maurice Blanchot defines the latter as 'the reception of what escapes attention, an opening upon the unexpected, a waiting that is the unawaited of all waiting.'[31] This book has addressed a number of exhibits to which visitors cannot attend directly. Perhaps the most suggestive of these is Marcus Schinwald's *Bob* (2007) within *The World as a Stage*. Looking at this work indirectly, visitors perceive that this piece brings together the temporal and the static, the displayed and the performed, within one object.

Trisha Donnelly's *The Redwood and the Raven* (2004) appears too in a space between the photographic document and transient performance, exhibiting in its variable curation instability between stasis and momentum, temporality and perpetuity, while Ulla von Brandenburg's *Kugel* (2007) speaks specifically to the interrelation of display and performance through its juddering motionlessness. Comparably, the slowed body of Kira O'Reilly within *Marina Abramović Presents...* and the performances of Marie Cool Fabio Balducci move ambiguously across terrains, susceptible to more than one meaning and conceptualisation. The filmic works addressed in this book follow this model too. Douglas Gordon's *24 hour psycho back and forth and to and fro* (2008), for example, bestows on moving images something like the conventional stillness of a museum object only to exceed this in protracted, yet still present, motion. In all of these examples the act of becoming irregular, of functioning intermittently or intermediately between the displayed and the performed, works, borrowing from Lefebvre, to 'produce a lacuna, a hole in time, to be filled by an invention, a creation.'[32] Within *theanyspacewhatever* this lacuna is occupied by Douglas Gordon and Rirkrit Tiravanija's *Cinema Liberté/Bar Lounge* (2008), a space presented to me as a 'lull in the action', an intermission in which visitors receive attention and remain still. The practices returning in Chapter 3 work through and signal a sort of museological interruption of disappearing artistic forms. By returning to the relational, *theanyspacewhatever* and *Double Agent* intervene within the linearity of an art historical genealogy.

Moving between two case studies in each chapter, linked to a few particular theoretic texts, this book traces different characterisations of the intersection between display and performance. In Chapter 1, the intermittency is between the pictorial and the theatrical; in Chapter 2, between the representational and the actional; in Chapter 3, and the relational returns it encodes, between the symbolic and the social, and specific interrelations both produced and represented; and in Chapter 4 in the visualisation and performative potential of visitors' perceptions. Invested in 'the necessity of the interval', within the case studies this book recollects, as in Blanchot's theory, 'attention is between the one and the other' and intermittently constructs these associations of objects as displayed and performed.[33] Moving from one form to another according to visitors' perceptions, the exhibitions addressed in this book operate like Rita McBride's *Arena* (1997) within *The World as a Stage*. Presenting original relations between practices of display and performance, my analysis has shown how acts of curation, visitation, and attention operate between the paradigms of these modes of expression and therefore within a dual temporality, which incorporates discontinuous composition, referential returns, and belated encounters. In this way, *Theatre, Exhibition, and Curation* presents a model of performance which flickers between material object and performed enactment so that, by assessing and critiquing these events, the potential of performance as something not restricted to or arrested within a single rhythmic formulation, temporal moment, or structure might begin to be imagined.

'Dancing: Dancing as visual arts material.'[34]

Emerging through an etymology which itself has the implication of movement from one state of being to another, the 'events' (from the Latin *evenire*) which this book describes come forth, emerge through the re-framing of the concept of exhibition as something which is defined by the intersection of processes that originate with display and performance. Communicating in terms outside of the expansion of concepts of the latter which the prevalence of a certain kind of 'staging of staging' enables, these exhibition events also offer the opportunity, as I suggested in the introduction to this book, to reflect on how specific large-scale and high-profile institutions of display are currently conceptualising their own processes and potential. Jon McKenzie has reminded us that 'terms frequently employed as synonyms for performance are *capability, operation, function,* and *efficiency*.'[35] In relation to ideas of purpose and productivity, it is noteworthy to observe in the final moments of this book an increasing presence of dance in contemporary art institutions with regards to which *Move* represents just one example. Dance has had a strong presence in Catherine Wood's performance programmes at Tate, prominent within the Tank's first season, *Art in Action* (2012), with contributions from Nina Beier, Anne Teresa De Keersmaeker, Boris Charmatz, and others, and more recently Wood has collaborated with the latter for the 2015 proposition *If Tate Modern was Musée de la danse?* In another sphere, Frieze London 2014 also accommodated a new 'Live' section of performance-based installations, including work by Franz Erhard Walther, also represented in *Move*, within its commercial vistas.

While many dance practitioners exhibit a preference for showing their work in gallery contexts, at the same time dance, it seems to me, is being called on by art institutions to stand in for broader categories of live work and to perform as a kind of synecdoche or referent of other forms of performance. 'In the past two decades,' writes Lepecki, but most prominently over the past 10 years, dance and choreography have become inescapable forces in contemporary art.' Lepecki's attitude to this association is hopeful, focused on the ways in which dance might offer to the visual arts techniques of political empowerment, 'not mere conceptual propositions but actual *possibilities* for action.'[36] Claire Bishop's stance is less optimistic. While observing too that dance in the museum has 'displaced all talk about performance as a component of parallel programming to exhibitions,' Bishop suggests that the specific lineages of dance embraced by arts institutions have an aesthetic well-suited to 'visual art's critique of theatricality, while offering an austere, pared-down beauty that also supplies a plenitude missing from so much contemporary visual art performance, with its preference for the authenticity of the unrehearsed.'[37] From either position, this emphasis on dance within the museum seems to follow too neatly a theoretical preference for dematerialisation and a linear transition from object to performance (to dance) which Senior Curator of International Art (Performance) Catherine Wood, from the position of battling for a museological place for the latter, has also critiqued.

My experience of *If Tate Modern was Musée de la danse?* – initiated by Wood and Director of Musée de la danse, choreographer and dancer Boris Charmatz – began on the fourth floor of Tate Modern in a gallery titled 'Structure and Clarity.' Dancer Asha Thomas is performing something of Alvin Ailey's *Revelations* (1960) for me and for a friend who are the only other people in the room and have thereby, somehow, identified ourselves as spectators. It is extraordinary to see this dance performed, but moreover, it is extraordinary to see this dance performed in this context. The dancer's movements seem to open up the gallery somehow and bring new ways of attending to a venue usually without musical accompaniment. I notice anew the height of the ceilings and that the paintings take up only the bottom quarter of the walls. And Thomas seems to be lifting, carrying, and thickening the rest of the space with her movement. In her essay on 'People and Things in the Museum' (2014), Wood suggests that the increasing presence of live performance in art galleries 'somehow also prompts a bigger question about the absolute de-attachment of this artwork from the world of material things.' That question might be, in Wood's words: 'Instead of conceiving of a progression evolving away from object towards action, as certain thinking about the recent increase of attention towards "performance" does, how might we pause and focus on the reality of our more complex ecology in which objects and actions are imperfectly co-existent, even inseparable, and certainly mutually influencing?'[38] This book might offer one such approach, the possibility of an experience and understanding of performance constructed not only in an ephemeral 'live' moment but through other media and in different forms, something found in a lacuna between the performed and displayed which may be encountered anew and imagined again through acts of theatre, exhibition, and curation.

Notes

1. Ian Hacking, *Historical Ontology* (Harvard: Harvard University Press, 2002), 1.
2. Ibid., 2.
3. Ibid.

4. Ibid., 18.
5. Ibid., 8.
6. P. A. Skantze, *Stillness in Motion in the Seventeenth-Century Theatre* (London and New York: Routledge, 2003), 19.
7. Joe Kelleher, *The Illuminated Theatre: Studies on the Suffering of Images* (London and New York: Routledge, 2015), 13. Original emphasis.
8. Johannes Birringer, 'Dancing in the Museum,' *PAJ: A Journal of Performance and Art* 99 (2011), 45.
9. Ibid., 47.
10. André Lepecki and Stephanie Rosenthal, 'Archive: Introduction,' in *Move: Choreographing You* [Exhibition Catalogue], ed. by Stephanie Rosenthal, (London: The Hayward Gallery, 2010), 133.
11. André Lepecki, 'Zones of Resonance: Mutual Formations in Dance and the Visual Arts Since the 1960s,' in *Move: Choreographing You* [Exhibition Catalogue] ed. by Stephanie Rosenthal, 156.
12. Erin Brannigan, 'Dance and the Gallery: Curation as Revision,' *Dance Research Journal* 47:1 (2015), 14.
13. Lepecki, 'Zones of Resonance,' 157.
14. Lepecki and Rosenthal, 'Archive: Introduction,' 133.
15. The subtitles in this concluding chapter refer to subsections of the interactive digital archive co-curated by Stephanie Rosenthal and André Lepecki as part of the exhibition *Move: Choreographing You* (Hayward Gallery, London, 2010–11). These final pages draw on Rosenthal and Lepecki's archival categories to structure some final remarks and reflections.
16. Lepecki, 'Zones of Resonance,' 157.
17. Ibid., 154.
18. Stephanie Rosenthal, 'Choreographies in the Visual Arts,' in *Move: Choreographing You* [Exhibition Catalogue], ed. Stephanie Rosenthal, 11–12 and 17.
19. Ibid., 8.
20. Nicolas Bourriaud, *Relational Aesthetics*, trans. Simon Pleasance, Fronza Woods, and Mathieu Copeland, (Dijon: les presses du réel, 2002), 16.
21. Henri Lefebvre, *Rhythmanalysis: Space, Time and Everyday Life*, trans. Stuart Elden and Gerald Moore (London: Bloomsbury 2013 [1992]), 17.
22. The subtitles in this concluding chapter refer to subsections of the interactive digital archive co-curated by Stephanie Rosenthal and André Lepecki as part of the exhibition *Move: Choreographing You* (Hayward Gallery, London, 2010–11). These final pages draw on Rosenthal and Lepecki's archival categories to structure some final remarks and reflections.
23. Lepecki, 'Zones of Resonance,' 158.
24. Bourriaud, *Relational Aesthetics*, 28.
25. Rosenthal, 'Choreographies in the Visual Arts,' 10.
26. Lepecki, 'Zones of Resonance,' 152.
27. The subtitles in this concluding chapter refer to subsections of the interactive digital archive co-curated by Stephanie Rosenthal and André Lepecki as part of the exhibition *Move: Choreographing You* (Hayward Gallery, London, 2010–11). These final pages draw on Rosenthal and Lepecki's archival categories to structure some final remarks and reflections.
28. Ibid., 158.
29. Henri Bergson, *Matter and Memory*, trans. Nancy M. Paul and W. Scott Palmer (London: George Allen & Unwin Ltd, 1950 [1911]), 128.

30. Hal Foster, *The Return of the Real: The Avant-Garde at the End of the Century* (Cambridge, Mass.: MIT Press 1996), 28.
31. Maurice Blanchot, *The Infinite Conversation*, trans. Susan Hanson (Minneapolis and London: University of Minnesota Press, 1993 [1969]), 121.
32. Lefebvre, *Rhythmanalysis*, 44.
33. Blanchot, *The Infinite Conversation*, 75 and 213.
34. The subtitles in this concluding chapter refer to subsections of the interactive digital archive co-curated by Stephanie Rosenthal and André Lepecki as part of the exhibition *Move: Choreographing You* (Hayward Gallery, London, 2010–11). These final pages draw on Rosenthal and Lepecki's archival categories to structure some final remarks and reflections.
35. Jon McKenzie, *Perform or Else: From Discipline to Performance* (London and New York: Routledge, 2002), 97.
36. Lepecki, 'Zones of Resonance,' 155. Original emphasis.
37. Claire Bishop, 'The Perils and Possibilities of Dance in the Museum: Tate, MoMA, and Whitney,' *Dance Research Journal* 46:3 (2014), 63 and 72.
38. Catherine Wood, 'People and Things in the Museum,' in *Choreographing Exhibitions*, ed. Mathieu Copeland (Dijon: Les presse du réel, 2014), 115 and 118.

Primary Curated Exhibition and Performance Sources

Marina Abramović and Hans Ulrich Obrist, *Marina Abramović Presents...* presented at the Whitworth Art Gallery, Manchester from 3 to 19 July 2009.

Claire Bishop and Mark Sladen, *Double Agent*, presented at the Institute of Contemporary Arts (ICA), London from 14 February to 6 April 2008.

Nicholas Cullinan and Iria Candela, The Unilever Series: *FILM* by Tacita Dean, presented at Tate Modern, London from 11 October 2011 to 11 March 2012.

Elmgreen & Dragset and Tim Etchells, *Drama Queens*, performed at the Old Vic Theatre, London on 12 October 2008.

Stephanie Rosenthal, *Move: Choreographing You*, presented at the Hayward Gallery, London from 13 October 2010 to 9 January 2011.

Nancy Spector, *theanyspacewhatever*, presented at the Solomon R. Guggenheim Museum, New York from 24 October 2008 to 7 January 2009.

Catherine Wood and Capucine Perrot, *BMW Tate Live 2012: Performance Room*, curated by Tate Modern, London from 22 March to 28 June 2012.

Catherine Wood and Jessica Morgan, *The World as a Stage*, presented at Tate Modern, London from 24 October 2007 to 1 January 2008.

Barnaby Wright, *Frank Auerbach: London Building Sites 1952–62* presented at the Courtauld Gallery, London from 16 October 2009 to 17 January 2010.

Barnaby Wright, *Renoir at the Theatre: Looking at La Loge* presented at the Courtauld Gallery, London from 21 February to 25 May 2008.

Bibliography

Agamben, Giorgio. 'Notes on Gesture.' In *Infancy & History: Essays on the Destruction of Experience*. Translated by Liz Heron, 133–140. London and New York: Verso, 1993.

———. *Potentialities: Collected Essays in Philosophy*. Translated by Daniel Heller-Roazen. Stanford: Stanford University Press, 1999.

———. *The Signature of All Things: On Method*. Translated by Luca D'Isanto and Kevin Attell. New York: Zone, 2009.

———. 'What is the Contemporary?' In *What Is an Apparatus?: And Other Essays*. Translated by David Kishik and Stefan Pedatella, 39–54. Stanford: Stanford University Press, 2009.

Alpers, Svetlana. 'The Museum as a Way of Seeing.' In *Exhibiting Cultures: The Poetics and Politics of Museum Display*. Edited by Ivan Karp and Steven D. Lavine, 26–32. Washington, DC, and London: Smithsonian Institution Press, 1991.

Althusser, Louis. 'Ideology and Ideological State Apparatuses (Notes towards an Investigation).' In *Lenin and Philosophy and Other Essays*. Translated by Ben Brewster, 127–186. New York: Monthly Review Press, 1971.

Artaud, Antonin. *The Theatre and Its Double*. Translated by Victor Corti. London: Alma Classics, 2013 [1964].

Augé, Marc. *Non-places: Introduction to an Anthropology of Supermodernity*. Translated by John Howe. London and New York: Verso, 1995.

Auslander, Philip. *From Acting to Performance: Essays in Modernism and Postmodernism*. London and New York: Routledge, 1997.

———. *Liveness: Performance in a Mediatized Culture*. London and New York: Routledge, 1999.

———. 'The Performativity of Performance Art Documentation.' *Performing Arts Journal* 84 (2006): 1–10.

Barker, Emma. 'Introduction' to *Contemporary Cultures of Display*. Edited by Emma Barker, 8–21. London: Yale University Press in association with the Open University, 1999.

———, ed. *Contemporary Cultures of Display*. London: Yale University Press in association with the Open University, 1999.

Batchelor, David. *Minimalism*. London: Tate Gallery Publishing, 1997.

Battcock, Gregory, ed. *Minimal Art: A Critical Anthology*. London: Studio Vista, 1969.

Baudelaire, Charles. 'The Painter of Modern Life' [1863]. In *Baudelaire: Selected Writings on Art and Artists*. Translated by P. E. Charvet, 390–436. Cambridge: Cambridge University Press, 1972.

————. 'The Movement of Embodied Thought: The Representational Game of the Stage Zero of Signification in *Jérôme Bel*.' *Performance Research* 13:1 (2008): 35–41.

Bauer, Una. 'Jérôme Bel: An Interview.' *Performance Research* 13:1 (2008): 42–48.

Baxandall, Michael. 'Exhibiting Intention: Some Preconditions for the Visual Display of Culturally Purposeful Objects.' In *Exhibiting Cultures: The Poetics and Politics of Museum Display*. Edited by Ivan Karp and Steven D. Lavine, 33–41. Washington, DC, and London: Smithsonian Institution Press, 1991.

Benjamin, Walter. 'The Work of Art in the Age of Mechanical Reproduction' [1936]. In *Illuminations*. Edited by Hannah Arendt and translated by Harry Zohn, 211–244. London: Jonathan Cape Ltd, 1970.

————. *The Arcades Project*. Translated by Howard Eiland and Kevin McLaughlin. Cambridge, Mass., and London: Belknap Press, 1999.

Bennett, Susan. *Theatre Audiences: A Theory of Production and Reception*. London and New York: Routledge, 1990.

————. *Theatre & Museums*. Houndmills: Palgrave Macmillan, 2012.

Bennett, Tony. 'The Exhibitionary Complex.' In *Thinking About Exhibitions*. Edited by Reesa Greenberg, Bruce W. Ferguson, and Sandy Nairne, 81–113. London and New York: Routledge, 1996.

Bergson, Henri. *Matter and Memory*. Translated by Nancy M. Paul and W. Scott Palmer. London: George Allen and Unwin, 1950 [1911].

Biesenbach, Klaus. 'Sympathy for the Devil.' In *Douglas Gordon: Timeline*. Edited by Douglas Gordon and Klaus Biesenbach, 10–31. New York: The Museum of Modern Art, 2006.

Birringer, Johannes. 'Interactive Environments and Digital Perception.' In *A Cosmology of Performance: Testimony from the Future, Evidence of the Past*. Edited by Judie Christie, Richard Gough, and Daniel Peter Watt, 87–93. London: Routledge, 2006.

———— 'Dancing in the Museum.' *PAJ: A Journal of Performance and Art* 99 (2011): 44–52.

Bishop, Claire. 'Antagonism and Relational Aesthetics.' *October* 110 (2004): 51–79.

————. *Artificial Hells: Participatory Art and the Politics of Spectatorship*. London and New York: Verso, 2012.

————. 'The Perils and Possibilities of Dance in the Museum: Tate, MoMA, and Whitney.' *Dance Research Journal* 46:3 (2014): 62–76.

Bishop, Claire, and Phil Collins. 'Staging a Terrain of Shared Desire.' In *Double Agent* [Exhibition Catalogue]. Edited by Claire Bishop and Silvia Tramontana, 28–33. London: ICA, 2008.

Bishop, Claire, and Mark Sladen. 'Discussion with Donelle Woolford at the ICA.' In *Double Agent* [Exhibition Catalogue]. Edited by Claire Bishop and Silvia Tramontana, 78–91. London: ICA, 2008.

Bishop, Claire, and Silvia Tramontana, eds. *Double Agent* [Exhibition Catalogue]. London: ICA, 2008.

Blake, Bill. *Theatre & the Digital*. Houndmills: Palgrave Macmillan, 2014.

Blanchot, Maurice. *The Infinite Conversation*. Translated by Susan Hanson. Minneapolis and London: University of Minnesota Press, 1993 [1969].

Blazwick, Iwaona and Simon Wilson, eds. *Tate Modern: The Handbook*. London: Tate Publishing, 2000.

Bleeker, Maaike. *Visuality in the Theatre: The Locus of Looking.* Houndmills: Palgrave Macmillan, 2008.

Bochner, Mel. 'Serial Art, Systems, Solipsism' [1967]. In *Minimal Art: A Critical Anthology.* Edited by Gregory Battcock, 92–102. London: Studio Vista, 1969.

Bourriaud, Nicolas. *Relational Aesthetics.* Translated by Simon Pleasance, Fronza Woods, and Mathieu Copeland. Dijon: les presses du réel, 2002.

——— 'The Reversibility of the Real: Nicolas Bourriaud on Pierre Huyghe.' *Tate Etc.* 7 (2006). Accessed 4 August 2015. http://www.tate.org.uk/context-comment/articles/reversibility-real.

Brannigan, Erin. 'Dance and the Gallery: Curation as Revision.' *Dance Research Journal* 47:1 (2015): 5–25.

Brendan, Roy, Amy Budd, Tom Jones, et al. 'Transcript of *Instant Narrative (IN)*, 2006–2008.' In *Double Agent* [Exhibition Catalogue]. Edited by Claire Bishop and Silvia Tramontana, 40–47. London: ICA, 2008.

Brine, Daniel, ed. *The Live Art Almanac.* London: Live Art Development Agency, 2008.

Brook, Peter. *The Empty Space.* London: Penguin, 1990 [1968].

Brown, Bill. *Thing Theory.* In *Things.* Edited by Bill Brown. Chicago and London: University of Chicago Press, 1–16.

———, ed. *Things.* Chicago and London: University of Chicago Press, 2004.

Cage, John. *Silence: Lectures and Writings.* Middletown, Conn.: Wesleyan University Press, 1973.

Candela, Emily. '*Double Agent* Teachers' Pack.' Accessed 4 August 2015. https://www.ica.org.uk/sites/default/files/downloads/ICA%20Educator's%20Resource%20Pack%20Double%20Agent.pdf.

Carlson, Marvin. *The Haunted Stage: The Theatre as Memory Machine.* Ann Arbor: University of Michigan Press: 2003.

Casey, Valerie. 'Staging Meaning: Performance in the Modern Museum.' *TDR: The Drama Review* 49:3 (2005): 78–95.

Cherix, Christophe. 'Preface' to *A Brief History of Curating.* Edited by Hans Ulrich Obrist, 5–9. Zurich: JRP/Ringier & les presses du réel, 2008.

Christie, Judie, Richard Gough, and Daniel Peter Watt, eds. *A Cosmology of Performance: Testimony from the Future, Evidence of the Past.* London: Routledge, 2006.

Clifford, James. *The Predicament of Culture: Twentieth-Century Ethnography, Literature, and Art.* Harvard: Harvard University Press, 1988.

Cool, Marie and Fabio Balducci, eds. *Marie Cool Fabio Balducci: Untitled (Prayers) 1996–2005.* Translated by Julien Bismuth, Charles Penwarden and Simon Turner. London: South London Gallery, 2005.

Copeland, Mathieu, ed. *Choreographing Exhibitions.* Dijon: les presses du réel, 2014.

Courtauld Gallery. *Frank Auerbach: London Building Sites 1952–62* [Exhibition Leaflet]. Produced on the occasion of the *Frank Auerbach: London Building Sites 1952–62* exhibition, London, 16 October 2009–17 January 2010.

———. '*Renoir at the Theatre: Looking at La Loge.*' Accessed 20 August 2015. http://courtauld.ac.uk/gallery/what-on/exhibitions-displays/archive/renoir-at-the-theatre-looking-at-la-loge.

Crary, Jonathan. *Techniques of the Observer: On Vision and Modernity in the Nineteenth Century.* Cambridge, Mass., and London: MIT Press, 2001 [1992].

Crimp, Douglas. 'Pictures' [1977]. *X-tra Contemporary Art Quarterly* 8 (2005): 17–30.

Čufer, Eda. 'Don't!' In *A Bigger Splash: Painting after Performance* [Exhibition Catalogue]. Edited by Catherine Wood, 23–29. London: Tate Publishing, 2012.

Danby, Charles, ed. *The Tanks Programme Notes*. London: Pureprint Group, 2012.

Daston, Lorraine, 'Introduction: Speechless.' In *Things That Talk: Object Lessons from Art and Science*. Edited by Lorraine Daston, 9–26. New York: Zone, 2004.

———, ed. Things That Talk: Object Lessons from Art and Science. New York: Zone, 2004.

de Certeau, Michel. *The Practice of Everyday Life*. Translated by Steven Rendell. Berkeley: University of California Press, 1984.

———. *The Practice of Everyday Life, Volume 2: Living & Cooking*. Translated by Timothy Tomasik. Minneapolis: University of Minnesota Press, 1998.

Deleuze, Gilles. *Cinema 1: The Movement – Image*. Translated by Barbara Habberjam and Hugh Tomlinson. London: Continuum, 1986.

———. *Francis Bacon: The Logic of Sensation*. Translated by Daniel W. Smith, London and New York: Continuum, 2004 [1981].

DeLillo, Don. *Point Omega*. London: Pan Macmillan, 2010.

Dercon, Chris. 'An Open Manifesto: 15 Weeks of Art in Action.' In *The Tanks Programme Notes*. Edited by Charles Danby, 2. London: Pureprint Group, 2012.

———.'Foreword' to *A Bigger Splash: Painting after Performance* [Exhibition Catalogue]. Edited by Catherine Wood, 6–7. London: Tate Publishing, 2012.

Didi-Huberman, Georges. *Confronting Images: Questioning the Ends of a Certain History of Art*. Translated by John Goodman. Pennsylvania: Pennsylvania State University Press, 2005.

Dixon, Steve. *Digital Performance: A History of New Media in Theater, Dance, Performance Art, and Installation*. Cambridge, Mass., and London: MIT Press, 2007.

Downey, Anthony. 'Towards a Politics of (Relational) Aesthetics.' *Third Text* 21:3 (2007), 267–275.

Dutton, Richard, ed. *The Oxford Handbook of Early Modern Theatre*. Oxford: Oxford University Press, 2009.

Elmgreen, Michael and Dragset, Ingar. 'The Incidental Self' [Art Review Artist Publication]. *Art Review* 26 (2008).

Elmgreen, Michael, Ingar Dragset, and Tim Etchells. *Drama Queens: A Play by Elmgreen & Dragset with Text by Tim Etchells*. London: The Old Vic, 2008.

Etchells, Tim. *Certain Fragments: Contemporary Performance and Forced Entertainment*. London and New York: Routledge, 1999.

Feaver, William. *Frank Auerbach*. New York: Rizzoli, 2009.

Fenves, Peter. *Arresting Language: From Leibniz to Benjamin*. Stanford: Stanford University Press, 2001.

Ferguson, Bruce W., Reesa Greenberg, and Sandy Nairne, 'Introduction' to *Thinking about Exhibitions*. Edited by Reesa Greenberg, Bruce W. Ferguson, and Sandy Nairne, 1–3. London and New York: Routledge, 1996.

———, eds. *Thinking About Exhibitions*. London and New York: Routledge, 1996.

Flusser, Vilém. *Towards a Philosophy of Photography*. Translated by Anthony Mathews. London: Reaktion Books, 2000.

Foster, Hal. *The Return of the Real: The Avant-Garde at the End of the Century*. Cambridge, Mass.: MIT Press, 1996.

Fowler, James. 'Collecting Live Performance.' In *Museums and the Future of Collecting*. Edited by Simon J. Knell, 242–249. Aldershot: Ashgate, 2004.

Fried, Michael. 'Art and Objecthood' [1967]. In *Minimal Art: A Critical Anthology.* Edited by Gregory Battcock, 116–147. London: Studio Vista, 1969.

Giannachi, Gabriella. *Virtual Theatres: An Introduction.* London and New York: Routledge, 2004.

———. 'The Making of Empty Stages by Tim Etchells and Hugo Glendinning.' *Leonardo Electronic Almanac (Mish Mash)* 17:1 (2011): 102–117.

Gillick, Liam. 'Contingent Factors: A Response to Claire Bishop's "Antagonism and Relational Aesthetics".' *October* 115 (2006): 95–107.

Goldberg, Roselee. *Performance: Live Art Since the 60s.* London: Thames and Hudson, 1998.

———. 'One Hundred Years' In *Live: Art and Performance.* Edited by Adrian Heathfield, 176–180. London: Tate Publishing, 2004.

———. *Performance Art: From Futurism to the Present.* London and New York: Thames and Hudson, 2011 [1979].

Goumarre, Laurent. In *Marie Cool Fabio Balducci: Untitled (Prayers) 1996–2005.* Edited by Marie Cool and Fabio Balducci. Translated by Julien Bismuth, Charles Penwarden and Simon Turner, 5–15. London: South London Gallery, 2005.

Greenhalgh, Paul. Ephemeral Vistas: The Expositions Universelles, Great Exhibitions and World's Fairs, 1851–1939. Manchester: Manchester University Press, 1988.

Groys, Boris. *Art Power.* Cambridge, Mass., and London: MIT Press, 2008.

Guy, Georgina. 'Out of Sync: Curation, Participation and Reactional Pathways.' *Performance Research* 16:3 On Participation and Synchronization (2011): 89–93. http://www.tandfonline.com/.

———. 'NOTES on a return: Durations of the Missed and the Previously Unvisited.' *Performance Research* 17:5 On Duration (2012): 135–139.

Hacking, Ian. *Historical Ontology.* Harvard: Harvard University Press, 2002.

Hao, Sophia Yadong and Matthew Hearn, eds. *NOTES on a return* [Exhibition Catalogue], Sunderland: Art Editions North, 2010.

Harvie, Jen. 'Agency and Complicity in "A Special Civic Room": London's Tate Modern Turbine Hall.' In *Performance and the City.* Edited by D.J. Hopkins, Shelley Orr and Kim Solga, 204–217. Houndmills: Palgrave Macmillan, 2009.

———. 'Democracy and Neo-liberalism in Art's Social Turn and Roger Hiorns's *Seizure*.' *Performance Research* 16:2 Performing Publics (2011): 113–123.

———. *Fair Play – Art, Performance and Neoliberalism.* Houndmills: Palgrave Macmillan, 2013.

Heathfield, Adrian, ed. *Small Acts: Performance, the Millennium and the Marking of Time.* London: Black Dog Publishing, 2000.

———. 'Alive.' In *Live: Art and Performance.* Edited by Adrian Heathfield, 6–13. London: Tate Publishing, 2004.

——— and Amelia Jones, ed. *Perform, Repeat, Record: Live Art in History.* London: Intellect, 2012.

———, ed. *Live: Art and Performance.* London: Tate Publishing, 2004.

Herzog, Jacques. 'From an Industrial Underground.' In *The Tanks Programme Notes.* Edited by Charles Danby, 34–35. London: Pureprint Group, 2012.

Hibberd, Sarah and Richard Wrigley, ed. 'Introduction' to *Art, Theatre, and Opera in Paris, 1750–1850: Exchanges and Tensions,* 1–16. London: Ashgate, 2014.

Hoffman, Jens and Joan Jonas. *Perform.* London: Thames and Hudson, 2005.

House, John, Ernst Vegelin van Claerbergen and Barnaby Wright, 'Catalogue.' In *Renoir at the Theatre: Looking at La Loge* [Exhibition Catalogue]. Edited by Ernst Vegelin van Claerbergen and Barnaby Wright, 64–90. London: The Courtauld Gallery and Paul Holberton Publishing, 2008.

——. 'Modernity in Microcosm: Renoir's *Loges* in Context.' In *Renoir at the Theatre: Looking at La Loge* [Exhibition Catalogue]. Edited by Ernst Vegelin van Claerbergen and Barnaby Wright, 26–43. London: The Courtauld Gallery and Paul Holberton Publishing, 2008.

Institute of Contemporary Arts (ICA). '*Double Agent*' [Gallery Guide]. Produced on the occasion of the *Double Agent* exhibition, London, 14 February–6 April 2008.

——. '*Double Agent*.' Accessed 4 August 2015. https://www.ica.org.uk/whats-on/double-agent.

Ireson, Nancy. 'The Lure of the *Loge*.' In *Renoir at the Theatre: Looking at La Loge* [Exhibition Catalogue]. Edited by Ernst Vegelin van Claerbergen and Barnaby Wright, 10–25. London: The Courtauld Gallery and Paul Holberton Publishing, 2008.

Jackson, Shannon. *Professing Performance: Theatre in the Academy from Philology to Performativity*. Cambridge: Cambridge University Press, 2004.

——. *Social Works: Performing Art, Supporting Publics*. New York and London: Routledge, 2011.

——. 'Working Publics.' *Performance Research* 16:2 Performing Publics (2011): 8–13.

Jones, Amelia. '"Presence" in Absentia: Experiencing Performance as Documentation.' *Art Journal* 56:4 (1997): 11–18.

——. '"The Artist is Present": Artistic Re-enactments and the Impossibility of Presence.' *TDR/The Drama Review*, 55:1 (2011): 16–45.

——. 'Timeline of Ideas: Live Art in (Art) History, a Primarily European-US-based Trajectory of Debates and Exhibitions Relating to Performance Documentation and Re-enactments.' In *Perform, Repeat, Record: Live Art in History*. Edited by Adrian Heathfield and Amelia Jones, 425–434. London: Intellect, 2012.

Jones, Caroline A. 'Talking Pictures: Clement Greenberg's Pollock.' In *Things That Talk: Object Lessons from Art and Science*. Edited by Lorraine Daston, 329–374. New York: Zone, 2004.

Joseph, Branden W. 'Angela Bulloch: Ambivalent Objects.' In *theanyspacewhatever* [Exhibition Catalogue]. Edited by Nancy Spector, 31–38. New York: Solomon R. Guggenheim Museum, 2008.

Karp, Ivan and Steven D. Lavine, eds. *Exhibiting Cultures: The Poetics and Politics of Museum Display*. Washington, DC, and London: Smithsonian Institution Press, 1991.

Karp, Ivan, Corinne A. Kratz, Lynn Szwaja, and Tomás Ybarra-Frausto, eds. *Museum Frictions: Public Cultures/Global Transformation*. Durham and London: Duke University Press, 2006.

Kaye, Nick. *Site-Specific Art: Performance, Place and Documentation*. London and New York: Routledge, 2000.

Kelleher, Joe. *The Illuminated Theatre: Studies on the Suffering of Images*. London and New York: Routledge, 2015.

Kelsey, John. '*theanyspacewhatever*.' *Artforum* (2009). Accessed 4 August 2015. http://artforum.com/inprint/id=22123.

Kermode, Frank. *Forms of Attention: Botticelli and Hamlet*. Chicago: University of Chicago Press, 2011 [1985].

Kirshenblatt-Gimblett, Barbara. 'Objects of Ethnography.' In *Exhibiting Cultures: The Poetics and Politics of Museum Display*. Edited by Ivan Karp and Steven D. Lavine, 386–443. Washington, DC, and London: Smithsonian Institution Press, 1991.

——. *Destination Culture: Tourism, Museums, and Heritage*. Berkeley: University of California Press, 1998.

———. 'Exhibitionary Complexes.' In *Museum Frictions: Public Cultures/ Global Transformation.* Edited by Ivan Karp, Corinne A. Kratz, Lynn Szwaja, and Tomás Ybarra-Frausto, 35–45. Durham and London: Duke University Press, 2006.

———. 'World Heritage and Cultural Economics.' In *Museum Frictions: Public Cultures/ Global Transformation.* Edited by Ivan Karp, Corinne A. Kratz, Lynn Szwaja, and Tomás Ybarra-Frausto, 161–202. Durham and London: Duke University Press, 2006.

Knell, Simon J., ed. *Museums and the Future of Collecting.* Aldershot: Ashgate, 2004.

Koerner, Joseph Leo. 'Bosch's Equipment.' In *Things That Talk: Object Lessons from Art and Science.* Edited by Lorraine Daston, 27–66. New York: Zone, 2004.

Kraak, Menno-Jan. 'Geovisualization and Time – New Opportunities for the Space-Time Cube.' In *Geographic Visualization: Concepts, Tools and Applications.* Edited by Martin Dodge, Mary McDerby and Martin Turner, 293–306. London: Wiley, 2008.

Krauss, Rosalind. 'LeWitt in Progress.' *October* 6 (1978): 46–60.

———. *Passages in Modern Sculpture.* Cambridge, Mass., and London: MIT Press, 1981 [1977]).

———. 'Rosalind Krauss on Tacita Dean's FILM.' Tate. Last modified 8 March 2012. http://www.tate.org.uk/context-comment/video/rosalind-krauss-on-tacita-deans-film.

Krens, Thomas. 'Preface' to *theanyspacewhatever* [Exhibition Catalogue]. Edited by Nancy Spector, 6–7. New York: Solomon R. Guggenheim Museum, 2008.

Kuburović, Branislava. 'Sta(i)r Falling.' *Performance Research* 16:1 (2011): 91–101.

Lange, Christy. 'Douglas Gordon: Ten Years Ago Today.' In *theanyspacewhatever* [Exhibition Catalogue]. Edited by Nancy Spector, 65–72. New York: Solomon R. Guggenheim Museum, 2008.

Laurenson, Pip and Vivian van Saaze. 'Collecting Performance-based Art: New Challenges and Shifting Perspectives.' In *Performativity in the Gallery: Staging Interactive Encounters.* Edited by Outi Remes, Laura MacCulloch, and Marika Leino, 27–41. Bern: Peter Lang, 2014.

Lefebvre, Henri. *Rhythmanalysis: Space, Time and Everyday Life.* Translated by Stuart Elden and Gerald Moore. London: Bloomsbury 2013 [1992].

Lepecki, André. 'Zones of Resonance: Mutual formations in Dance and the Visual Arts Since the 1960s.' In *Move: Choreographing You* [Exhibition Catalogue]. Edited by Stephanie Rosenthal, 152–163. London: The Hayward Gallery, 2010.

Lepecki, André, and Stephanie Rosenthal. 'Archive: Introduction.' In *Move: Choreographing You* [Exhibition Catalogue]. Edited by Stephanie Rosenthal, 133. London: The Hayward Gallery, 2010.

Lind, Maria, 'Performing the Curatorial: An Introduction.' In *Performing the Curatorial: Within and Beyond Art.* Edited by Maria Lind, 8–20. Berlin: Sternberg Press, 2012.

———, ed. Performing the Curatorial: Within and Beyond Art. Berlin: Sternberg Press, 2012.

Lippard, Lucy. *Six Years: The Dematerialization of the Art Object from 1966 to 1972.* Berkeley: University of California Press, 1997 [1973].

Manchester International Festival. 'Marina Abramović Presents...' Accessed 16 July 2009. http://mif.co.uk/event/marina-abramovic-presents/.

Massey, Doreen. *For Space.* London and Thousand Oaks, Calif.: SAGE, 2005.

McKenzie, Jon. *Perform or Else: From Discipline to Performance*. London and New York: Routledge, 2002.

Meisel, Martin. *Realizations: Narrative, Pictorial, and Theatrical Arts in Nineteenth-Century England*. Princeton: Princeton University Press, 1984.

Mondzain, Marie-José. 'Chapter 1 (Excerpt) The Images That Give Birth To Us.' Translated by Patrick Ffrench for Mondzain's presentation at *Caves*, an event convened by Alan Read in the Anatomy Theatre and Museum, King's College London on 14 February 2011. This section is published in French as 'Les images qui nous font naître,' in *Homo Spectator*. Paris: Bayard, 2007.

Monks, Aoife. *The Actor in Costume*. Houndmills: Palgrave Macmillan, 2010.

———. 'Collecting Ghosts: Actors, Anecdotes and Objects at the Theatre.' *Contemporary Theatre Review* 23.2 (2012): 146–152.

Morgan, Jessica. 'The World as a Stage.' In *The World as a Stage* [Exhibition Catalogue]. Edited by Jessica Morgan and Catherine Wood, 7–11. London: Tate Publishing, 2007.

Morgan, Jessica and Catherine Wood, eds. 'It's All True.' *Tate Etc.* 11 (2007): 71–75.

———. *The World as a Stage* [Exhibition Catalogue]. London: Tate Publishing, 2007.

Mulvey, Laura *Death 24x a Second: Stillness and the Moving Image*. London: Reaktion Books, 2006.

Murray, Timothy. *Digital Baroque: New Media Art and Cinematic Folds*. Minneapolis: University of Minnesota Press, 2008.

Noble, Kathy. '*Marina Abramović Presents*.' *Frieze*. Last modified 21 August 2009. http://blog.frieze.com/marina_abramovic_presents/.

Norden, Linda. 'Night at the Museum.' *Artforum* (2008). Accessed 4 August 2015. http://artforum.com/diary/id=21388.

Obrist, Hans Ulrich, ed. *A Brief History of Curating*. Zurich: JRP/Ringier and les presses du réel, 2008.

Obrist, Hans Ulrich, and Daniel Birnbaum. 'Philippe Parreno: Dust.' In *theanyspacewhatever* [Exhibition Catalogue]. Edited by Nancy Spector, 99–104. New York: Solomon R. Guggenheim Museum, 2008.

O'Doherty, Brian. *Inside the White Cube: The Ideology of the Gallery Space*. Expanded Edition. Berkley: University of California Press, 1999 [1976].

O'Neill, Paul. 'The Curatorial Turn: From Practice to Discourse.' In *Issues in Curating Contemporary Art and Performance*. Edited by Judith Rugg and Michèle Sedgwick, 13–28. Bristol: Intellect, 2007.

O'Reilly, Kira. 'Notes for Whitworth Art Gallery Staircase (North).' Accessed 10 November 2011. http://www.kiraoreilly.com/blog/?p=216.

Oxford University Press. *OED Online*. Accessed 2008–present. http://www.oed.com.

Performa. 'Why Dance in the Art World? Jérôme Bel and RoseLee Goldberg in Conversation.' Last modified 13 September 2012. http://performa-arts.org/magazine/entry/why-dance-in-the-art-world-jerome-bel-and-roselee-goldberg-in-conversation.

Phelan, Peggy. *Unmarked: The Politics of Performance*. London and New York: Routledge, 1993.

———. 'Marina Abramović: Witnessing Shadows.' *Theatre Journal* 56:4 (2004): 569–577.

———. 'Shards of a History of Performance Art: Pollock and Namuth Through a Glass, Darkly.' In *A Companion to Narrative Theory*. Edited by James Phelan and Peter J. Rabinowitz, 499–514. Oxford: Blackwell, 2005.

———. 'Moving Centres.' In *Move: Choreographing You* [Exhibition Catalogue]. Edited by Stephanie Rosenthal, 22–31. London: The Hayward Gallery, 2010.

Preziosi, Donald and Claire J. Farago. 'General Introduction: What Are Museums For?' In *Grasping the World: The Idea of the Museum*. Edited by Donald Preziosi and Claire J. Farago, 1–21. Aldershot: Ashgate, 2004.

———, eds. Grasping the World: The Idea of the Museum. Aldershot: Ashgate, 2004.

Proust, Marcel. *In Search of Lost Time Volume III: The Guermantes Way*. Trans. by C. K. Scott Moncrieff and Terence Kilmartin. London: Vintage, 2000.

Rancière, Jacques. *The Politics of Aesthetics: The Distribution of the Sensible*. Trans. Gabriel Rockhill. London and New York: Continuum, 2004.

Read, Alan. *Theatre, Intimacy and Engagement: The Last Human Venue*. Houndmills: Palgrave Macmillan, 2009.

———. Theatre in the Expanded Field: Seven Approaches to Performance. London: Bloomsbury, 2013.

Reason, Matthew. 'Archive or Memory?: The Detritus of Live Performance.' *New Theatre Quarterly*, 19:1 (2003), 82–89.

———. 'Still Moving: The Revelation or Representation of Dance in Still Photography.' *Dance Research Journal*, 35–36 (2-1) (2003–2004): 43–67.

Remes, Outi, Laura MacCulloch, and Marika Leino, eds. *Performativity in the Gallery: Staging Interactive Encounters*. Bern: Peter Lang, 2014.

Rendell, Jane. *Art and Architecture: A Place Between*. London: I. B. Tauris, 2006.

Ribeiro, Aileen. 'The Art of Dress: Fashion in Renoir's *La Loge*.' In *Renoir at the Theatre: Looking at La Loge* [Exhibition Catalogue]. Edited by Ernst Vegelin van Claerbergen and Barnaby Wright, 44–63. London: The Courtauld Gallery and Paul Holberton Publishing, 2008.

Ridout, Nicholas. 'You look charming. You look enchanting. You look dazzling. You look breathtaking. You look unique. But you don't make an evening. You are not a brilliant idea. You are tiresome. You are not a rewarding subject. You are a theatrical blunder. You are not true to life.' *Tate Etc.* 11 (2007): 104–107.

———. 'Performance in the Service Economy: Outsourcing and Delegation.' In *Double Agent* [Exhibition Catalogue]. Edited by Claire Bishop and Silvia Tramontana, 126–131. London: ICA, 2008.

Rogozinski, Luciana. 'Winter Peacock.' In *Marie Cool Fabio Balducci: Untitled (Prayers) 1996–2005*. Edited by Marie Cool and Fabio Balducci. Translated by Julien Bismuth, Charles Penwarden and Simon Turner, 23–31. London: South London Gallery, 2005.

Rokem, Freddie. *Performing History: Theatrical Representations of the Past in Contemporary Theatre*. Iowa City: University of Iowa Press, 2000.

———. Philosophers & Thespians: Thinking Performance. Stanford: Stanford University Press, 2010.

Roms, Heike. 'Eye and Ear, Foot and Mouth: Mapping Performance in Three Journeys and One Withdrawal.' In *A Cosmology of Performance: Testimony from the Future, Evidence of the Past*. Edited by Judie Christie, Richard Gough and Daniel Peter Watt, 10–14. London: Routledge, 2006.

Rosenthal, Stephanie. 'Choreographies in the Visual Arts.' In *Move: Choreographing You* [Exhibition Catalogue]. Edited by Stephanie Rosenthal, 8–21. London: The Hayward Gallery, 2010.

———, ed. Move: Choreographing You [Exhibition Catalogue]. London: The Hayward Gallery, 2010.

Rugg, Judith, and Michèle Sedgwick, eds. *Issues in Curating Contemporary Art and Performance*. London: Intellect, 2007.

Sayre, Henry M. *The Object of Performance: The American Avant-Garde Since 1970*. Chicago and London: University of Chicago Press, 1989.

Schechner, Richard. *Performance Studies: An Introduction*. Second Edition. London and New York: Routledge, 2002.

Schneider, Rebecca. 'Performance Remains.' *Performance Research* 6:2 On Maps an Mapping (2001): 100–108.

———. 'The Document Performance.' In *The Live Art Almanac*. Edited by Daniel Brine, 117–120. London: Live Art Development Agency, 2008.

———. *Performing Remains: Art and War in Times of Theatrical Reenactment*. London and New York: Routledge, 2011.

Searle, Adrian. 'Marina Abramović Presents the "Unnerving and Unforgettable" at Manchester International Festival. Last modified 7 July 2009. http://www.theguardian.com/culture/video/2009/jul/06/marina-abramovic-manchester-festival-adrian-searle.

Serota, Nicholas. *Experience or Interpretation: The Dilemma of Museums of Modern Art*. London: Thames and Hudson, 2013 [1996].

Shalson, Lara. 'On Duration and Multiplicity.' *Performance Research* 17:5 On Duration (2012): 98–106.

Shepherd, Simon and Mick Wallis. *Drama/Theatre/Performance*. London and New York: Routledge, 2004.

Skantze, P.A. *Stillness in Motion in the Seventeenth-Century Theatre*. London and New York: Routledge, 2003.

Smithson, Robert. 'Earth' (excerpts from a symposium at the Andrew Dickson White Museum of Art, Cornell University, in 1969). In *Robert Smithson: The Collected Writings*. Edited by Jack Flam, 177–187. Berkeley: University of California Press, 1996.

Social Research Association. *Ethical Guidelines*. Accessed 10 January 2012. http://the-sra.org.uk/wp-content/uploads/ethics03.pdf.

Sofer, Andrew. 'Properties.' In *The Oxford Handbook of Early Modern Theatre*. Edited by Richard Dutton, 560–574. Oxford: Oxford University Press, 2009.

Solomon R. Guggenheim Museum. '*theanyspacewhatever*.' Accessed 4 August 2015, http://www.guggenheim.org/new-york/exhibitions/past/exhibit/1896.

———. '*theanyspacewhatever* Online Exhibition.' Accessed 4 August 2015, http://web.guggenheim.org/exhibitions/anyspace/exhibition.html.

Spector, Nancy. '*theanyspacewhatever*: An Exhibition in Ten Parts.' In *theanyspacewhatever* [Exhibition Catalogue]. Edited by Nancy Spector, 13–27. New York: Solomon R. Guggenheim Museum, 2008.

———, ed. *theanyspacewhatever* [Exhibition Catalogue]. New York: Solomon R. Guggenheim Museum, 2008.

Tate. 'BMW Tate Live 2012: Performance Room.' Accessed 15 July 2015. http://www.tate.org.uk/whats-on/tate-modern/eventseries/bmw-tate-live-2012-performance-room.

———. 'BMW Tate Live 2015: Performance Room.' Accessed 15 July 2015. http://www.tate.org.uk/whats-on/tate-modern/eventseries/bmw-tate-live-2015-performance-room.

———. 'BMW Tate Live: Performance Room – Jérôme Bel.' Accessed 15 July 2015. http://www.tate.org.uk/whats-on/tate-modern/music-and-live-performance/bmw-tate-live-performance-room-jerome-bel-shirtology.

———. 'BMW Tate Live: Performance Room – Pablo Bronstein.' Accessed 15 July 2015. http://www.tate.org.uk/whats-on/tate-modern/music-and-live-performance/bmw-tate-live-performance-room-pablo-bronstein.

———. 'BMW Tate Live: Performance Room – Harrell Fletcher.' Accessed 15 July 2015. http://www.tate.org.uk/whats-on/tate-modern/music-and-live-performance/bmw-tate-live-performance-room-harrell-fletcher.

———. 'BMW Tate Live: Performance Room – Emily Roysdon.' Accessed 15 July 2015. http://www.tate.org.uk/whats-on/tate-modern/music-and-live-performance/bmw-tate-live-performance-room-emily-roysdon-i-am.

———. 'BMW Tate Live: Screening of Performance Room series.' Tate. Accessed 15 July 2015. http://www.tate.org.uk/whats-on/tate-modern/film/bmw-tate-live-screening-performance-room-series.

———. 'Curator, Catherine Wood on Performance Art.' Last modified 20 March 2012. http://www.tate.org.uk/context-comment/video/curator-catherine-wood-on-performance-art.

———. 'New Tate Modern Tanks open to the public.' Last modified 16 July 2012. http://www.tate.org.uk/about/press-office/press-releases/new-tate-modern-tanks-open-public.

———. 'Rita McBride Interview by Discoteca Flaming Star.' In *UBS Openings: Saturday Live – Arena* [Event Leaflet], Saturday 27 October 2007, Tate Modern, London.

———. 'Tacita Dean on FILM: Interview.' Accessed 15 July 2015. http://www.tate.org.uk/whats-on/tate-modern/exhibition/unilever-series-tacita-dean-film.

———. 'The Unilever Series 2011: Tacita Dean.' Last modified 10 October 2011. http://www.tate.org.uk/about/press-office/press-releases/unilever-series-2011-tacita-dean.

———. *The World as a Stage* [Exhibition Leaflet]. Produced on the occasion of *The World as a Stage* exhibition, Tate Modern, London, 24 October 2007–1 January 2008.

———. 'The World as a Stage.' Accessed 20 August 2015. http://www.tate.org.uk/node/237078/default.shtm.

Taylor, Diana. *The Archive and the Repertoire: Performing Cultural Memory in the Americas*. Durham: Duke University Press, 2003.

Todoli. Vicente. 'Foreword' to *The World as a Stage* [Exhibition Catalogue]. Edited by Jessica Morgan and Catherine Wood, 5. London: Tate Publishing, 2007.

Vegelin van Claerbergen, Ernst, and Barnaby Wright, eds. *Renoir at the Theatre: Looking at La Loge* [Exhibition Catalogue]. London: The Courtauld Gallery and Paul Holberton Publishing, 2008.

Verhagen, Marcus. 'Elmgreen & Dragset: Inconvenient Truths.' *Art Review* 26 (2008): 74–91.

Visser, Barbara. 'About.' Accessed 4 August 2015. http://www.barbaravisser.net/about/.

Weber, Samuel. *Theatricality as Medium*. Bronx: Fordham University Press, 2004.

Whitworth Art Gallery. *Exhibitions and Events May – August 2009* [Gallery Brochure].

———. *Marina Abramović Presents...* [Exhibition Leaflet]. Produced on the occasion of the *Marina Abramović Presents...*, Manchester, 3–19 July 2009.

Wiles, David. *A Short History of Western Performance Space*. Cambridge: Cambridge University Press, 2003.

Wilkie, Fiona. 'The Production of "Site": Site-Specific Theatre.' In *A Concise Companion to Contemporary British and Irish Drama*, edited by Nadine Holdsworth and Mary Luckhurst, 87–106. Oxford: Blackwell, 2008.

Wilson, James Andrew. 'When is a Performance?: Temporality in the Social Turn.' *Performance Research* 17:5 On Duration (2012): 110–118.

Wood, Catherine, 'Art Meets Theatre: The Middle Zone.' In *The World as a Stage* [Exhibition Catalogue]. Edited by Jessica Morgan and Catherine Wood, 18–25. London: Tate Publishing, 2007.

———. 'In Context: The Sublevel.' In *The Tanks Programme Notes*. Edited by Charles Danby, 38–39. London: Pureprint Group, 2012.

———. 'Painting in the Shape of a House.' In *A Bigger Splash: Painting after Performance* [Exhibition Catalogue]. Edited by Catherine Wood, 10–22. London: Tate Publishing, 2012.

———. 'People and Things in the Museum.' In *Choreographing Exhibitions*. Edited by Mathieu Copeland, 113–122. Dijon: les presse du réel, 2014.

———, ed. *A Bigger Splash: Painting after Performance* [Exhibition Catalogue]. London: Tate Publishing, 2012.

Worthen, W. B. *Drama: Between Poetry and Performance*. Oxford: Wiley-Blackwell, 2010.

Wright, Barnaby. *Frank Auerbach: London Building Sites 1952–1962* [Exhibition Catalogue]. London: The Courtauld Gallery and Paul Holberton Publishing, 2009.

Index